OFF THE BEATEN PATH® SERIES

ELEVENTH EDITION

OFF THE BEATEN PATH®
VIRGINIA

A GUIDE TO UNIQUE PLACES

JUDY COLBERT

gpp®
travel

Guilford, Connecticut

All the information in this guidebook is subject to change. We recommend that you call ahead to obtain current information before traveling.

To buy books in quantity for corporate use
or incentives, call **(800) 962-0973**
or e-mail **premiums@GlobePequot.com.**

Editor: Kevin Sirois
Project Editor: Heather M. Santiago
Layout: Joanna Beyer
Text design: Linda R. Loiewski
Maps: Equator Graphics © Morris Book Publishing, LLC

ISSN 1539-8110
ISBN 978-0-7627-7330-5

Printed in the United States of America
10 9 8 7 6 5 4 3 2

Contents

About the Author

Judy Colbert is a native Washingtonian (DC, not the state) whose mother grew up in a large family in Virginia's Tidewater or Hampton Roads area. Family visits were frequent and much of the history and attractions (natural and manmade) of the state seeped in as if by osmosis. "One activity my mother loved was 'getting lost,' and I relished those days when we drove around and explored and were misplaced almost beyond belief. We always knew someone would be around the corner to tell us how to make it back home," says Judy.

A natural-born storyteller who has honed her craft for many years, Judy is thrilled when someone says, "I didn't know that" about a place that's right down the street or across the county line. Judy likes to wander into restaurants, libraries, and even beauty parlors to listen to the locals as they tell her to "Go talk to Uncle Fred. He invented the wooden leg." "I don't know if that's true or they're pulling mine. It doesn't matter," she says.

Judy is an award-winning writer and photographer who has been writing about the mid-Atlantic and other areas for decades and is the author of *Maryland & Delaware Off the Beaten Path, Insiders' Guide to Baltimore, Chesapeake Bay Crabs Cookbook, Country Towns of Maryland and Delaware, Fun Places to Go With Children in Washington, D.C., Peaceful Places Washington, D.C., It Happened in Maryland, It Happened in Delaware,* and *It Happened in Arkansas.* She has written hundreds, if not thousands, of articles that have appeared in international, national, regional, and local publications and websites, including www.FreeFunGuides.com and *Howard County Times.* She thanks the Virginia Division of Tourism and all the wonderful Virginians who took the time to assist her in researching and updating *Off the Beaten Path Virginia.*

After thoroughly exploring the mid-Atlantic, Judy would like to spend a year or two on a cruise ship exploring other parts of the world.

She is a member of the American Society of Authors and Journalists, Society of Professional Journalists, Screen Actors Guild, and American Federation of Television Arts and Sciences.

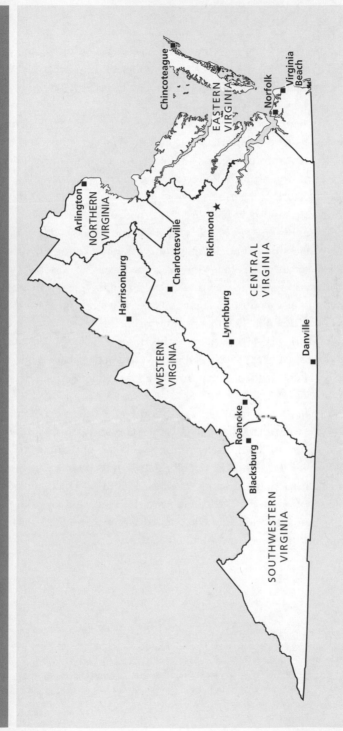

VIRGINIA

Chincoteague

EASTERN VIRGINIA

Virginia Beach

Norfolk

Arlington

NORTHERN VIRGINIA

Charlottesville

Richmond

CENTRAL VIRGINIA

Harrisonburg

WESTERN VIRGINIA

Lynchburg

Danville

Roanoke

Blacksburg

SOUTHWESTERN VIRGINIA

Introduction

Whatever frame of mind you're in, there's a place for you in Virginia. From mountains to beaches, from cosmopolitan to country, from great dining and fine lodging to down-home cooking and rustic campsites, you can look to Virginia for a special time in your life.

In fact, if you rearrange "getaway" it becomes "gateway" and Virginia certainly is the gateway to so many fascinating and unusual attractions and events.

Virginia's famed tourism slogan, "Virginia Is for Lovers," means that Virginia is for lovers of mountain climbing, catching some rays, or seeing innovative modern architecture or log cabins from a previous century. It was modified to "Live Passionately" and now it's "Virginia, Where Love Lives." The modification may change, but the gist is still Virginia Is for Lovers. With more than 700 museums, you're sure to find an interesting exhibit covering the history of your favorite subject. It means that Virginia is for lovers of horseback riding, auto racing, outlet shopping, covered bridges, gristmills, great wineries, and just about anything else you can imagine. Okay, so it's not great for extreme skiing, but you can downhill and cross-country ski.

You can find the most bodacious barbecue and a library designed by noted postmodernist architect Michael Graves. Varieties of tomatoes and cantaloupes are grown here that are grown nowhere else. Smithfield ham can only come from Smithfield, Virginia.

Remember, whatever you love in a vacation you can find in Virginia.

Virginia is the fourth largest South Atlantic state and 35th in size among all the states. It extends 200 miles from north to south and about 430 miles from east to west. It's the 12th most populous state in the country, with nearly three-fourths of the population living in cities. Within its woodlands are 12 varieties of oak, 5 of pine, and 2 of walnut, as well as locust, gum, and poplar. Its indigenous mammals include the white-tailed Virginia deer, elk, black bear, bobcat, woodchuck, raccoon, opossum, and nutria.

Falling in Love

We've already covered the "Virginia is for Lovers" slogan, so this is for people who want a short getaway as the leaves are turning and trees are getting ready for winter's grip. The state tourism people have organized a number of fall getaways that might include mountain biking, a Segway tour in Norfolk, vineyard hopping, and then they let you know that accommodations and dining options are reduced for the package. Check the www.virginia.org/fall website.

Among the many "firsts" of Virginia was the establishment of a state-wide birding and wildlife trail so visitors can view some of the 400 species of birds, 250 species of fish, 150 species of terrestrial and marine mammals, 150 species of amphibians and reptiles, and who knows how many aquatic and terrestrial invertebrates. Three guides are available: a 200-page Mountain Area (everything west of US 29), an 84-page Piedmont Area (central portion), and the 100-page Coastal Area (eastern Virginia and the Eastern Shore). It's a partnership between the Department of Game and Inland Fisheries and the Virginia Tourism Corporation. In promoting Mother Nature's fall foliage fashion show, the VTC joined with the Virginia Department of Forestry and Virginia State Parks.

Operation Wildflower is a combined program of the Virginia Department of Transportation and the Virginia Federation of Garden Clubs, Inc., that has grown from 25 plots of wildflowers planted in 1976 to hundreds of acres of assorted species planted along state highways today. From April through October, you'll see (seasonally) black-eyed Susans, New England asters, oxeye sunflower, New York ironweed, butterfly weed, lance-leaved coreopsis, purple coneflower, tickseed-sunflower (all native to Virginia), Indian blanket (central United States), plains coreopsis (southern United States), sulphur cosmos and mixed cosmos (Mexico), and corn poppy (Europe). If you don't know a sunflower from an aster, pick up a *Wildflowers Color Virginia* brochure at a welcome station; or call (804) 371-6825 or (800) 774-3382.

Home-grown Goodness

Fall is the time to pick that perfect pumpkin or wonderful apples for pies and more. Many farms offer a pick-your-own option, nature studies for your young ones without being in a classroom, and fun outdoor activities. As many of these farms now earn more from two months of corn or hay maze and related sales than they do from farming all year, the options have grown exponentially. Check www.pumpkinpatchesandmore.org/vapnorthen.php for a list of farms that offer pumpkin patches, corn mazes, hay rides, and more. This list, as of this writing, includes farms in Culpeper, Fairfax, Fauquier, Frederick, Loudoun, Page, Prince William, Rappahannock, Shenandoah, Spotsylvania, and Stafford Counties.

Check www.pumpkinpatchesandmore.org/vapalbe.php for farms in Central Virginia, including Albemarle, Amherst, Appomattox, Augusta, Fluvanna, Greene, Madison, Nelson, Orange, Rockbridge, and Rockingham Counties, and the cities of Harrisonburg and Lynchburg.

For farms in the southwestern part of the state, check www.pumpkin patchesandmore.org/vapwest.php, including Bedford, Botetourt, Halifax,

Montgomery, Patrick, Pittsylvania, Russell, Scott, Tazewell, Washington, Wise, and Wythe Counties and the city of Roanoke.

And, for eastern and southeastern parts of the state, check www.pumpkin patchesandmore.org/vapsoutheast.php for farms in Caroline, Chesterfield, Dinwiddie, Gloucester, Hanover, Henrico, James City, King William, Mathews, Northampton, Nottoway, Surry, Westmoreland, and York Counties, and the cities of Chesapeake, Charles, Hampton, Richmond, Virginia Beach, and Portsmouth.

You will be wise to verify activities, hours of operation, and fees. You can also find links for fruit and vegetable and Christmas tree farms.

Wineries

There were 192 wineries in Virginia as of April 2011. That's up from 130 wineries in 2009. Yes, this is a growth industry and most wineries are open for tours and tastings. Even the front south garden of the Governor's Mansion in Richmond now has some grapevines. Planted in March 2011 by First Lady Maureen McDonnell, the 10 Chambourcin vines follow an original dictate that every settler in Jamestown should plant at least 10 grape vines.

Wine trails have been established that help you explore the wines of Virginia as you tour throughout the state—Northern, Shenandoah Valley, Central, Eastern, Chesapeake Bay, Blue Ridge Highlands, Hampton Roads, Heart of Appalachia, Southern, the six American Viticultural Areas of Shenandoah Valley, Monticello, Eastern Shore, Washington Birthplace, North Fork, and Rocky Nob (www.virginiawine.org).

Look for wine-related events almost throughout the year, regardless of the season. Some programs include Valentine's Day–themed wine pairings, an *annual wine expo* (www.virginiawineexpo.com), a "Wines and Wags" event that includes showing off dogs and wines, a wine and bluegrass festival, a wine and garlic festival, hot air balloon and wine festival, and the *annual state wine fest* (www.virginiawinefest.com). That is only a sip out of a barrelful of occasions. The *Virginia Wine of the Month Club* can help highlight individual wines for you; (800) 826-0534 or (434) 985-9709; www.vawineclub .com. A statewide organization, the *Virginia Wine Board Marketing Office,* has valuable information about the wineries, recipes using local wines, tours, and festivals in their Richmond office; on their website, www.virginiawine.org; or by calling (804) 344-8200.

Re-enactments

You may have heard (almost impossible not to) that 2011 has seen the start of a multiyear celebration of the *sesquicentennial of the American Civil War and Emancipation* (or the War Between the States or the War of Northern Aggression or whatever else you might have heard it called). You are likely to see re-enactments of famed battles scheduled throughout the next four years.

Two questions, at least, may come to mind about the way wars were fought in those days. Why the soldiers stood shoulder-to-shoulder as they marched across the field becomes an understandable approach when you realize smokeless gunpowder had not been invented, and the only way they could be sure they weren't aiming at their fellow soldier was to be standing next to him. You may also wonder why they wore heavy wool uniforms when the South had fields of cotton and that's why they needed slaves. And then you learn that cotton was very flammable while wool could resist the stray spark that flew from a firearm that had just been discharged.

A list of re-enactment activities in your neighborhood or where you want to visit is available at www.civilwarnews.com. You can also look for historic and art-related exhibits at museums and historical societies.

Just remember that you don't want to buy any swords or souvenirs claiming to be original if they are stamped "First Battle of Bull Run" or "First Battle of Manassas" because no one knew there would be a second battle when the first one took place.

Shenandoah's Birthday

Both the *Shenandoah National Park* and the *Virginia State Parks* celebrated 75 years of existence in 2011. President Franklin D. Roosevelt dedicated the Shenandoah in 1936. This land preservation act means you can explore the 200,000 acres with more than 500 miles of trails (your dog may join you on almost all of those miles). If you want to see the park without becoming too personally involved, drive any or all of the 105 miles of *Skyline Drive,* a 2-lane road that has 75 overlooks so you can enjoy the views. Also started in

Rails-to-Trails

Virginia has been very active in the Rails-to-Trails program that converts the old railroad right-of-way into a pedestrian-friendly trail. Because the trains had to be able to climb any incline, you can figure the trails will be fairly flat and any incline will be moderate. *The Rails-To-Trails Conservancy Guidebook* for the mid-Atlantic area includes 17 trails in Virginia for walkers, hikers, history buffs, and bicycle riders. They go through Civil War battlefields, wetlands, and small and large towns. You can purchase a guidebook covering the Rail-Trails for Delaware, Maryland, Virginia, West Virginia, and Washington, DC, through the Conservancy website, www.railstotrails.org.

1936, the Virginia State Park system now has 34 parks in the system ranging from sandy beaches to what we consider tall mountains.

General Notes

As this book highlights unique places, there is less emphasis on the major tourism destinations and sites. Some of them are mentioned, with a focus on what's unique about those popular sites and destinations. To find those roads more traveled, call (800) VISIT-VA (847-4882) for a Virginia vacation guide, or write to the *Division of Tourism* at 901 E. Byrd St., Richmond 23219. The tourism division (804-786-4484; www.virginia.org) can also provide more specific information about a particular area. They have many special-interest brochures that will help you in your search for the perfect bed-and-breakfast, African-American and Hispanic sites and events, and other destinations.

Many museums, zoos, and other public places have an exchange or reciprocal program. Become a member at one and that allows you free admission to other members of their program when you pay for a specific level membership at the first museum. Although many of the attractions listed here are too small or ask for donations, you might want to see if your favorite home attraction or one place you'll be visiting on your travels participates and it would be worthwhile joining. Look for North American Reciprocal Museum Program, Association of Science and Technology Centers Passport Program, Association of Children's Museums, Association of Zoos & Aquariums, American Public Gardens Association, Wildflower Organization, Council of American Jewish Museums, Modern and Contemporary Reciprocal Program, and probably others. Additionally, the Blue Star Museum program has provided free admission to more than 900 museums to active members of the military and their families during the summers of 2010 and 2011. Check to see if that program has been extended.

Much of Virginia is old, and many buildings were constructed before wheelchair access and special needs were a public concern. While most, if not all, public buildings have been made accessible or comply with the Americans With Disabilities Act, this is not always the case. A building in Williamsburg may not have an elevator to the second floor. It probably will have a narrated video of the areas you can't access that you can watch instead. For specific information about public accessibility, check the *Virginia Travel Guide for Persons with Disabilities* at www.acccessiblevirginia.org.

This is not always the case with accommodations. Even a bed-and-breakfast that's on one floor may have steps to a porch. As I have limited the number of chain hotels and motels listed in this book and made an emphasis on individually owned and operated accommodations, you may find properties that are not accessible. Restaurants, too, may be downstairs or upstairs or have tables set close to each other. Sometimes, they will offer to carry a person in a wheelchair (sitting in the chair) to a table.

Be sure to call any place you plan to visit to determine whether the facility is wheelchair accessible or if there are special provisions for those who have visual or hearing impairments. (The TDD number is 804-371-0327.)

Tobacco farming and cigarette manufacturing have been providing a huge chunk of Virginia's economy for almost 400 years, ergo, it has been slow to adopt a statewide ban against smoking in restaurants, stores, offices, and other

birthplace of presidents

You may have heard that Virginia is the birthplace of presidents because eight men from this state held that office—George Washington, Thomas Jefferson, James Madison, James Monroe, William Henry Harrison, John Tyler, Zachary Taylor, and Woodrow Wilson. A ninth Virginian, Joseph Jenkins Roberts, became the first African-American governor (president) of the colony of Liberia, Africa, in 1841.

public places. As of December 1, 2009, legislation adopted earlier that year and signed by then-Governor Timothy M. Kaine prohibited smoking in restaurants (and bars) that are open to the public with a few exceptions. One exception is an outdoor area that doesn't have a temporary enclosure. Private clubs are also exempt. Therefore, if this is one of your hot-button issues (particularly if you come from an area with a more extensive no-smoking policy), then you should check the policies of the places you plan to visit. If you want more details, check this site from the **Virginia Department of Health:** www.vdh .virginia.gov/breatheeasy/faqs.htm.

Virginia has 95 counties, 40 independent cities, and 189 incorporated towns. This can be a little confusing, particularly when trying to locate and visit an independent city that's located within a county. You'd probably do well to avoid trying to figure out the difference between Fairfax County, Fairfax city, Alexandria, Arlington, etc. Just plug the location information into your GPS or find an online map. Persevere, please.

By the way, Virginia is a commonwealth—a term first used in Jamestown in 1619—not a state. Kentucky, Massachusetts, and Pennsylvania also use the term commonwealth.

When I started researching and writing the first edition of *Virginia Off the Beaten Path,* we did not have websites and the state certainly didn't have four telephone area codes. Now, almost every place listed has a presence on the Internet, growing from being part of a regional organization to individual sites. Some places have entered the 21st century and can be found on Facebook,

Twitter, Foursquare, and other social networking sites. The URLs, addresses, phone numbers, prices, rates, and times of operation listed in this guidebook were confirmed at press time. Note that many places are closed for national holidays. We recommend that you call establishments before traveling to obtain current information.

Virginia Tourism Resources

VIRGINIA TOURISM

Virginia Tourism Corporation, 901 E. Byrd St., Richmond 23219; (804) 545-5572, (800) 732-5827, or (800) VISIT-VA (847-4882); fax (804) 371-0327; TTY/TTD (804) 371-0327; www.virginia.org

VIRGINIA VISITOR CENTERS

Northern Virginia

Alexandria Visitors Center, 221 King St., Alexandria 22314; (703) 746-3301 or (800) 388-9119; www.funside.com

Arlington Convention and Visitors Services, 1100 N. Glebe Rd., Suite 1500, Arlington 22201; (800) 677-6267 or (703) 228-5720; www.stayarlington.com

Fairfax Museum & Visitors Center, 10209 Main St., Fairfax 22030; (800) 545-7950 or (703) 385-8414; www.fairfaxva.gov/museumvc/mvc.asp

Fairfax County Convention & Visitors Corporation, 7927 Jones Bridge Dr., South Wing 100, McLean 22102; (703) 752-9500; www.fxva.com

Fredericksburg Visitor Center, 706 Caroline St., Fredericksburg 22401; (800) 678-4748 or (540) 373-1776; www.visitfred.com

Herndon Dulles Visitor's Center, Old Train Depot, 717 Lynn St., Herndon 20170; (703) 437-6366; www.visitherndon.com

Loudoun County Visitors Center, 112-G South St. Southeast, Leesburg 20175; (800) 752-6118 or (703) 771-2671; www.visitloudoun.org

Manassas Visitors Center, Train Depot, 9431 West St., Manassas 20110; (703) 361-6599; www.visitmanassas.org

Northern Neck Tourism Commission, P.O. Box 1707, Warsaw 22572; (804) 333-1919; www.northernneck.org

Prince William County, Manassas Convention Visitors Bureau, 10611 Balls Ford Rd., Suite 110, Manassas 20109; (703) 396-7130 or (800) 432-1792; www.visitpwc.com

Spotsylvania County Visitors Center, 4704 Southpoint Pkwy., Fredericksburg 22407; (540) 891-6670 or (800) 654-4118; www.spotsylvania.va.us

Stafford Visitors Center, 224 Washington St., Falmouth 22405; (540) 654-1015; www.umw.edu/gari_melchers/visit/default.php

Virginia Welcome Center at Fredericksburg, I-95S, mile marker 131, Fredericksburg 22404; (540) 786-8344; www.virginia.org

Virginia Welcome Center at Manassas, I-66W, mile marker 48, 9915 Vandor Lane, Manassas 20109; (703) 361-2134; www.virginia.org

Warrenton–Fauquier County Visitors Center, 33 N. Calhoun St., Warrenton 20186; (540) 341-0988 or (800) 820-1021; www.visitfauquier.com

Eastern Virginia

Assateague Island National Seashore, Toms Cove Visitor Center, 8586 Beach Rd., Chincoteague 23336; (757) 336-6577; www.nps.gov/asis

Chincoteague Chamber of Commerce and Visitor Center, 6733 Maddox Blvd., Chincoteague Island 23336; (757) 336-6161; www.chincoteaguechamber .com

Colonial Beach Visitor Center, 106 Hawthorne St., Colonial Beach 22443; (804) 224-8145; www.colonialbeach.org

Greater Williamsburg Chamber & Tourism Alliance, 421 N. Boundary St., Williamsburg 23187; (800) 368-6511 or (757) 229-6511; www.visitwilliamsburg .com

East Coast Gateway Welcome Center, I-64E, mile marker 213, New Kent 23124; (804) 966-7450; www.virginia.org

Eastern Shore of Virginia Tourism, P.O. Box 72, Tasley 23441; (757) 787-8268; www.esvatourism.org

Hampton Visitors Center, 1919 Commerce Dr., Hampton 23666; (800) 487-8778 or (757) 727-1222; www.visithampton.com/go/visitors

Mathews County Visitor & Information Center, Sibley's General Store, 239 Main St., Mathews 23109; (804) 725-4BAY; www.visitmathews.com

Newport News Visitor Center, Newport News Park, 13560 Jefferson Ave., Newport News 23603; (888) 493-7386 or (757) 886-7777; www.newport-news .org

Visit Norfolk Today, 232 E. Main St., Norfolk 23510; (800) 368-3097 or (757) 664-6620; www.visitnorfolktoday.com

Portsmouth Visitor Information Center, 801 Crawford St., Portsmouth 23704; (757) 393-8000; www.visitportsva.com

Suffolk Visitor Center, 524 N. Main St., Suffolk 23434; (866) SEE-SUFK or (757) 514-4130; www.suffolk-fun.com

Smithfield and Isle of Wight Convention & Visitor Bureau, 319 Main St., Smithfield 23431; (800) 365-9339 or (757) 357-8084; www.visitsmithfieldisleof wight.com

Virginia Beach Convention & Visitors Bureau, 2100 Parks Ave., Virginia Beach 23451; (800) 822-3224; www.visitvirginiabeach.com/visitors

Virginia Welcome Center at New Church, US 13, New Church 23415; (757) 824-5000; www.virginia.org

Central Virginia

Appomattox Visitor Information Center, 214 Main St., Appomattox 24522; (434) 352-8999; www.tourappomattox.com

Ashland–Hanover Visitor Information Center, 101 Thompson St., Ashland 23005; (804) 798-9219; www.town.ashland.va.us

Bedford Area Welcome Center, 816 Burks Hill Rd., Bedford 24523; (540) 587-5682 or (877) HI-PEAKS (447-3257); www.visitbedford.com

Charlottesville Visitor Center, 610 E. Main St., Charlottesville 22902; (877) 386-1103 or (434) 293-6789; www.pursuecharlottesville.com

Culpeper Visitor's Center, 111 S. Commerce St., Culpeper 22701; (540) 727-0611; www.visitculpeperva.com

Danville Tourism, 645 River Park Dr., Danville 24540; (434) 793-4636; www.visitdanville.com

Gloucester Visitor Center, 6509 Main St., Gloucester 23061; (804) 693-0014 or (866) 847-4887; www.gloucesterva.info/

Henrico County Tourist Information Center, 3812 Nine Mile Rd., Henrico, 23228; (804) 652-3406; www.co.henrico.va.us

Hopewell Visitor Center, 4100 Oaklawn Blvd., Hopewell 23860; (800) 863-TOUR (863-8687) or (804) 541-2461; www.hopewellva.gov

Lynchburg Visitors Center, 216 12th St. at Church, Lynchburg 24504; (800) 732-5821 or (434) 847-1811; www.discoverlynchburg.org

Madison County Chamber of Commerce, 110 N. Main St., #A, Madison 22727; (540) 948-4455; www.madison-va.com

Martinsville-Henry County Visitor Center, 54 W. Church St., Martinsville 24112; (888) PACE-4YU (722-3498) or (276) 632-8006; www.visitmartinsville.com

Nelson County Convention & Visitors Bureau, 8519 Thomas Nelson Hwy. (US 29), Lovingston 22949; (800) 282-8223; www.nelsoncounty.com

Orange County Visitors Center, 122 E. Main St., Orange 22960; (877) 222-8072 or (540) 672-1653; www.visitorangevirginia.com

Petersburg Visitors Center, 425 Cockade Alley, Petersburg 23803; (804) 733-2400 or (800) 368-3595; www.petersburg-va.org/tourism

Piedmont Crossroads Visitor Center—Louisa, Fluvanna & Orange Counties, 135-A Wood Ridge Terrace, Zion Crossroads 22942; (540) 832-0555; www.louisacounty.com

Pulaski County Visitor Center, 4440 Cleburne Blvd., Dublin 24084; (540) 674-1991; www.pulaskicounty.org

Richmond Bell Tower Visitor Center, 101 N. 9th St., Richmond 23219; (804) 545-5584; www.virginia.org

Richmond Metropolitan Convention and Visitors Bureau, 401 N. 3rd St., Richmond 23219; (800) 370-9004; www.richmondva.org

Rockfish Gap Tourist Information Center, 20 Afton Circle, Afton 22920; (540) 943-5187 or (540) 942-6644; www.visitwaynesboro.net

Smith Mountain Lake Visitors Center, 16430 Booker T. Washington Hwy., Unit 2, Moneta 24121; (540) 721-1203; www.visitsmithmountainlake.com

South Hill Tourist Information Center, 201 S. Mecklenburg Ave., South Hill 23970; (800) 524-4347 or (434) 447-4547; www.southhillchamber.com

Town of Hillsville Visitor's Center, 410 N. Main St., Hillsville 24343; (276) 728-2128 or (276) 730-3100; www.townofhillsville.com

Virginia's Heartland Regional Visitor Center, 121 E. 3rd St., Farmville 23901; (434) 392-1482; www.co.prince-edward.va.us/travel.shtml

Virginia Welcome Center at Bracey, I-85, mile marker 1, Bracey 23919; (434) 689-2295; www.virginia.org

Virginia Welcome Center at Bristol, I-81, mile marker 0, 66 Island Rd., Bristol 24201; (276) 466-2932

Virginia Welcome Center at Lambsburg, I-77 northbound, mile marker 0, Lambsburg 24351; (276) 755-3931; www.virginia.org

Virginia Welcome Center at Rocky Gap, I-77, mile marker 61, Rocky Gap 24366; (276) 928-1873; www.virginia.org

Virginia Welcome Center at Skippers, I-95, Skippers 23879; (434) 634-4113; www.virginia.org

Western Virginia

Alleghany Highlands Travel Council, 241 W. Main St., Covington 24426; (540) 962-2178; www.ahchamber.com/visitus.htm

Blacksburg/Christiansburg Visitor Center, 103 Professional Park Dr., Blacksburg 24060; (540) 552-2636 or (877) 367-4843; www.virginianaturally.com

Blue Ridge HOST, Inc. Visitors Center, 7648 Fancy Gap Hwy., Fancy Gap 24328; (276) 398-3207; www.blueridgehost.com

Blue Ridge Plateau Regional Visitor Center, 235 Farmers Market Rd., Hillsville 24343; (276) 730-3100; www.visittheblueridge.com

Blue Ridge Visitor Center in Patrick County, 2577 Jeb Stuart Hwy., Meadows of Dan 24120; (276) 694-6012; www.patrickchamber.com

Buena Vista Regional Visitor Center, 595 E. 29th St., Buena Vista 24416; (540) 261-8004; www.lexingtonvirginia.com

Cedar Creek Battlefield Visitors Center, 8437 Valley Pike, Middletown 22645; (540) 869-2064; www.cedarcreekbattlefield.org

E. Lee Trinkle Regional Visitors Center, 975 Tazewell St., Wytheville 24382; (276) 223-3441 or (800) 446-9670; www.virginiablueridge.org

Front Royal–Warren County Visitor Center, 414 E. Main St., Front Royal 22630; (800) 338-2576 or (540) 635-5788; www.frontroyalva.com

Greene County Visitor's Center, 9661 Spotswood Trail, Stanardsville 22973; (434) 985-9756; www.greeneva.com/tourism/index.htm

Harrisonburg Tourism and Visitor Services, 212 S. Main St., Harrisonburg 22801; (540) 434-8937; www.harrisonburgtourism.com

Highland County Visitor's Center, Highland Inn, Main Street, Monterey 24465; (540) 468-2550; www.highlandcounty.org

Hopewell Tourism and Visitor Center, 4100 Oaklawn Blvd., Hopewell 23860; (800) 863-8687 or (804) 541-2461; www.ci.hopewell.va.us

Lexington, Buena Vista, and Rockbridge County Visitor's Center, 106 E. Washington St., Lexington 24450; (877) 453-9822 or (540) 463-3777; www.lexingtonvirginia.com

Luray–Page County Visitor Center, 18 Campbell St., Luray 22835; (540) 743-3915 or (888) 743-3915; www.luraypage.com

Rappahnnock Office of Tourism, 290 Gay St., Washington 22747; (540) 675-5330; www.visitrappahannockva.com

Roanoke Valley Convention and Visitors Bureau, 101 Shenandoah Ave. Northeast, Roanoke 24016; (540) 342-6025; www.visitroanokeva.com

Salem Visitors Center, Salem Civic Center, 1001 Boulevard, Salem 24153; (888) VA-SALEM (725-2536) or (540) 375-4044; www.visitsalemva.com

Staunton Travel Information Center, 1290 Richmond Rd., Staunton 24401; (800) 332-5219 or (540) 332-3972; www.visitstaunton.com

Staunton Visitors Center, 35 S. New St., Staunton 24401; (800) 342-7982; www.visitstaunton.com

Virginia Welcome Center at Clear Brook, I-81S, mile marker 320, Clear Brook 22624; (540) 722-3448; www.virginia.org

Virginia Welcome Center at Covington, mile marker 2, 1 Welcome Center Dr., Covington 24426; (540) 559-3010; www.virginia.org

Waynesboro Department of Tourism, 301 W. Main St., Waynesboro 22980; (540) 942-6512; www.visitwaynesboro.net.html

Winchester–Frederick County Visitors Center, 1400 S. Pleasant Valley Rd., Winchester 22601; (877) 871-1326 or (540) 542-1326; www.visitwinchester va.com

Southwestern Virginia

Abingdon Visitors Center, 335 Cummings St., Abingdon 24210; (800) 435-3440 or (276) 676-2282; www.abingdon.com/visitor-center

Bristol Convention and Visitors Bureau, 20 Volunteer Pkwy., Bristol, TN 37620; (423) 989-4850; www.visitbristoltnva.org

Carroll County Office of Tourism and Blue Ridge Plateau Regional Visitor Center, 235 Farmers Market Rd., Hillsville 24343; (276) 730-3100; http://itsourstyle.com/index.php

Depot Welcome Center, 55 Franklin St., Rocky Mount 24151; (540) 489-0948

Grayson County Tourist Information Center, 107 E. Main St., Box 217, Independence 24348; (276) 773-2000; www.graysoncountyva.com

Lonesome Pine Tourist Info Center, 619 Gilley Ave. East, Box 236, Big Stone Gap 24219; (540) 523-2060; www.bigstonegap.org

Tazewell County Visitors Center, 200 Sanders Lane, Bluefield 24605; (276) 322-1345; www.visittazewellcounty.org

USEFUL WEBSITES

Metropolitan Washington Airports, www.metwashairports.com
National Park Service, www.nps.gov
Virginia Tourism Corporation, www.virginia.org

MAJOR NEWSPAPERS

Alexandria Gazette Packet, 1606 King St., Alexandria 22314; (703) 821-5050; www.connectionnewspapers.com/

Bristol Herald-Courier/Virginia-Tennessean, 320 Morrison Blvd., Bristol 24201; (276) 669-2181; www2.tricities.com

Charlottesville Daily Progress, 685 Rio Rd. West, Charlottesville 22901; (434) 978-7200; www.dailyprogress.com

Culpeper Star–Exponent, 471 James Madison Hwy., Suite 201, Culpeper 22701; (540) 825-0771; www.starexponent.com

Danville Register & Bee, 700 Monument St., Danville 24541; (434) 793-2311; www.registerbee.com

Free Lance–Star, 616 Amelia St., Fredericksburg 22401; (540) 374-5000; www.freelancestar.com

Lynchburg News & Advance, 101 Wyndale Dr., Lynchburg 24501; (434) 385-5440 or (800) 275-8830; www.newsadvance.com

Manassas Journal Messenger, 9009 Church St., Manassas 20110; (703) 368-3101; www.manassasjm.com

News Leader, 11 N. Central Ave., Staunton 24402; (540) 885-7281 or (800) 793-2459; www.newsleader.com

News-Virginian, 544 W. Main St., Waynesboro 22980; (540) 949-8213 or (540) 886-3400; www.newsvirginian.com

Richmond Times Dispatch, 300 E. Franklin St., Richmond 23219; (804) 649-6000 or (800) 468-3382; www.timesdispatch.com

Roanoke Times, 201 W. Campbell Ave., Roanoke 24070–2491; (540) 981-3140 or (800) 346-1234; www.roanoke.com

Washington Post, 1150 15th St. Northwest, Washington, DC 20071; (202) 334-6000; www.washingtonpost.com

PUBLIC TRANSPORTATION

Amtrak, (800) USA-RAIL (872-7245), (888) 268-7251 or (888) AMTRAK1; www.amtrak.com

Norfolk International Airport, 2200 Norview Ave., Norfolk 23518; (757) 857-3351; www.norfolkairport.com

Newport News–Williamsburg International Airport, Jefferson Avenue, Newport News 23602; (757) 877-0221; www.nnwairport.com

Richmond International Airport, Richmond 23231; (804) 226-3000; www.flyrichmond.com

Roanoke Airport, 5202 Aviation Dr. Northwest, Roanoke 24012; (540) 362-1999; www.roanokeairport.com

Ronald Reagan National Airport, Arlington 22210; (703) 417-8600; www.metwashairports.com

Virginia Railway Express (VRE), 1500 King St., Suite 202, Alexandria 22314; (703) 684-1001 or (800) RIDE-VRE (743-3433); www.vre.org

Washington Dulles International Airport, Herndon 22204; (703) 572-2700; www.metwashairports.com

Fast Facts About the Old Dominion

Area (land): 39,598 square miles; rank: 35

Capital: Richmond

Largest city: Virginia Beach, population 439,467

Number of counties: 95

Highest elevation: 5,729 feet, Mount Rogers

Lowest elevation: sea level, at the Atlantic Ocean

Population: 8,001,024 (2010 census)

Population distribution: 88.5 percent in urban areas, 11.5 percent rural

Institutions of higher education: 97

Median family income: $59,372 (2009)

Statehood: June 25, 1788; the 10th state

Nickname: Old Dominion, Mother of Presidents

State flower: dogwood flower

State tree: dogwood

State motto: Sic Semper Tyrannis ("Thus Always to Tyrants")

State bird: northern cardinal

State shell: oyster shell

State fossil: *Chesapecten jeffersonius*

State dog: American foxhound

State drink: milk

State insect: tiger swallowtail butterfly

State folkdance: square dancing

State boat: Chesapeake Bay Deadrise

State fish: brook trout

Climate Overview

Virginia's weather depends on the region and the season. The Tidewater area is relatively mild in the winter but can be quite humid in the summer. Northern Virginia also has hot, humid summer days but receives an average 20 inches of snow each winter. The mountains can receive severe winter storms and then enjoy delightful summer days.

Famous Sons & Daughters of Virginia

Richard Arlen, actor
Arthur Ashe, tennis champion
Stephen F. Austin, Texas founder
Pearl Bailey, singer
Russell Baker, columnist
Phil Balsley, singer

Warren Beatty, actor
George Bingham, painter
Richard Evelyn Bird, naval officer/ explorer
Jeff Burton, NASCAR driver
Maybelle Carter, singer

June Carter Cash, singer

Willa Cather, novelist

Spencer Christian, TV weatherman

Roy Clark, country music artist

William Clark, soldier/explorer

Henry Clay, orator and statesman

Patsy Cline, singer

Joseph Cotten, actor

Ella Fitzgerald, jazz singer

Jimmy Fortune, singer

William Henry Harrison, US president

Patrick Henry, statesman

Sam Houston, political leader

Thomas Jefferson, US president

Henry "Light-Horse Harry" Lee,
  public official

Robert E. Lee, Confederate general

Meriwether Lewis, explorer

Shirley MacLaine, actress

James Madison, US president

John Marshall, US chief justice

Dave Matthews, singer

Cyrus Hall McCormick, inventor

James Monroe, US president

Wayne Newton, entertainer

Opechancanough, Powhatan leader

John Payne, actor

Pocahontas, Indian princess

Walter Reed, army surgeon

Harold Reid, singer

Tim Reid, actor/director

Matthew Ridgway, army chief of staff

Joseph Jenkins Roberts, first president
  of Liberia

Bill "Bojangles" Robinson, dancer
  and actor

George C. Scott, actor

Willard Scott, TV weatherman

Kate Smith, singer

Sam Snead, golfer

Statler Brothers, singing group

James "Jeb" Stuart, Confederate army
  officer

Thomas Sumter, army officer

Zachary Taylor, S. president

Nat Turner, leader of slave uprising

John Tyler, US president

Blair Underwood, actor

Booker T. Washington, educator

George Washington, US president

James E. West, inventor

Thomas Woodrow Wilson, US
  president

Tom Wolfe, journalist

NORTHERN VIRGINIA

Poor Northern Virginia. Other than those who follow Civil War history, there probably aren't many visitors who say, "Oh, I'm going to Northern Virginia for my vacation." They say they're going to Washington, DC, and decide to stay in the neighboring state across the Potomac River. That's all well and good for the restaurants and hotels—their managements love it. But it's not fair to the visitor who could be missing a spectacular Virginia museum, an unusual spot to get away from it all for a few hours, or a significant link to history.

When you stay on this side of the river, you can visit an old gristmill, see where the George Washington cherry tree fable originated, or check out an apothecary that seems frozen in time.

Note: Because of the spread of the **emerald ash borer** you are **not allowed** to remove firewood from the state parks in Arlington, Fairfax, Fauquier, Loudoun, and Prince William Counties and the cities of Alexandria, Fairfax City, Falls Church, Manassas, and Manassas Park.

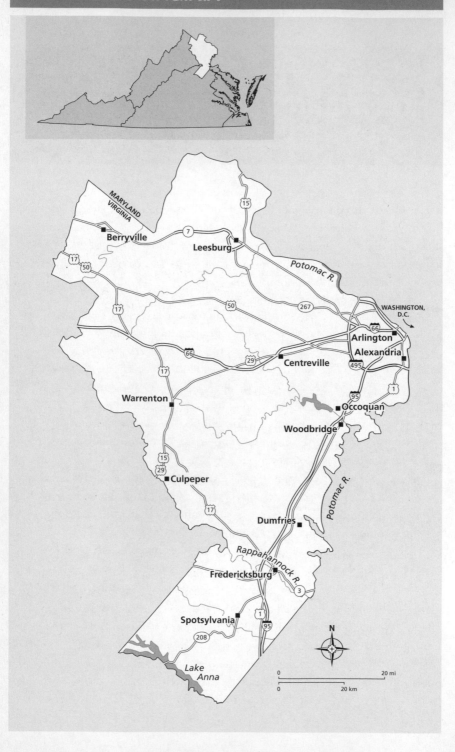

MARYLAND
VIRGINIA

Berryville

Leesburg

15

7

Potomac R.

17
50

17

50

267

WASHINGTON, D.C.

66

Arlington

Alexandria

495

66

29

Centreville

17

1

Warrenton

95

Occoquan

Woodbridge

15

29

Culpeper

17

Potomac R.

Dumfries

Rappahannock R.

Fredericksburg

3

1

Spotsylvania

95

208

Lake Anna

N

0   20 mi
0   20 km

Arlington

If you aren't a local resident, the chances are good that you flew into **Reagan National Airport** (although Dulles International Airport and Baltimore-Washington International Airport are almost as convenient), so our visit will start in Arlington.

Arlington is the smallest county in the United States that is self-governing. New York County, New York (22 square miles), is smaller, but, as the borough of Manhattan, it is not a separate jurisdictional entity. Established March 13, 1847, as Alexandria County, the name was changed to Arlington on March 16, 1920. The county is named for the estate where George Washington Parke Custis lived before he built the house currently known as Arlington House in Arlington National Cemetery. The estate had been named to honor England's Earl of Arlington.

For brochures and specific information, contact the **Arlington Convention and Visitors Services Center,** which is open daily from 9 a.m. to 5 p.m. 1100 N. Glebe Rd., Suite 1500, Arlington 22201; (703) 228-5720 or (800) 677-6267; www.stayarlington.com. As social media and discount shopping are entering our lives like so many IV drips, stop by the www.shoparlington.com website or follow them on Twitter or Facebook for discounts on shopping and dining.

Now, on to touring and learning about Arlington.

Near Arlington National Cemetery, the Iwo Jima Memorial, and the Netherlands Carillon is **Fort Myer,** home of the oldest military division in the United

Honoring the Last Full Measure

In 1992, Merrill Worcester, owner of Worcester Wreath Company of Harrington, Maine, donated several thousand surplus wreaths to decorate the headstones at Arlington National Cemetery for the winter holiday season. This continued until 2005 when a photo of the wreaths and snow covering the headstones went viral on the Internet and people started requesting a wreath on a headstone at a particular cemetery or a cemetery-wide project. This became **Wreaths Across America** and, in 2006, wreaths were placed at 150 cemeteries and that grew to more than 300 in 2008 in every state, Puerto Rico, and foreign countries. The number has increased to more than 100,000 wreaths. The program with the mission of "Remember, Honor and Teach" accepts donations and welcomes volunteers who will place the wreaths on the second Saturday of December. If you'd like to participate, either at Arlington or in another area, want to donate, or you want to use this as a teaching moment, check for information at www.wreathsacrossamerica.org.

AUTHOR'S FAVORITES IN NORTHERN VIRGINIA

Annual Historic Garden Week
April, statewide
(804) 644-7776
www.vagardenweek.org

18th-century Craft Fair
September, Mount Vernon
(703) 780-2000
www.mountvernon.org

US Marine Corps War Memorial (Iwo Jima Memorial)
Arlington
(703) 289-2500
www.nps.gov/gwmp/marinecorps
warmemorial.htm

Wolf Trap Farm Park for the Performing Arts
Vienna, (703) 938-1900
www.wolftrap.org

States, the Third U.S. Infantry Division. This is the ceremonial unit for Arlington Cemetery.

The caissons, stables, and the *Old Guard Museum* in the fort are often open to the public on weekdays. Blackjack, the riderless horse whose symbolism was so moving during the funerals of Presidents John F. Kennedy and Dwight D. Eisenhower as well as more than 150 other funerals, is buried on the marching grounds. Look for the plaque and flowering bushes marking his grave. A stable has been dedicated as a museum to him. The rest of the museum, which is the only US Army museum in the Washington, DC, area, is dedicated to the regiment that began its history in 1784. It has been undergoing a renovation and relocation, and as of this writing, they don't have a scheduled opening date. Check the website or give them a call.

For additional information, contact the Old Guard Museum, Building 249, Sheridan Avenue, Fort Myer, Arlington 22211. The museum is open Mon through Sat 9 a.m. to 4 p.m. and Sun from 1 to 4 p.m. Admission is free. Call (703) 696-6670 before your arrival to schedule a 40-minute guided tour.

Free concerts by the US Army Band and guest artists are held on a regular schedule in Brucker Hall. For more information call (703) 696-3399 (a recorded concert hotline) or (703) 696-3718, or visit www.army.mil/armyband.

Restaurants in Virginia have been quick to jump on the farm-to-table program that helps support local farmers while providing that unmistakable taste of fresh-from-the-field food to appreciative diners. The *Lost Dog Cafe and Gourmet Pizza Deli* and the *Stray Cat Cafe* serve real milkshakes, gluten-free pizza for only $4 more than the regular, and have about a dozen beers on tap and maybe 200 more in bottles. That's all well and good, but there's another reason to visit the Lost Dog or Stray Cat—owners Ross Underwood and Pam McAlwee participate in another valuable community program. They have been rescuing stray dogs and cats and, through a nonprofit foundation they started, placing nearly 2,000 abandoned and homeless critters into loving homes. Each pet has been spayed or neutered before adoption. You can help their cause by dining at one of their three restaurants or volunteering at or donating to the foundation (www.lostdogrescue.org). 5876 Washington Blvd., Arlington 22205, (703) 237-1552; 2920 Columbia Pike, Arlington 22204, (703) 553-7770; or 1690A Anderson Rd., McLean 22102, (703) 356-5678; www .lostdogcafe.com.

funfacts

Women in Military Service for America Memorial, located at the ceremonial entrance to Arlington National Cemetery, is dedicated to all military women—past, present, and future. The views from the memorial are impressive (that's Arlington House above it as you're approaching the memorial), and just listening to the stories of the battles

Arlington National Cemetery
covers 624 acres and conducts nearly 7,000 funerals a year. It has the second largest number of people interred, more than 300,000. The Calverton National Cemetery on Long Island is the largest of the 130 national cemeteries.

fought to create the memorial, particularly the architectural ones, is almost as impressive as learning about the battles these women fought for more than two centuries, from Revolutionary days to the present. You can search for women who have served, either in person or online. There's a gift shop; rotating exhibits of artifacts, photographs, documents, memorabilia, and uniforms; a film, *In Defense of a Nation;* a computerized register with the stories of some 250,000 military women (and accepting more); and a monthly children's program. The Women's Memorial is open daily from 8 a.m. to 5 p.m. Oct through Mar; to 7 p.m. Apr through Sept, closed December 25. Children are welcome, and it's wheelchair accessible. Women in Military Service for America Memorial, Department 560, Washington, DC 20042-0560; (800) 222-2294 or (703) 533-1155; www.womensmemorial.org.

It seems there's a museum for and about everything, and now there's one about drugs—not pharmaceuticals meant to save your life, but dope drugs. It's the **Drug Enforcement Administration's Museum and Visitors Center** at DEA headquarters (700 Army-Navy Dr., Arlington 22202; 202-307-3463; www .deamuseum.org) in Pentagon City (across from the Pentagon City Metro stop).

On display are 150 years of drug and alcohol abuse paraphernalia, including bent spoons, bongs, hash pipes, hookahs, marijuana, photos, and old syringes. It also follows the history of the DEA and its predecessors, starting in 1906 when the government began regulating drugs. The display, contained in a narrow 2,200-square-foot room, is fairly small, and there is a gift shop, run by the Association of Former Federal Narcotics Agents Foundation. Just as the Mint doesn't give samples of the paper money it prints, the DEA museum doesn't offer drug samples. But you can pick up a DEA sweatshirt, coffee mug, miniature lapel badge, badges in Lucite, pens, key chains, or a Beanie bear with a DEA shirt. You also can drop off expired, unused, and unwanted prescription drugs during the annual take-back day in April (no questions asked about where, how, or why you obtained the drugs). The museum is open Tues through Fri from 10 a.m. to 4 p.m.

funfacts

The escalator at the Rosslyn Metro station is the third longest (194 feet, 8 inches) in the Washington, DC, Metro system and takes 140 seconds to ride. The two longer escalators are at Wheaton (230 feet) and Bethesda (213 feet, 10 inches), Maryland. The disks placed on the metal surface between the escalators were installed so people would not try to slide down them.

When you stop by the 17-acre *Lyndon Baines Johnson Memorial Grove,* off the George Washington Memorial Parkway, you will find white pine, dogwoods, numerous flowering bushes, and a tape recording of Lady Bird Johnson's remarks at the dedication ceremony in 1976. Her speech is played through an outdoor speaker installed at one end of the footbridge that connects the grove to the Pentagon parking lot. There is also a 43-ton obelisk that was brought in from Marble Falls Quarry, near the LBJ Ranch in Johnson City, Texas. It looks rough intentionally, just as Johnson was rough.

Five-sided News

The **Pentagon** is 3,705,793 square feet large, or twice the size of the Merchandise Mart in Chicago. There are 131 stairways, 19 escalators, 13 elevators, 17.5 miles of corridors (the Pentagon says it takes only 7 minutes to walk between any two points), 691 water fountains, and 284 restrooms. Guided 1-hour walking tours (yes, the guides walk backwards) are offered daily from 9 a.m. to 3 p.m. and start at the Pentagon Metro station entrance; reservations should be made from 8 to 90 days ahead of time. (703) 697-1776. More details are available at http://pentagon.afis.osd .mil/tour-guidelines.html.

The **Pentagon Memorial,** dedicated to the 184 people who died from the attack on September 11, 2001, is open to the public every day. Support staff is available from 10 a.m. to 8 p.m. during standard time and until 10 p.m. during daylight saving time. You reach it by following the marked path from the Pentagon Metro station. www .whs.mil/memorial.

Precious Stones

The 15-foot pinkish granite archway monument at 540 S. Washington St. in Falls Church honors two African Americans, *Joseph Tinner* and *Edwin B. Henderson,* who started the fight for civil rights in 1915. They founded what was the first rural NAACP branch. Tinner worked in a quarry, and the stone excavated there was used for the foundations of many Falls Church buildings. As they were demolished, local residents claimed the old stone and used it in their gardens. When the monument was approved, the residents gave up their stones to the tune of 16 tons from 26 different sites. Future plans for honoring these leaders include constructing a replica of the house where Tinner lived, on the then-called *Tinner Hill,* to be used as a black history museum. (703) 241-4109; www.tinnerhill.org.

There are no quotations or citations proclaiming Johnson's victories while in office. There are just peace and tranquility and natural beauty signifying the Johnsons' contribution to our national park system and the highway beautification program. For additional information, call the National Park Service, (703) 289-2500; www.nps.gov/lyba.

The *Upton Hill Regional Park Mini Golf Course* is where you'll find one of the longest minigolf holes in the world. The 140-foot hole is part of the course designed by Jim Bryant, one of the world's foremost designers of miniature golf courses. These holes have more exotic themes than you find in your normal miniature golf course.

The course is open seasonally and if that's not your favorite activity, you can enjoy the water park, bocce ball, horse shoes, hiking (three trails), batting cages, playground, picnicking, or just being in a wooden oasis that's a donut hole inside a severely heavily populated area. Fees are charged for admission and activities, often with residents receiving a discounted rate over non-residents. The main park is open year-round. 6060 Wilson Blvd., Arlington 22205; (703) 534-3437; www.nvrpa.org/park/upton_hill.

To get away from museums and traffic, stop by Arlington's *Bon Air Memorial Rose Garden,* with its selection of roses (more than 157 varieties, of which 32 have been awarded the American Rose Society's "E" award for Excellence), azaleas, ornamental tree garden, and wildflower area. The park isn't huge, but it's nice, and there are benches for sitting and enjoying the gardens. It is open from sunrise to a half hour after sunset. Wilson Boulevard and N. Lexington Avenue, Arlington; (703) 228-6525; www .arlingtonva.us.

Clarendon—a small corner of north Arlington, which until 1846 was the rest of the diamond shape of the District of Columbia—was named in 1899 for

Daisy, Daisy

At 100 feet wide, the **W&OD Trail** is one of the skinniest in all of Virginia. Measuring 45 miles of rails-to-trails path from Arlington to Purcellville for bikers, hikers, and others makes it one of the longest. It's accessible in Falls Church, Vienna, Reston, Herndon, and Leesburg. You may walk, hike, jog, bike, or in-line skate along the trail. Or horseback riders may use a bridle path that parallels the trail for 32.5 miles from Vienna to Purcellville. www.wodfriends.org. Check the site for tidbits about the railroad, towns along the trail, old houses within a long stone's throw of the trail, flora and fauna, and so much more.

the Earl of Clarendon (1609–1674). Catch the Metro (orange line) to Clarendon Station under the intersection of Fairfax Drive, Washington Boulevard, and Wilson Boulevard. Wander out to see the **American Legion War Memorial** monument, or go to the Court House stop and enjoy the variety of restaurants, pubs, coffeehouses, and shops reflecting the multiethnic (Japanese, Chinese, Korean, Moroccan, Indian, Cuban, Greek, Peruvian, Persian, Mexican, Irish, Salvadoran) population of the area.

Not far from the Virginia Square Station is the **Arlington Arts Center,** home of exhibits, classes, and live theater. 3550 Wilson Blvd., Arlington 22201; (703) 248-6800; www.arlingtonartscenter.org.

The **Ball-Sellers House,** a log house built around 1742, is Arlington's oldest residence and is believed to be typical of the way many early settlers lived in Colonial Virginia. John Ball built the one-room house on a 166-acre land grant, along Four Mile Run, from Lord Thomas Fairfax. It has a loft and an attached lean-to room at the rear that has its original logs, clapboard roof, and pegged floorboards. Ball, his wife, and their five daughters lived here until Ball's death in 1766. It was donated to the Arlington Historical Society in 1975; it's open Sat from 1 to 4 p.m., Apr through Oct and by appointment. There's no admission charge, but donations are appreciated. 5620 3rd St. South, Arlington 22210; (703) 379-2123; www.arlingtonhistorical society.org.

Alexandria

The **Alexandria Visitors Center at Ramsay House** (Alexandria Convention & Visitors Bureau) is the place to start your Alexandria touring. It's open daily 9 a.m. to 5 p.m. 221 King St., Alexandria 22314; (703) 746-3301 or (800) 388-9119; www.funside.com.

You can find a calendar of events, discount coupons, and special offers from Alexandria's shops and restaurants at www.holidaysinalexandria.com.

One of the biggest things to happen to the Alexandria area in years was the opening of **National Harbor and Gaylord National Resort and Convention Center,** which are actually across the Potomac River from Old Town. The **Potomac Riverboat Company** (www.potomacriverboatco.com) provides a shuttle service (fee) between the two destinations. The *Awakening* statue that used to grace Hains Point is now in the sand at National Harbor, and you can find a few one-of-a-kind shops there and in the Gaylord resort. Alexandria spent more than $2 million dollars to spruce up the marina and expand its marketing materials and services in anticipation of visitors from National Harbor.

If you enjoy walking tours and ghost tales, call **Alexandria Colonial Tours** for their "Ghosts & Graveyards" tour, presented from the first weekend in April through November. During the tour you'll hear legends, folklore, and twisted tales, starting with George Washington's time, and you'll end up in a cemetery! Tours are presented by colonial-clad guides. Other tours include a history tour of Alexandria, an African-American, Christmas, and Women's (the latter two about Washington). Group reservations are required. Call (703) 519-1749 or visit www.alexcolonialtours.com for additional information; or write 201 King St., 3rd Floor, Alexandria 22314.

As you wander around the historic section of town, you'll notice cobblestone streets (the 100 block of Prince Street and the 600 block of Princess Street), brick sidewalks, and vintage streetlamps. You can see the narrowest houses in Alexandria in the 400 block of Prince Street and the 500 block of Queen Street. These were alley houses built between two other houses. Sometimes they were called *"spite houses"* or *"mother-in-law houses."*

Alexandria features an architectural style that may be unique, called a **Flounder house.** A typical house was cut in half the long way, was usually much taller and narrower than normal, and was probably built to satisfy a provision of the sale of the lots that the property would be improved within two years. People who envisioned building something grander started with the Flounder, which became a minor wing when the larger front part was constructed. The original section usually was

phoning it in

Northern Virginia phones have been assigned to one of two area codes, 703 and 571 (703 being the original code). All telephone calls to and from Northern Virginia phones must include the area code (but not a "1"), even if you're calling across the street or next door.

built without windows because of taxes on glass. Besides the Flounder house, you can find examples of Georgian (starting about 1700 and ending around the time of the Revolutionary War), Federal (late 18th century), Greek Revival (late 1840s), Victorian (1860–1900), Gothic Revival, Italianate (1820–1885), Second Empire (1885–1900), Richardson Romanesque (1880–1900), and Queen Anne (1880–1910) architecture.

After the exhausting sightseeing and shopping, stop by **Hank's Oyster Bar,** a new restaurant operated by chef/owner Jamie Leeds. In September 2010 Jamie announced a partnership with Bruce Wood and Kenny Hobar of Dragon Creek in Montrose, Virginia, whereby the guys would help develop an oyster in Nomini Creek that is unique to Hank's. They're also collecting the oyster shells to be returned to local waters to help repopulate the oyster crop. Because the creek has a low salinity factor, the oyster has a wonderfully sweet flavor, great for on the half-shell, baked, or fried. 1026 King St., Alexandria 22314; (703) 739-HANK (4265); www.hanksdc.com.

One of the most widely imitated art forms is the transformation of an old factory into an arts center. One of the first was the **Torpedo Factory Arts Center** (a 1918 factory where torpedo shell cases were manufactured), housing more than 80 artists and 6 galleries in 3 floors of studio space. You can buy original artwork (weavings, paintings, musical instruments, pots, prints, sculptures, jewelry, glassworks, and photographs), talk with the artists, attend lectures, take art classes, and take part in a variety of other activities. You can also see an MK-14 torpedo on display on the first floor. An annual jury for studio space is held each March. All artists working in fine arts and fine crafts are eligible. The Torpedo Factory Arts Center, 105 N. Union St., Alexandria 22314, is open daily 10 a.m. to 5 p.m. and until 9 p.m. on Thurs, except major holidays. Studio and gallery hours vary; (703) 838-4565; www.torpedofactory.org.

The **Alexandria Archaeology Museum** and research lab (105 N. Union St., #327, Alexandria 22314) are located on the third floor of the Torpedo

Public Art

Three Metro stations in Northern Virginia feature public arts projects. At the **Huntington station** (yellow line), you'll see **Metropolitan Scene,** a painted mural about urban congestion and mass transit efficiency, by David Chung, installed in 1990. The **Rosslyn station** (orange and blue lines) has another David Chung–painted mural that's 88 feet by 4 feet portraying stylized images of local architecture, installed in 2000. Elizabeth Ryland Mears created the stained and architectural glass panels titled **Tunnel of Light** installed at the **Franconia-Springfield station** in 2004.

It's a Photo Moment

I'm always looking for that perfect or unusual photo, particularly when it comes to views of Washington. If you didn't see enough of the Washington skyline as you landed at Reagan National Airport (perhaps you came in from the south approach or you were on an inside seat, or maybe you drove), there are some great spots with amazing views of downtown Washington, with its marble monuments and greenery. Try *Freedom Park;* the *Iwo Jima Memorial; Arlington House at Arlington Cemetery;* the *Windows Over Washington* restaurant (dinner on Sat and Sun evenings only) on the 14th floor of the Doubletree Hotel in Arlington; and the *Vantage Point Restaurant and Lounge* at the Holiday Inn Rosslyn. The *George Washington Masonic National Memorial,* the most visible sight in Alexandria, also provides a most spectacular view of the city and of Washington, DC, 6 miles away. You'll want to bring your widest and longest camera lenses to shoot from the observation tower of this 333-foot building.

Factory Arts Center. In addition to the rotating exhibits on the archaeological history of the area, they might have a Family Dig Day where children, their families, and friends enjoy a hands-on experience with the past while screening for artifacts on an excavation site. Two weeklong day camps are held in the summer for 12- to 15-year-olds. The museum is open Tues through Fri 10 a.m. to 3 p.m., Sat 10 a.m. to 5 p.m., and Sun 1 to 5 p.m. There is no admission fee. Call (703) 838-4399 for more information or visit www.alexandriava .gov/archaeology.

The *Alexandria Old Town Farmers' Market,* on the south plaza of City Hall at 301 King St., was established in the original lot sale of July 1749, when two lots were designated for the purpose. The farmers' market started in 1753 and is said to be the nation's oldest continually operating market. George Washington, born near Fredericksburg, spent his young adult life in this area and is said to have sent produce here to be sold. The market moves indoors during winter to the lobby of City Hall. Farmers come early, about 5 a.m., as do wise shoppers. You might see notices that it's open until 11 a.m., but by that time your selections will be slim, if any. For more information call (703) 746-3200; http://alexandriava.gov.

Four other farmers' markets worth checking out include *Del Ray Farmers' Market* (E. Oxford and Mount Vernon Avenue) on Sat from 8 a.m. to noon; *Four Mile Run Farmers' and Artisans Market,* (4109 Mount Vernon Ave.) on Sunday mornings from April 1 through October 31; *Upper King Street Fresh Farmers' Market* (1806 King St. at King Street Gardens Park) on Wednesday afternoons from May through October; and the *West End*

Farmers' Market (4800 Brenman Park Dr. at Ben Brenman Park) on Sunday mornings from May through November.

John Gadsby was an Englishman who operated a tavern and an inn in the late 18th century. What is now *Gadsby's Tavern* was the center of all that was political, social, and commercial. Meetings, dances, and theatrical and musical presentations all found a home here. Dentists treated their patients here, and merchants sold their wares.

The buildings were used as a tavern and hotel until the late 19th century and then housed a variety of businesses, eventually falling into disrepair and near-demolition. Fortunately the American Legion Post 24 bought and saved the buildings in 1929, but it wasn't until 1972 that they were given to the city of Alexandria.

Both structures, restored to their late-18th-century splendor, are open for viewing, and an Early American–style restaurant serves visitors in three of the tavern rooms.

The *Gadsby's Tavern Museum* is open Tues through Sat 10 a.m. to 5 p.m., and Sun and Mon 1 to 5 p.m. from Apr through Oct; Wed through Sat 11 a.m. to 4 p.m. and Sun 1 to 4 p.m. Nov through Mar. Guided tours are offered at quarter past and quarter of the hour and last 30 minutes, with the final tour starting 15 minutes before closing. Gadsby's has been raising funds for interpretive signs and other improvements to the ice well area so a raffle was held in the winter of 2010–11 to see who could guess when a large ice block, covered with straw and otherwise protected with 18th century methods would melt. Prizes for the winning ticket included diamonds, crystal, and icy drinks. The progress was visible through the museum's webcam on their website.

Admission to the museum is $5 for adults; $3 for children (5 through 12); with discounts to AAA members, Gadsby's Tavern restaurant diners, and those who have coupons issued by other museums. Society members, AAM members, and Alexandria City employees are free. 134 N. Royal St., Alexandria 22314; (703) 838-4242; http://oha.alexandriava.gov/gadsby.

Civil War history buffs will delight in visiting *Fort Ward Museum and Historic Site.* Because Virginia was a Southern state, Union troops occupied Alexandria and Arlington Heights at the beginning of the war. They began construction of 162 earthen forts around Washington, with Fort Ward the fifth largest of the fortifications and supply bases. Named for Commander James Harmon Ward, the first Union naval officer to be killed in the war, the fort had 36 guns mounted in 5 bastions.

Major preservation work started on the fort in 1961 as part of a Civil War Centennial project (boy, 50 years sure have flown by). The Northwest Bastion was restored, with a reconstructed ceremonial gate marking the entrance to the fort. Young soldiers can let their imaginations go wild with the defense displayed here. A reconstructed Officers' Hut represents a typical fort dwelling of that time.

Exhibits on a number of Civil War subjects are in the museum, which was opened in 1964. Interpretive programs, tours, and lectures are offered throughout the year.

The museum is open Tues through Sat 10 a.m. to 5 p.m. and Sun noon to 5 p.m. The historic site is open daily 9 a.m. to sunset. There is no admission charge, but donations are accepted. 4301 W. Braddock Rd., Alexandria 22304; (703) 746-4848; http://alexandriava.gov/historic/fortward/default.aspx.

The Americana in the *Collingwood Library of and Museum on Americanism* deals with patriotism and the collection includes copies of the US Constitution, a Sioux chief's headdress, presidential china, and a library of about 7,000 books on military history. The books are available for research.

Originally part of George Washington's farm, the estate eventually was divided for a streetcar line and then Mount Vernon Parkway, built in 1932. The building was converted into this library and opened in 1977. It is named for British Admiral Lord Cuthbert Collingwood, the hero of the Battle of Trafalgar.

The museum is located at Collingwood on the Potomac, 8301 E. Boulevard Dr., Alexandria 22308. It is open Mon and Wed through Sat 10 a.m. to 4 p.m., and Sun 1 to 4 p.m. There is no admission charge. Guided tours are available and last as long as you're interested. The museum is wheelchair accessible. Call (703) 765-1652 or visit www.collingwoodlibrary.com for additional information.

The *George Washington Masonic National Memorial* houses a collection about Washington's life from his days as a surveyor to his first inauguration. Over the front doors is a frieze of Washington in profile. The main lobby features two 46-by-18-foot murals by Allyn Cox, one depicting the laying of the cornerstone of the United States Capitol in September 1793, and one of General Washington at a religious service on St. John's Day 1778 in Christ Church, Philadelphia. There's a 17-foot-3-inch bronze statue of George Washington in the Memorial Hall and a collection of Washington memorabilia, including the clock that stopped by itself when he died, the family Bible, and sabers used at his funeral. The auditorium is surrounded by granite columns and bronze medallions of the US presidents who have been Freemasons. The Parade Room contains an elaborate display of a mechanical parade of miniature uniformed Shrine Units.

The memorial is open Mon through Sat, 10 a.m. to 4 p.m. and on Sun from noon to 4 p.m., from October 1 through March 31, and opens at 9 a.m. Mon through Sat the rest of the year. Admission to the first and second floor exhibits is free and $5 per adult for the tower exhibits and observation deck. Guided 1-hour tours are offered Mon through Sat at 10 and 11:30 a.m. and 1:30 and 3 p.m. and at noon and 1:30 and 3 p.m. on Sun. Groups should reserve at least two weeks in advance.

There's plenty of free parking, and it's also within walking distance (uphill) of the King Street Metro station. Although it is not wheelchair accessible, Masons visiting the shrine will be helped by the brothers. The memorial is at 101 Callahan Dr., atop Shooters Hill at the west end of King Street, Alexandria 22301; (703) 683-2007; www.gwmemorial.org.

The town of **Del Ray,** which celebrated its 100th anniversary in 2008, has been cited as an exceptional living community. One of its successful ventures is First Thursday, held from 6 to 9 p.m. from May through Sept, when Del Ray throws a community theme party. You should notice the red caboose on the grounds of the Mount Vernon Community School, a salute to the 1890s, when Del Ray became the home of the first interurban streetcar (and probably the first commuting suburb) in the United States. Perhaps the latest buzzword has no historical significance and, yet, "Meet me at the Egg" refers to a new 15-ton marble and limestone sculpture called **Three Eggs in Space,** created by Karen Bailey. Contact the Delray Citizens Association; www.delraycitizen.org.

As you travel through the enclave, make sure you stop by **Artfully Chocolate** featuring Kingsbury Confections. It's an art gallery, orchid shop, and purveyor of all things chocolate, including a cocoa bar and production kitchen, and a new shop, **Artful Chef,** which sells kitchen supplies and ingredients for working and cooking with chocolate.

There are lots of art galleries in Alexandria, so owner Eric Nelson knew he had to do something different. He teamed with Rob Kingsbury of Kingsbury Chocolates, some other artisan chocolatiers, and Mothers Macaroons to create this heavenly smelling shop. Edward Hart, his partner, wanted orchids, so they were included. Look for chocolate in the shape of voodoo dolls, golf balls, crayons, racing cars, roses, and more. Or you can try the chocolate smoothies, chocolate-scented spa products, and books extolling the wonders of chocolate. Then, they opened **Artfully Paper** a few blocks away. It specializes in cards, origami, and art. The shop is open Tues through Thurs and Sun from 10 a.m. to 9 p.m.; Fri and Sat from 10 a.m. to 10 p.m. 2003A Mt. Vernon Ave., Alexandria 22301; (703) 635-7917; www.artfullychocolate.com.

Still another viewpoint of the area can be found along the **Mount Vernon Trail,** which parallels the George Washington Memorial Parkway from Mount

Vernon to Theodore Roosevelt Island in the Potomac River. Starting south at the **Arlington Memorial Bridge** (dedicated in 1932 to symbolize the union of the North and South following the Civil War and connecting the Lincoln Memorial to the Lee home), you'll go past the **Lyndon Baines Johnson Memorial Grove** in Lady Bird Johnson Park; the **Navy-Marine Memorial** (the Ernesto Begni del Platta statue honoring Americans who served at sea, dedicated in 1934); **Gravelly Point,** which is a terrific place to view the takeoffs and landings at Reagan National Airport; **Old Town Alexandria; Jones Point Lighthouse** (in service from 1836 to 1925); and **Dyke Marsh** (a 240-acre wetland where more than 250 species of birds have been sighted). You can catch a look at **Fort Washington** (on the Maryland side) and end at **Mount Vernon.** Volunteers patrol the trail on bike periodically, usually more frequently on the weekends and super gorgeous days. They can help with questions, remind you about the helmet laws, and assist with minor first aid situations.

You can walk, jog, or bike the length of this 18.5-mile trail or just parts of it. Three areas along the trail are quite steep and might be a little strenuous for new bikers. There are plenty of places to picnic and to enjoy nature and history, and a physical fitness course helps you vary the type of exercise you're doing. Call (703) 289-2500 or visit www.nps.gov/gwmp/mtvernontrail.htm. Check with **Big Wheel Bikes** in Old Town, (703) 739-2300; www.bigwheel bikes.com/alexandria.htm about renting a bike for an hour or a day.

Among the numerous Alexandria cemeteries is the **African-American Heritage Park.** There are 6 identified headstones of about 21 burials that took place here. The wetlands part of the cemetery is a home for mallards,

Designer Library

Virginia has a Michael Graves–designed library—quite a difference from the structured architecture of Old Town Alexandria, and one you're sure to remember. The **Charles E. Beatley Jr. Central Library** (named after the city's long-serving mayor, who died in December 2003) is located at the intersection of Duke and Pickett Streets, south of the Old Holmes Run Channel. At 60,200 square feet, it's more than twice as large as the Barrett Branch, which had been the central library. Special features include a full-service library for the blind, speaking computer terminals with OptiVoice artificial speech and enlarged type capabilities, and dataports at carrels for personal laptops. The precast stone clock on the south side, the Duke Street facade, weighs 5 tons. The library is open Mon through Thurs, 9 a.m. to 9 p.m., Fri, 9 a.m. to 6 p.m., Sat, 9 a.m. to 5 p.m., and Sun, 1 to 5 p.m., if you want to view the interior. The library is at 5005 Duke St., Alexandria 22304; (703) 746-1702; www.alexandria .lib.va.us/branches/beatley.html.

painted turtles, beavers, and crayfish. ***Truths that Rise from the Roots Remembered,*** a bronze sculpture of trees by Jerome Meadows, is a tribute to the contribution of African Americans to Alexandria. A number of other statues are placed throughout the cemetery. The park is located at 902 Wythe St., Alexandria 22314, and is open during daylight hours. The museum is open Tues through Sat, 10 a.m. to 4 p.m. and admission is $2. (703) 746-4356; http:// alexandriava.gov/blackhistory.

It isn't often that you can see what a Quaker pharmacy of 200 years ago looked like, but you can at the ***Stabler-Leadbeater Apothecary Shop.*** Edward Stabler opened his shop in 1792, when Alexandria was a bustling port city with about 300 homes. The family operated the business through the War of 1812, an 1821 yellow fever epidemic, the Civil War, the Spanish-American War, and World War I, before succumbing to the Great Depression and closing the store in 1933.

Fortunately, Stabler was a master pack rat; miraculously, more than 8,000 herbs, potions, pill rollers, mortars and pestles, drug mills, medical glassware, documents, journals, letters, and paper labels are still around. Volunteers have gone through the boxes of deteriorating books and letters, finding a note from Martha Washington, a letter to Robert E. Lee, prescriptions for curing everything from gout to hams, and much more. Among the changes that took place over the lifetime of the apothecary are the introduction of prescription forms, the hypodermic needle, pills, and controlled-substance regulations. This is the only old apothecary museum in the country where the shop sold retail, wholesale, and manufactured products. It is open Tues through Sat from 10 a.m. to 5 p.m. and on Sun and Mon from 1 to 5 p.m., from Apr through Oct; it's open Wed through Sat from 11 a.m. to 4 p.m. and Sun from 1 to 4 p.m. the rest of the year. The admission fee is $5 for adults and $3 for children (5 through 12); children under 5 are free, or buy a multi-site pass if you'll be visiting other historic sites. 105–107 S. Fairfax St., Alexandria 22314; (703) 746-3852; http://alexandriava.gov/apothecary.

George Washington's Mount Vernon Estate and Gardens is one of the more popular "off the beaten path" sites in Northern Virginia. Frequent special events make a visit even more interesting and delightful. Here are just a few:

In February you can have "breakfast with George" on the weekend around his birthday. His favorite breakfast is said to have been "hoecakes swimming in butter and honey," and you can sample this delicacy (while supplies last) and then participate in "America's Smallest Hometown Parade" in the afternoon. Enjoy a fife-and-drum corps, 18th-century music, and wish the "General" a happy birthday. Admission is free if you're named George or if your birthday is February 22. Yes, if your name is Martha or you were born on June 2, you also receive free admission on that day. Mrs. Washington is available for photographs on Mother's Day in May and shares her thoughts on motherhood in the late 18th century.

As noted in the introduction, there are more than 190 wineries throughout Virginia, and more than a dozen of them are featured at the Spring Wine Festival and Sunset Tour in mid-May. Samples are offered, accompanied by live jazz music, and the rarely opened wine cellar can be toured. Another wine festival is held in the fall.

July Fourth, as can be imagined, is a daylong celebration with patriotic music, a reading of the Declaration of Independence (by "George" himself), a band concert, and birthday cake (while supplies last).

By far, the annual 18th-century **Craft Fair,** held in mid-September, is one of the highlights of the year. You can watch Colonial-attired crafters create baskets, leather goods, woodcarvings, paper cuttings, and other items from the period, and you can buy them for a most unusual souvenir.

Mount Vernon is a constantly changing destination, so if you saw it 10 or 20 years ago, it's different now. "Mount Vernon is now the only site in the country that shows how whiskey was made in the 18th century," said Jim Rees, executive director of Mount Vernon. "But more important, the Distillery is a colorful, interesting way for visitors to learn about George Washington as farmer and entrepreneur."

Fans of *National Treasure: Book of Secrets* crowded Mount Vernon for the first few weeks of 2008 as the tour included the tunnel-like cellar where Nicholas Cage kidnaps the president. This was so popular they now offer an entire *National Treasure* tour that includes information about the filming. It's available at 9:30 and 11:30 a.m. and 1 and 3 p.m. from March 1 through October 31, and at 11 a.m. and 1 p.m. the rest of the year. This tour fills up quickly, so purchase your ticket online.

Sealed with a Kiss

Postage stamp collectors probably are familiar with the work of **Howard Paine** of Delaplane. Paine was involved in the design or as art director for such stamps as the one dedicated to jazz (issued March 26, 2011), Kansas statehood (issued January 27, 2011), Raoul Wallenberg, big bands, and the Leonard Bernstein commemorative stamp issued on July 10, 2001. The first US postage stamp to honor the favorite pastime of cruciverbalists was issued in February 1998 as part of the Celebrate the Century series. The stamp was issued to commemorate the publication of the first crossword puzzle and is in the sheet for the decade of 1910 to 1919. Paine designed this stamp also.

Mount Vernon is open daily from 8 a.m. to 5 p.m. Apr through Aug; 9 a.m. to 5 p.m. Mar, Sept, and Oct; and 9 a.m. to 4 p.m. Nov through Feb. Note: That's at least an hour earlier than other attractions, so if you're an early riser and want to cram as much as possible into your sightseeing day, start with Mount Vernon. Adult admission is $15, senior tickets (62 and above) are $14, and children 6 through 11 (with an adult) are $7. An annual pass is $25 for adults and an additional $10 for a youth annual pass. Check the site for discount options. (703) 780-2000 or (703) 799-8121 (TDD); www.mount vernon.org.

Washington's Gristmill is a reconstruction of George Washington's 1772 stone mill on Dogue Creek, built when the creek was still navigable. Located in the George Washington's Gristmill Historic State Park, it's in a beautiful scenic setting, just 3 miles from Mount Vernon. The mill has a 16-foot waterwheel and millstones that weigh a thousand pounds each. The foundation cornerstone of Washington's mill is shown at the beginning of the tour. During the careful excavation, part of the wheel, bearings for the wheel, part of the trundlehead, complete wheel buckets, and other items were found. Open daily 10 a.m. to 5 p.m. April 1 through October 31, the mill is at 5514 Mount Vernon Memorial Hwy., Mount Vernon 22079. Regular admission is $4 for adults and $2 for children, or you can buy a joint Mount Vernon and gristmill ticket for $2 more for adults and $1.50 for children. www.mountvernon.org/visit/plan/index.cfm/pid/356/.

Okay, **Dulles International Airport** isn't exactly off the beaten path (unless you live in Maryland and then it seems like the other side of the world) and millions of people fly into and out of this facility annually. However, the AeroTrain (not to be confused with airport architect Eero Saarinen) started operation in late January 2010, so it's new if you haven't been there in a while. The train system consumed about $1.5 billion and is designed to whisk you between plane and terminal more quickly than the previous mobile lounges (they will be used for international flights). The underground system will depart from the "B" gate station and slink along underground until just past the "C" gates. From there, you will take a people mover back to the "C" gates. This was done in anticipation of more "C" gates being added at some future time. Construction of the almost 4-mile-long network took 8 years. www.metwash airports.com/dulles.

However, thousands shun the airport physically to flock to the Smithsonian Institution's National Air and Space Museum's facility for the display and preservation of its collection of historic aviation and space artifacts. Named the **Steven F. Udvar–Hazy Center** (the museum's major donor), this new space provides display room for a lot of things that couldn't be included in the

Smithsonian's National Air and Space Museum on the National Mall in Washington, DC. It opened in December 2003 in honor of the 100th anniversary of the Wright brothers' first powered flight.

There are more than 80 aircraft and dozens of space artifacts here, including an SR-71 Blackbird reconnaissance aircraft, the Dash 80 prototype of the Boeing 707, the Superfortress *Enola Gay,* and a deHavilland Chipmunk, which is an aerobatic plane.

A 2011 addition to the collection is the **Space Shuttle Discovery.** As the longest-serving orbiter in the shuttle fleet, it will be prepared and then delivered to the James S. McDonnell Space Hangar. It will replace the Space Shuttle *Enterprise,* which will be moved to the Intrepid Sea, Air and Space Museum in New York City.

You can walk among the artifacts on the floor and look into space or stroll along skyways to see the hanging displays. Some of the airliners, engines, helicopters, rockets, satellites, ultralights, and experimental flying machines are on display for the first time in a museum setting. There's also the **Donald D. Engen Observation Tower** (164 feet high) for a view of the area and planes taking off and landing, and an IMAX theater. If you've contributed to this museum, you should be able to find your name on a permanent memorial at the entrance.

There is no admission fee to the museum, which is open daily from 10 a.m. to 5:30 p.m. except December 25. There is a fee for the IMAX films; tickets can be purchased online. Parking is available for $15 a car. 14390 Air & Space Museum Pkwy., Chantilly 20151; (202) 633-1000; www.nasm.si.edu.

Outside Washington

In May 1997 the renovated 3-story brick *Aldie Mill* was opened to the public on a regular basis for the first time since 1981. Now, every Sat from noon to 5 p.m. and Sun from 1 to 5 p.m. spring through Oct, tours are given through the 1807 mill, showing the early machinery used to grind wheat and corn. Further work has been and continues to be done, including clearing of the head and tail races, stabilizing the archaeological sites, and creating pedestrian trails and interpretive signs. The Aldie Mill, which was restored in October 2010 with help from the Loudoun Preservation Society, is Virginia's only known gristmill powered by twin overshot wheels (the water pours over the wheel, making the wheel

funfacts

The two-lane Aldie Stone Bridge, crossing Little River on US 50, was constructed in 1824 and is one of two stone bridges still in use in Loudoun County.

turn forward, instead of "down" the wheel, which would make it turn backward). Admission is $4 for adults and $2 for seniors and children. The Aldie Mill is located west of Aldie on US 50; 39401 John Mosby Hwy., Aldie 20105; (703) 327-9777; www.nvrpa.org/park/aldie_mill_historic_park.

Within the historic district known as Leesburg is the historic **Norris House Inn,** built in 1760. Carol and Roger Healey now offer bed-and-breakfast accommodations, with full use of the dining room, parlor, library, sunroom, and a rambling veranda overlooking the gardens. The bedrooms are appointed with antiques and brass and feather 4-poster beds, and 3 guest rooms have working fireplaces. Tea service is available on weekend afternoons in the inn's compound in the Old Stone House Tea Room. Guests may use the fitness facilities (indoor pool, fitness room, gym, etc.) at the nearby Ida Lee Park Recreation Center for free. Room rates run from $110 for a weeknight to $199 a night on weekends, including a full country breakfast. Special weekday and weekly rates are available. The inn is located at 108 Loudoun St. Southwest, Leesburg 20175; (703) 777-1806 or (800) 644-1806; www.norrishouse.com.

Since 1833, ferryboats have been moving travelers across the Potomac River between **White's Ferry** (on the Maryland side) and the Leesburg, Virginia, area. There used to be 100 ferries crossing the Potomac; this is the only one left. It used to be known as Conrad's Ferry, but after the Civil War a Confederate officer, Colonel Elija V. White, bought and renamed it. For three decades the *Jubal Early* (named for the Confederate general) carried about six cars a trip, but the demand became so heavy that owner Malcolm Brown installed a new 30-ton vessel in mid-1988 that can carry as many as 24 cars.

The ferry is propelled by a small diesel boat on the upriver side. When the ferry reaches the far side, the ferry pilot casts off a line, and the current carries the small boat around to point it in the right direction for the return trip. There is a general store on the Maryland side, open only in summer.

The ferry charge is $4 for cars one-way or $6 round-trip (50 cents for pedestrians, $1 for bicyclists, and $2 for motorcycles), and the ferry operates

Who's Bluffing Now?

On October 21, 1861, troops from the North and the South met at **Ball's Bluff,** outside of Leesburg, for one of the first Union battle disasters of the war. There are 25 graves holding the remains of 53 unknowns and one known (grave 13) soldier. The Ball's Bluff Battlefield and National Cemetery is the smallest national cemetery in the nation and is open from dawn to dusk. Guided tours are offered on weekends from early May through October. Ball's Bluff Road, Leesburg; (703) 779-9372; www.nps .gov/nr/travel/journey/bnc.htm.

A Rustic Retreat

Despite the mini-skyscraper and multi-mall population of Tysons Corner, you have only to go to Loudoun County for a taste of the rustic and a wooded view of the Potomac River. In *Algonkian Park,* just 15 miles west of Tysons Corner, are a dozen furnished, air-conditioned cabins accommodating four to 10 people. There are decks for watching the scenery and fully equipped kitchens. Relax in a unit with a fireplace or one of the more elegant models, complete with hot tub. Can't unwind quite that much? There's an 18-hole golf course, boat landing, large swimming pool, and miniature golf within walking distance. Rentals start at $135, Mon through Thurs, and from $140 on weekends. 47001 Fairway Dr., Sterling 20165; (703) 450-4655; www.nvrpa.org/algonkian.

on call from 5 a.m. to 11 p.m. daily as water levels permit. Call (301) 349-5200 to be sure the ferry is in service, unless you're just planning to take a pretty ride and you're not dependent upon the ferry taking you across the river. Take US 15 north out of Leesburg to the signs. 24801 White's Ferry Rd., Dickerson, Maryland 20842; (301) 349-5200; http://canal.mcmullans.org/whites_ferry.htm.

Fairfax County

The *Fairfax Museum and Visitor Center* is housed in the former Fairfax Elementary School, built in 1873. It was the first 2-story school in Fairfax County and is listed on the National Register of Historic Places. This is where you can see fascinating exhibits on the area's history, sign up for walking tours of the historic district (spring and fall), and obtain information about places to visit and shop and where to eat and stay. The center is open daily from 9 a.m. to 5 p.m. 10209 Main St., Fairfax 22030; (703) 385-8414 or (800) 545-7950; www.fairfaxva.gov/museumvc/mvc.asp.

The *Fairfax Station Railroad Museum* includes, naturally enough, a museum of railroad memorabilia, complete with a Norfolk & Western railroad line caboose. Clara Barton, founder of the Red Cross, nursed many Civil War wounded on a neighboring hill, and there's an exhibit area dedicated to her pioneering work. One of the most enjoyable parts of the museum is when a group of "N" gauge railroaders from the Northern Virginia NTRAK club come in every Sunday to display their trains from 1 to 4 p.m. Constructed in the 1850s, the museum opened in 1989 and is open regularly on the third Sun of the month from 1 to 4 p.m. Admission is $2 for adults and $1 for children (4 to 10). The museum, which is wheelchair accessible, is located at 11200 Fairfax

Station Rd., Fairfax Station 22039 (look for the caboose in the front yard); (703) 425-9225; www.fairfax-station.org.

Transportation is as important today as it was years ago as evidenced by the expansion of the *Metro* system to Dulles International Airport. Even as earth was dug and rails were laid, the Fairfax County Board of Supervisors was working on the names of the eight new stations so they reflect the geographical features and be no longer than 19 characters. As of March 2011, the selected names are Tysons-McLean, Tysons I & II, Spring Hill Road, Reston-Wiehle Avenue, Reston Town Center, Herndon- Reston West, and Herndon-Dulles East. From that selection process, the names had to be approved by the Metro board of directors. A recent estimate I saw said changing a station name costs about $400,000 (maps, signs, website, etc.), so they want to make sure it's right. That also explains why the Waterfront-SEU station still carries that name even though Southeastern University closed in 2009. (202) 637-7000; www.wmata.com.

Combining beauty, conservation, education, and more, the 95-acres of *Meadowlark Visitor Botanical Gardens* have large ornamental gardens, native plants (including wildflowers), walking trails, lakes, shade garden, gazebos, and so much more. Within the visitor center are displays about conservation and plant diversity with an indoor tropical garden in the atrium—great for meetings and events. The latest to-do has been the establishment of a Korean bell garden, funded by the Korean American Cultural Committee (to the tune of about $1 million). The garden will have Korean trees, a meandering path, and, as you might imagine, a bell pavilion and bell. Check their schedule for gardening and horticulture workshops, field trips, and other activities. 9750 Meadowlark Gardens Ct., Vienna 22182; (703) 255-3631; www.nvrpa.org/park/meadowlark_botanical_gardens.

As you head west toward Dulles International Airport, you travel past a lot of shopping centers (areas that were corner grocery stands just a few years ago)

Blast from the Past

Nostalgia buffs might want to visit the *29 Diner* in Fairfax, built in 1947 and listed on the National Register of Historic Places. Clad in blue and silver porcelain enamel and stainless steel, the interior is complete with a marble counter and terrazzo floor. Blue Naugahyde seats, tile, and Formica highlight the decor. It's had a storied past that seems to have settled a little bit, but the details on the diner's website make for fascinating reading. The diner is open 24 hours a day, 7 days a week, except from 10 p.m. to 6 a.m. Mon night through Tues morning. 10536 Lee Hwy. (Route 29), Fairfax 22030; (703) 591-6720; www.29diner.com.

A Town of Firsts

Clifton, a town of about 200 people (although other residential areas nearby have glommed onto the Clifton zip code for its cachet), located at the junction of the railroad tracks and Route 645, southwest of Fairfax, was the first community in the area to have electricity—from the Bull Run Power Company—in 1925. It also had the first high school whose students commuted by train from other parts of Fairfax County.

and brainy think tanks. But you can spend a day at ***Colvin Run Mill Park*** and not begin to realize you're only moments away from the hustle and bustle of the commercial Tysons Corner area. This is a particularly good place to bring preschoolers on puppet show day, where the docent will speak of the Little Red Hen who took her grain to the miller; you'll meet Marvin the Miller, Fred the Farmer, Matilda the farmer's wife, and Alvin the Apprentice and discuss where grain comes from and how it's ground into flour.

The restored early-19th-century mill usually is in operation (call to make sure, if that's the primary reason for your visit), and you can tour a miller's house (built by Philip Carper), walk through a dairy barn, and stop to buy a few things from the general store.

Programs include grain grinding on the first and third Sun of Apr through Oct from noon to 3 p.m., blacksmithing demonstrations on Sat from 11 a.m. to 2 p.m., ghost tales around Halloween time, spring and fall dulcimer concerts, and fall scarecrow making. There are also beautiful picnic grounds and ducks to feed.

Colvin Run Mill Park is located off Leesburg Pike (Highway 7) at 10017 Colvin Run Rd., Great Falls 22066, 5 miles west of Tysons Corner. It's open daily except Tues, 11 a.m. to 4 p.m., from Mar through Dec; until 4 p.m. in Jan and Feb, with tours starting on the hour and the last tour starting at 3 p.m. The tours cost $6 for adults, $5 for students 16 years and up with ID, $4 for seniors (65 and up) and children younger than 16. For more information call (703) 759-2771 or visit www.co.fairfax.va.us/parks/crm.

Prince William County

From Occoquan on the east to Manassas on the west, from the storyteller of George Washington's life to the largest tourist attraction in the state (yes, ***Potomac Mills Outlet Mall*** attracts as many as a quarter of a million shoppers in a weekend) to Civil War battlefields, Prince William County has just about everything a traveler could want. There are two welcome centers. One is located in Occoquan, just off I-95, at 200 Mill St., (703) 491-4045. A second is located in the western part of the county at 9431 West St., in the Railroad Depot; (703) 361-6599. Both are open daily from 9 a.m. to 5 p.m. www.visit pwc.com.

Now head south on I-95, where in addition to Potomac Mills, the outlet and off-price shopping mall with more than 200 stores and more visitors than any other place in all of Virginia, you can stop by the **Veterans Memorial Park.** It has a picnic area, lighted tennis and volleyball courts, ball fields, soccer fields, horseshoe pits, a playground area, a 50-meter outdoor pool and a water slide, hiking, and a community center where classes are offered. A roller hockey league is scheduled for practice and competition. And it's wheelchair accessible. You'll see lots of four-wheeling here, but it's of the skateboard variety. At the Scott D. Eagles skateboard facility, dedicated to a man who died young but immensely enjoyed his skateboarding while he was here (no, he didn't die of a skateboard accident), there are 7,200 square feet of bowls, bumps, moguls, a half-pipe, and smooth surfaces with sidewalk and street features for urban skaters. For those who've always wanted to try skateboarding but were reluctant to invest, skateboards can be rented at the park.

Located at 14300 Featherstone Rd., Woodbridge 22191, the park is open daily year-round during daylight hours, except in bad weather. The ranger office is closed on federal holidays; (703) 491-2183; www.pwcparks.org/vetspark.

For a very long time, the Washington area was known as the dinner theater capital of the world, well, maybe the country. The area had more dinner theaters per capita than any other region. Most of them are gone now, but

Order in the Court

The old **Prince William County Courthouse** in Brentsville started service in 1822 when there were 19 homes, 3 stores, 2 taverns, 1 house of entertainment, a church, and the clerk's office and jail located in this town, the geographic center of the county. At the time there were 130 people, including 3 attorneys and 3 physicians, residing in the area. The town served as the county seat from 1820 to 1894. During the Civil War the courthouse roof was destroyed and court records were burned for fuel. By 1894 the county seat had been moved to Manassas. Restoration of the courthouse has been under way for a few years, and the restored cupola was placed on top on December 17, 2001. The Brentsville Historic Trust estimated the exterior repairs will run about $1 million. 12239 Bristow Rd., P.O. Box 732, Bristow 20136; (703) 792-6600; www.brentsville.org.

The Stone Age

The trim on the **Aquia Episcopal Church,** which celebrated its semiquincentennial anniversary in 2001, is made of Aquia sandstone, or Aquia stone, also called free-stone because it could be freely carved in any direction. Aquia sandstone was also used for the original US Capitol—the center section with the dome—Mount Vernon, Gunston Hall, and some Philadelphia bridges. The church is on the National Historic Landmark register. 2938 Jefferson Davis Hwy., US 1, Stafford 22555; (540) 659-4007; www.aquiachurch.com.

luckily the *Lazy Susan Dinner Theater* (10712 Richmond Hwy., Woodbridge 22190) remains. It offers pleasant family entertainment—mostly musicals, but the 2011 season includes *Big River: The Adventures of Huckleberry Finn, Nunsense, Pirates of Penzance,* and *A Christmas Carol.* This has been a restaurant since the mid-1950s, when each table had a lazy Susan with homemade bread and other goodies. When Harold Gates and his son Glenn decided to go into the dinner theater business, they kept the name. The menu includes some Pennsylvania Dutch selections from the buffet table, and the decor is in wood paneling and Tiffany-style hanging lamps.

The Lazy Susan is at Route 1 at Furnace Road, just off I-95 at the Woodbridge exit; (703) 550-7384; www.lazysusan.com.

Occoquan is an Indian word meaning "at the end of the water," which is obvious once you visit the town. There are oodles of antiques and specialty stores, craft shops, and restaurants in the historic 4 blocks of town.

Start your visit at the Prince William County Visitor Center, 200 Mill St., Occoquan 22125 (703-491-4045), to pick up some information about Occoquan and Prince William County. It's open daily from 9 a.m. to 5 p.m.; www.occoquan.org. Craft lovers (both contemporary and country) should be sure to visit during the spring craft show, usually the first weekend of June, and the fall show, usually the last weekend of September. Call (703) 491-2168 for more information.

During your explorations, you'll pass the *Town Hall,* 314 Mill St., Occoquan 22125; (703) 491-1918. At the end of Mill Street, the main drag of Occoquan, is the *Merchants Mill Museum.* This was the site of the first automated gristmill in the nation. Ships and barges came to this mill along the Occoquan River with holds filled with grain, which was processed and then returned to the boats to be taken to Alexandria and the West Indies. The mill operated for 175 years, until fire destroyed it in 1924. The miller's office is now a museum operated by Historic Occoquan, with artifacts and displays about the town,

It's the Truth, by George!

Did you know:

- George Washington's real birthday was February 21, not 22.

- The Father of Our Country had no children of his own, but when he married widow Martha Custis, he adopted her children, John, age 4, and Martha, age 2.

- Washington never wore a wig, and his light auburn (not red) hair had started turning gray by the end of the Revolutionary War, when he was in his early 50s. He was also losing his vision.

- He never chopped down a cherry tree or said, "I cannot tell a lie." That story was the fabrication of Parson Mason Locke Weems, a minister and Washington biographer. You can sometimes buy a copy of his book, *Life of Washington,* at the **Weems-Botts Museum** in Dumfries; (703) 221-3346 or (703) 221-2218; www.dumfriesvirginia.org.

- George Washington "Washy" Parke Custis, Washington's grandson, was demonstrating Washington's strength by saying that his grandfather could throw a piece of slate across the Rappahannock River, which is not now, and never has been, as wide as the Potomac.

- Washington didn't sleep everywhere.

- He didn't design the layout for the city of Alexandria, but he did assist during an early (1749) survey of the town when he was 17.

- Washington's signature is not on the Declaration of Independence; he was busy fighting the war.

- It's said that Washington stood 6'2½", quite tall for that time, although it's also reported that when he was measured for a coffin, that figure was 6'3½". Washington was 67 when he died in 1799, quite a long life for those days.

including photographs of the damage done by Hurricane Agnes in 1972. Open 11 a.m. to 4 p.m. daily, there's no admission charge. It is located at 413 Mill St., Occoquan 22125; (703) 491-7525.

History and beauty and recreation combine at 500-acre **Leesylvania State Park.** It has a half-mile of sandy beach; a state-of-the-art boat launch into the Potomac that is one of the largest in the state; and fishing for bass, perch, catfish, and more. For landlubbers, there's hiking through miles of scenic trails through hardwood forests, wetlands, and coastal bluffs. It's also a residence for bald eagles, beaver, deer, and other birds and waterfowl. History buffs will appreciate the remains of a Civil War Confederate artillery battery built here to protect the Potomac River.

The Lee family plantation was built on this site in the mid-18th century, and it was home to Henry Lee II and his wife Lucy Grymes Lee. Eight Lee children were born and raised here, including General Robert E. Lee's father, Revolutionary War hero Henry "Light Horse Harry" Lee.

Stop by the visitor center that interprets the Potomac River environment and the history of the land that was the estate of Light Horse Harry and Robert E. Lee. There's a discovery room with touch tables, a weather station, children's activities, and a "legacy" room with historical and archaeological displays, area maps, and historical information.

There's also a 288-foot fishing pier; in addition to daytime fishing, the pier is available for night fishing Friday and Saturday and holidays from mid-May to mid-September. Admission and some other fees are charged. The park is at 2001 Daniel K. Ludwig Dr., Woodbridge 22191; (703) 570-0372; www.dcr.state .va.us/parks/leesylva.htm.

Dumfries, the oldest chartered town in Virginia, is another Scot-settled town that was a major seaport until the late 18th century. Now, pure-white whistling swans (perhaps as many as 200) return from Canada to Quantico Creek each year as early as mid-October and leave within 24 hours of March 19 (the same date as the Capistrano swallows out west). You can tell when they're getting ready to leave, for they gather in from the various creeks and very noisily talk things over, and then they all take off at the same time.

Just west of Quantico Creek is the **Weems-Botts Museum,** a four-room Colonial restoration. One half of the house was once the bookstore of Parson Mason Locke Weems, the biographer of George Washington, who created the legend of the cherry tree. The museum docent tells many little-known facts about George. Benjamin Botts, who lived from 1776 to 1811, bought the home from Weems in 1802. He became a prominent lawyer in Prince William County and was on the defense team for Aaron Burr at his treason trial.

Wolf Trap

One of the delights of attending a performance at Wolf Trap in Vienna is spreading a blanket on the lawn and enjoying a picnic. Perhaps the *Wolf Trap Foundation for Performing Arts* can help you with that with their **Four Seasons of Wolf Trap** cookbook ($19.95). Co-sponsored with Reico Kitchen and Bath, the 200-page book features 150 recipes including appetizers, salads, and soups; main dishes and sides; desserts and breads; and beverages, dressings, and sauces. The book can be purchased at the Wolf Trap gift shop or through their website, www.wolftrap.org, where you can also find information about upcoming shows.

Books on the history of the area from Colonial days to Civil War times are sold at the shop. A resource library is available for genealogical research. The museum is open Tues through Sat 10 a.m. to 4 p.m. The museum is open on Monday if it's a legal holiday. Admission is $4 for adults, $2.50 for seniors 55 and over and for children ages 6 through 12. 300 Duke St., Dumfries 22026; (703) 221-2218; www.dumfriesvirginia.org.

All 7 blocks of *Quantico* constitute the only town in the United States completely surrounded by the US Marine Corps; the only land access is through the *Quantico Marine Base.* For years the town has been totally landlocked, but a few years ago the government deeded 4.5 acres of waterfront property to Quantico to build a park, so now it can be reached by the Potomac River as well. The town has its own mayor, five council members, and its own police department. As an indication of the cooperation between the base and the town, Quantico is the only place in the world where Marines are allowed to wear their "utilities" (work uniforms) off base.

In the first year of operation, from November 2006 to November 2007, the *National Museum of the Marine Corps* had 650,000 people visit. Even if you aren't a Marine, you're likely to be intrigued by the building's design that's visible from I-95. The signature 210-foot stainless steel spire (designed by Fentress Bradburn Architects) soars over the tree line and is clearly visible, day and night. To some it emulates the iconic image of the raising of the American flag over Iwo Jima and to others it appears to be huge swords at salute, aircraft climbing to the heavens, or a howitzer at the ready. This privately operated facility features the history of the Marines from when they formed in 1775 through World War II, the Korean War, Vietnam, and the Global War on Terror, and an exhibit of Combat Art. The museum has been so successful and so much more popular than the "experts" predicted, that they had to add three more galleries. That addition provided more than 12,000 square feet of exhibit space that holds 250 new artifacts. In my thinking of awesome is the interactive

Snap This

Louis Lowery, World War II Marine combat photographer, took the famous picture of the US flag-raising atop Iwo Jima's Mt. Suribachi in 1945 (from which the monument was designed). He is among the 8,600 individuals buried at the *Quantico National Cemetery* on Joplin Road in Triangle. The cemetery was dedicated in 1983 and consists of 725 rolling, wooded acres. Hundreds of flags adorn the Memorial Pathway on national holidays. 18424 Joplin Rd., Route 619, Triangle 22172; (703) 221-2183 or (703) 690-2217.

Eyes Down

When you stop by the $1.9 million *Center for the Arts* in Manassas, on the site of the former Hopkins Candy Factory, take a look at the open floor area to see an exposed French drain and an adjacent trench that gave up some souvenirs of a massive fire that consumed the town in 1905. An archaeological dig was conducted during the summer of 2001 in hopes of finding Civil War relics, but the railroad tracks used for the drain were as far as they could research. There were thoughts that this might have been a bakery for Union troops, established by General John Pope. 9419 Battle St., Manassas 20110; (703) 333-ARTS; www.center-for-the-arts.org.

exhibit about John Philip Sousa, director of the President's Own Marine Corps Band, because you can experience a concert of your choosing.

Guided tours are conducted daily at 10 a.m., noon, and 2 p.m. (when a docent is available) and a free audio tour is available. The museum store carries a full line of Marine-themed merchandise, and food service is available. It is open daily from 9 a.m. to 5 p.m., except December 25. There is no admission fee. The museum is located at 18900 Jefferson Davis Hwy., Triangle 22172; (877) 635-1775; www.usmcmuseum.org.

Heading west in Prince William County, traveling from the I-95 corridor to the I-66 corridor, you'll find the *Manassas Museum,* set in a Victorian Romanesque 1896 building (the community's first national bank). It has a museum and a classroom for children to experience some natural and American history.

In the exhibit area you can see why this area, halfway between Washington, DC, and the Shenandoah Valley and the core of train transportation, spurred the region's development and why two of the Civil War's most famous battles were fought nearby. Collections include period photographs from the Civil War, children's toys of a century ago, and a major exhibit about the 1911 Peace Jubilee, which celebrated the 50th anniversary of the battle at Manassas. There's a gift shop with history books and souvenirs. The museum is open daily from 10 a.m. to 5 p.m. from Memorial Day through Labor Day, and Tues through Sun the rest of the year. It is at 9101 Prince William St., Manassas 20110; (703) 368-1873. Admission is $5 for adults and $4 for seniors older than 60 and students from 6 to 17. www.manassasmuseum.org.

The *Manassas Walking Tour,* which you can take at your leisure, includes the museum, the 1875 Presbyterian Church, the world's first military railroad, the defenses of Manassas and the Railroad Depot, the Candy Factory, Conner Opera House, and the Old City Hall. A brochure is available from the museum for this tour and the driving tour, which warns about the possible lack of parking at the historical markers and the heavy traffic.

Manassas was the site of the first and second battles of Manassas, and many of the events are marked in the *Manassas National Battlefield Park.* To assist your historical tour, pick up a *Prince William County Historical Marker Guide* at the welcome center or one of the museums. This will be a nice companion to John S. Salmon's *Guidebook to Virginia's Historical Markers,* published for the Virginia Landmarks Commission by the University Press of Virginia, Charlottesville.

The Battle of Manassas, also known as the Battle of Bull Run (you don't want souvenirs marked "the first Battle of Bull Run"), was the first major battle of the Civil War. It's commemorated at the Manassas National Battlefield Park with electronic battle maps, equipment displays, battle memorabilia, and interpretative presentations of the battlefield's history.

Start at the Henry Hill Visitor Center, 12521 Lee Hwy., Manassas 20109, (703) 361-1339, to view the museum, slide program, a 3-D map charting the strategies of the two battles, and a bulletin board listing the day's interpretive programs. The grounds are open daily from 8:30 a.m. to dusk. The center is open daily 8:30 a.m. to 5 p.m. except Thanksgiving and December 25. The Stone House, which served as a field hospital during the battles, is open from 10 a.m. to 4:30 p.m. on weekends Apr through Memorial Day and Labor Day weekend through Columbus Day weekend. Admission is $3 per adult. The park is located north of I-66 in Manassas; call (703) 361-1339; www.nps.gov/mana/index.htm

Stafford County

The *Globe and Laurel Restaurant* was opened in old-town Quantico in 1968 by Richard (Major, US Marine Corps, Ret.) and Gloria Spooner, but it burned, and the restaurant was reopened in Triangle in 1975. Now, due to the widening of US 1, the restaurant has moved again. Less than 2 miles from the Triangle location, in Stafford County, the new GL is five times the size, has more fireplaces, and all of the memorabilia.

Major Spooner was in the Marines for 29 years and 7 months and wanted a place with a pub atmosphere. You can read about some of the Major's battle experiences in his book, *The Spirit of Semper Fidelis: Reflections from the Bottom of an Old Canteen,* published in November 2004. The protagonist in the nearly 400-page book is named Pvt. Chic Yancey, but you can figure out that this is a historical novel.

Music of swing bands or bagpipes fills the air as you dine. Of historic note are Spooner's Purple Heart medals and the hundreds, maybe thousands, of police department badges on the ceiling from police forces across the United States and from about 30 other countries. Also of interest is the collection of former military insignia, many of which aren't in the possession of military historians, for apparently no one thought to save them; many date from the Civil War. If you have military buttons or other memorabilia, check with the Major before you throw them away. Meat lovers should definitely try the prime rib. The restaurant is located at 3987 Jefferson Davis Hwy., Stafford 22554; (703) 221-5763; www.theglobeandlaurel.com.

Fredericksburg

We're back along I-95. The Welcome Center at *Fredericksburg* (I-95S, mile marker 131; 540-786-8344), notes that it is historically the busiest in the state, with more than half a million travelers each year. That means the staff is used to helping people and assuage your thought that this is not off the beaten path.

In Fredericksburg itself, you're in an area that boasts that "George Washington slept in a lot of places, but he lived here." With 350 original buildings built before 1870, the area is steeped in history from colonial times and the Revolutionary and Civil Wars. It's possible to stay here several days without seeing everything. Be sure to get your free all-day parking pass at the *Fredericksburg Visitors Center,* see the audiovisual display, and obtain directions and operating hours for museums, the national parks, and other attractions.

A *Timeless Ticket,* at $32 for adults (one free student ages 6 to 18), provides discounted admission to several area attractions (the Fredericksburg

> **fun**facts
>
> There are 15,206 victims of the Civil War buried in the Fredericksburg National Cemetery.

The Apocryphal Stone's Throw

George Washington inherited *Ferry Farm* when he was 11 and spent his boyhood years on this property, 1 mile east of Fredericksburg and 38 miles south of Mount Vernon, on the banks of the Rappahannock River. Legend claims the cherry tree story ("I cannot tell a lie") and his powerful toss of a "silver dollar" across the Rappahannock took place here. George Washington's Ferry Farm, now a National Historic Landmark, is located on Route 3, 268 Kings Hwy., Fredericksburg 22405; (540) 370-0732; www.kenmore.org.

Area Museum, Mary Washington House, Rising Sun Tavern, Hugh Mercer Apothecary Shop, Belmont, the James Monroe Museum and Memorial Library, and the three area battlefields) with no expiration date. So, if you only make it through three or four on this visit, bring the ticket with you on your next visit and you can see some more. The price represents a 40 percent discount over individual prices. If you have but a short time and you're a member of AAA,

funfacts

The Masonic Lodge into which George Washington was initiated in 1752 is in Fredericksburg.

you will receive a 20 percent discount on admission. They're available at the visitor center and other selected sites. The visitor center is at 706 Caroline St., Fredericksburg 22401, and can be reached by calling (540) 373-1776 or (800) 678-4748; www.visitfred.com.

Riverby Books has three floors of used and rare books, with an emphasis on Civil War and Virginiana, in a pre–Civil War building. You'll also find philosophy, fiction, board books, and other topics within their 30,000 book selection. They're the largest of Fredericksburg's used book stores and will buy your unwanted books, whether it's one or an entire library. Say you saw an ad about the store and you'll receive a 20 percent discount on your purchase. 805 Caroline St., Fredericksburg 22301; (540) 373-6148; www.riverbybooks.com/fredstore.html.

Gourmet and wonderful are just a sampling of the superior food that's served at the *Poppy Hill Tuscan Kitchen* where Chef Scott Mahar creates noteworthy dishes in a great farm-to-table restaurant. Even if you aren't planning to visit Fredericksburg, Poppy Hill is worth a visit. The fresh-made daily pastas are worth a visit. Enjoy! 1000 Charles St., Fredericksburg 22401; (540) 373-2035; www.ciaopoppyhill.com.

By Women for a Woman

President Grover Cleveland unveiled the *Mary Washington monument,* at Washington Avenue and Pitt Street in Fredericksburg, in 1894. Mary Washington (George Washington's mother), who died in 1789 at the age of 81, was buried at her favorite spot near her daughter's home. President Andrew Jackson laid a cornerstone for the monument in 1883, but it was never finished. A new monument was commissioned in 1893 thanks to the efforts of a group of women called the Mary Washington Monument Association. The new monument was dedicated in 1894. It is the first monument ever erected to a woman by women; (800) 678-4748.

The tobacco-leaf–topped lamps in the historic area are not relics of the 1780s or an 1880s event. They were installed in 1980 and reflect Fredericksburg's part in the tobacco industry as the central licensing point for tobacco inspection for some years. Fredericksburg is home to *Mary Washington College,* so you can feel a historic or a more modern atmosphere depending on where you travel. For great souvenirs and items to ship to your friends, stop by John and Kathryn Mitchell's *Made in Virginia* store, where you can find wonderful edibles ranging from Brunswick stew to Graves' Mountain red raspberry preserves to Barboursville Cabernet Blanc wine. 920 Caroline St., Fredericksburg 22401; (540) 371-2030 or (800) 635-3149; www.madeinva.com.

An institution, even one that was started in 1947 by Carl Sponseller, doesn't have to be stodgy. It can be fun and tasty. Such is the case with *Carl's Frozen Custard.* You'll notice they have three flavors, chocolate, vanilla, and strawberry with lots of flavors to add into the custard. They do not have a cash register. Everyone's trained to do the math. Try the hot fudge milkshake. Carl's is open Sun through Thurs 11 a.m. to 11 p.m., and Fri through Sat 11 a.m. to 11:30 p.m., from Valentine's Day to Thanksgiving Day; 2200 Princess Anne St., Fredericksburg 22401; (540) 372-4457.

funfacts

Goolrick's, a great place for a sandwich and a refreshing drink, claims to be the oldest continuously operating soda fountain (since 1863) in the nation. It's located at 901 Caroline St., Fredericksburg 22401; (540) 373-3411 or (800) 471-8674.

Kenmore, a mid-Georgian structure, was built in 1752 by Colonel Fielding Lewis for his second wife, Betty, only sister of George Washington. Kenmore contains the finest ornamental plasterwork in America and authentic (but not original) furnishings of the period. (Lewis was providing munitions for the war and, not receiving payment, eventually was forced to auction the furnishings.)

You'll love the hot, fresh gingerbread and spiced tea at the end of the tour (from Mary Washington's original recipe, which you can purchase in the gift shop), and you can have tea in the kitchen or on the lawn. Stroll through the boxwood gardens, restored by the *Garden Club of Virginia.* There's a marvelous 9½-foot Daniel Hadley diorama of Colonial Fredericksburg, done in cooperation with the Hagley Museum in Delaware. If you've been taking the walking tour, been to the Stone House, and paid attention to all the details, you'll realize that there are some errors in the depiction, such as the height of Sophia Street compared to the river, and that the Baptist Church is the newer one, not the older one, but this is such a magnificent diorama that it shouldn't

And they swam and they swam . . .

On the chilly morning of February 23, 2004, thousands of spectators watched as the **Embrey Dam** on the Rappahannock River at Fredericksburg was destroyed. The 770-foot-wide dam was constructed in 1854 to provide power and a drinking water reservoir to the growing community. By the 1960s, the power plant was no longer in service and the movement was afoot to undo this insult to nature. Now the 184-mile Rappahannock is the longest free-flowing river leading into the Chesapeake Bay watershed and the shad can swim upstream to spawn.

be missed. The Lewis family tree is on display, filling a matrix that is 29 1-inch squares across and 49 1-inch squares down.

Besides being known for some of the most beautiful rooms in the country, Kenmore is cited as one of the first victories in the fight against suburban development. In 1922 a developer bought Kenmore and planned to demolish the house or convert it into apartments and subdivide the remaining 2 acres of land. His plans were thwarted by local historical preservationists. Kenmore has been undergoing an extensive multiyear renovation so if you were there before, you should return because a lot of changes have been made to take it back to its prime time.

Located at 1201 Washington Ave., Fredericksburg 22401, Kenmore is open 7 days a week, 10 a.m. to 5 p.m. Mar through Oct and from 10 a.m. to 4 p.m. Nov and Dec. It's closed Easter Sunday, December 24, 25, and 31 and January 1. Admission is $10 for adults; $5 for students, and combination tickets are available ($15 and $8) if you'll be visiting Ferry Farm, too. Discounts are available for seniors, AAA, active military, trolley passengers, and DAR members. Call (540) 373-3381 for more information; www.kenmore.org.

Fredericksburg is surrounded by battlefields and cemeteries, including Fredericksburg, Chancellorsville, Wilderness, and Spotsylvania Courthouse, each with programs run by the National Park Service. Descriptive audiotapes for driving tours are usually available at each headquarters building. Get directions from the Fredericksburg Visitors Center.

The **National Park Service Visitors Center,** the starting place for a self-guided tour through Fredericksburg and Spotsylvania Civil War battlefields, is open daily from 9 a.m. to 5 p.m. with extended hours during summer months. A small museum includes an orientation program and some exhibits. There is no admission charge. Guided tours of the Sunken Road are given three times daily in summer. You need permission from the National Park Service, but you can visit the place where Confederate general Thomas

Jonathan "Stonewall" Jackson's arm was buried after it was amputated on May 3, 1863.

During the Battle of Chancellorsville, Jackson was shot by friendly fire, and his left arm was amputated in a field hospital. It was taken to the family home, Ellwood Plantation, and a marker notes the spot. Jackson died a few days later and was buried in Lexington, Virginia. Stop by the visitor center for a map and a pass. For permission call (540) 371-0802. The visitor center is located at Lafayette Boulevard and Sunken Road. The Chancellorsville Battlefield Visitors Center is located off Route 3 West and is open from 9 a.m. to 5 p.m. daily. Write Fredericksburg and Spotsylvania National Military Park/Chatham Manor (headquarters for Civil War battlefields), 120 Chatham Lane, Fredericksburg 22405, or call (540) 654-5121; www.nps.gov/frsp.

Gari Melchers, one of America's finest impressionist painters, lived at *Belmont* from 1916 until his death in 1932. His former home now houses the *Memorial Gallery,* where spacious rooms are filled with antiques and paintings by Melchers and others, including Jan Brueghel, Frans Snyders, Auguste Rodin, and Berthe Morisot.

Belmont is open Thurs through Tues from 10 a.m. to 5 p.m. It's closed New Year's and Thanksgiving days, Easter Sunday, July 4, and December 24, 25, and 31. Admission fees are $10 for adults, $9 for AAA members and seniors, and free for up to two students (ages 18 and younger) with a paying adult. Belmont is located at 224 Washington St., Falmouth 22405; (540) 654-1015; www.umw.edu/gari_melchers/default.php.

funfacts

Gari Melchers painted the murals that adorn the walls of the Library of Congress in Washington, DC.

Gourmet and donuts may seem an oxymoron to you, but that might be because you've never tasted the offerings at *Eamonn's, A Dublin Chipper* ("Thanks be to Cod"). Yes, they serve super-tasty fried fish and chips, so it's difficult to save room for the fried dough balls, but you should try. If you're not a donut fan, you might want to try the fried Milky Way or fried bananas. They boast that they don't use any preservatives ("'cause it's just not good for yis"). It could be nothing stays around long enough to need them. They are located at 728 King St., Alexandria 22314; (703) 299-8384; www.eamonnsdublinchipper .com. It's about an hour drive from Fredericksburg, but it's worth it.

Culpeper County

A few miles west of Fredericksburg is the town of *Culpeper,* originally called Fairfax, founded in 1759 when George Washington (who was 17 at the time)

OTHER PLACES WORTH SEEING

ALEXANDRIA

Lee-Fendall House Museum &
Gardens
(703) 548-1789

Pope-Leighey House
(Frank Lloyd Wright)
(540) 780-4000

ARLINGTON

Arlington National Cemetery
(703) 607-8052
www.arlingtoncemetery.org

US Marine Corps War Memorial
(Iwo Jima Memorial)
(202) 289-2500

GREAT FALLS

Great Falls National Park
(703) 285-2966

MANASSAS

Manassas Industrial School/
Jennie Dean Memorial
(703) 368-1873

MOUNT VERNON

Woodlawn Plantation
(703) 780-4000

VIENNA

Wolf Trap Farm Park
for the Performing Arts
(703) 255-1900
www.wolf-trap.org

was commissioned to survey and plot the town and county of Culpeper. Over the years it thrived and suffered. During the Civil War, there were more than 100 battles and skirmishes in the area, primarily because its central railroad was vital to the North and the South. Homes became military lodging and hospitals, and over the years many farms, houses, historical artifacts, and, of course, lives were lost. About 100 years later, in the 1960s, the town was nearly devastated financially when a highway bypass was constructed, taking residential, commercial, and industrial growth away from the town center. A major Main Street project has strengthened and revitalized the historic core.

Stop by the depot, now the *Culpeper Visitors Center and Chamber of Commerce,* 109 S. Commerce St., for information about area activities and attractions. You can call (540) 825-8628 or (888) CULPEPER or visit the town's website at www.visitculpeperva.com.

More than 200,000 people visit the *Culpeper National Cemetery* every year as they follow Civil War events. Established on April 13, 1867, as a burial site for Union soldiers, the cemetery now is home to soldiers from all American wars and is listed on the National Register of Historic Places. Note the stone lodge/gatehouse near the entrance. Its mansard roof is unique in the Culpeper area but typical of cemetery architecture. Originally, the building was the residence and office of the cemetery's superintendent. The office is open weekdays from 8 a.m. to 4:30 p.m., and the grounds are open daily from dawn to dusk. 305 US Ave., Culpeper 22701; (540) 825-0027; www.cem.va.gov/cems/nchp/culpeper.asp.

You may have heard that the Library of Congress has been working to save original movies that were shot on nitrate film and other formats that date from more than 100 years ago. They are doing more than that. Specialists acquire, preserve, and provide access to what is immodestly called "the world's largest and most comprehensive collection of films, television programs, radio broadcasts, and sound recordings" at this state-of-the-art facility. Stored on 90 miles of shelving, the films and television programs are presented to the public in a 206-seat theater. Typical programs might feature *The Miracle of Morgan's Creek,* a 1944 film from Paramount that starred Eddie Bracken, Betty Hutton, William Demarest, and Diana Lynn; a 1926 silent black-and-white film, with music accompaniment by Andrew Simpson, from MGM entitled *Flesh and the Devil* with John Gilbert and Greta Garbo; or *Mister Buddwing* with James Garner, Suzanne Pleshette, and Jean Simmons in a film from MGM that was directed by Delbert Mann. These programs are presented at the **Packard Campus of the National Audio-Visual Conservation Center** in Culpeper on a 45-acre campus. The programs are free but you must make reservations by calling (540) 827-1079, ext. 79994 or (202) 707-9994; 19053 Mount Pony Rd., Culpeper 22701; www.loc.gov/avconservation/packard.

Many people think "old" when they think of Virginia, particularly those coming from the West Coast. At the **Museum of Culpeper History,** they're displaying "really old" with exhibits about dinosaur existence and activity, including tracks from a theropod, aetosaur, and pytosaur, that were discovered and removed from the Culpeper Stone Company Quarry. Also on display are artifacts from Native American life and the Civil War.

The museum is open Mon through Sat from 10 a.m. to 5 p.m. and on Sun from 1 to 5 p.m. Guided tours, by appointment only, can be arranged. The suggested admission is $3 for out-of-town adults. 803 S. Main St., Culpeper 22701; (540) 829-1749; www.culpepermuseum.com.

From spring through fall, you can see a variety of equestrian events at **Commonwealth Park,** including Grand Prix, Hunter, and Jumper events. This continues an equestrian history that started in 1897 and continued for the next 54 years. Show jumping returned to Culpeper in the 1980s, and some of the country's richest show jumping competitions have been held here. Children 12 and under are allowed in free. 13256 Commonwealth Pkwy., Culpeper 22701; (540) 825-7469; www.hitsshows.com.

TOP ANNUAL EVENTS

JANUARY

Alexandria Restaurant Week
(703) 746-3309
www.visitalexandriava.com

Fredericksburg Restaurant Week
(540) 372-1216
www.visitfred.com

FEBRUARY

Breakfast with George Washington
Mount Vernon
(703) 780-2000 or (800) 388-9119
www.mountvernon.org

George Washington Birthday Parade and Weekend Festivities
Alexandria
(703) 991-4474
www.washingtonbirthday.net/events

MARCH

Wine Week: Love by the Glass
(804) 344-8200
www.virginiawine.org

MARCH–APRIL

Easter Sunrise Service
Arlington
(202) 685-2851
www.arlingtoncemetery.org

APRIL

Annual Historic Garden Week
Statewide
(804) 644-7776 or (804) 643-7141
www.vagardenweek.org

JUNE–AUGUST

City of Fairfax Band Outdoor Concert Series
Veteran's Amphitheater at Fairfax City Hall; Thurs nights, Fairfax
(703) 757-0220
www.fairfaxband.org

JULY

World Championship Scottish Highland Games
Alexandria
(800) 388-9119 or (703) 912-1943
www.vascottishgames.org

AUGUST

Hot Air Balloon Festival
Bealeton
(540) 439-8661
www.flyingcircusairshow.com/balloon

SEPTEMBER

International Children's Festival
Wolf Trap Farm Park for the Performing Arts
(703) 642-0862
www.wolftrap.org

OCTOBER

Art on the Avenue
Del Ray
(703) 683-3100
www.artontheavenue.org

Loudoun Farm Color Tours
Leesburg
(703) 777-0426
www.loudounfarms.org

Waterford Homes Tour & Crafts Exhibit
Waterford
(540) 882-3018
www.waterfordva.org

DECEMBER

First Night
Alexandria
(703) 838-4200 or (800) 388-9119
www.funside.com

When it's time to eat, stop by **Baby Jim's Snack Bar,** a diner known for its burgers and shakes. For a "local" experience, go to the window and order "two dogs with the works, an order o' fries, and an RC." Just make sure you go early and join commuters preparing for a hard day's work in Washington, DC. Baby Jim's is open Mon through Sat 4:30 a.m. to 3 p.m. Established in the 1950s, Baby Jim's remains in the ownership of its founder's family. 701 N. Main St., Culpeper 22701; (540) 825-9212.

For doughnuts, éclairs, and other pastries, it's **Knakal's Bakery.** Founded by Joseph Knakal in 1935, the bakery is now run by Ken Whitt and family, who prepare at least a hundred dozen doughnuts every day, dozens of biscuits, and as many as a dozen wedding cakes every weekend. The aromas are enough to start the taste buds salivating for the cakes, pies, and cookies. Open Tues through Fri from 7 a.m. to 5:30 p.m. and Sat from 7 a.m. until 4 p.m. 146 E. Davis St., Culpeper 22701; (540) 825-8181; http://knakalsbakery.com.

Fauquier County

You'll be excused if you've not heard of **Remington** (unless you're a Civil War buff), for it's a town of 685 people (an additional population of about 60 people since 2000). The town's original name was Millview, then Bowenville, Rappahannock Station, and finally, in 1890, it became Remington. Whether it was named that because the townsfolk liked the sound of the name or whether it was named after a well-liked railroad conductor is unclear.

Civil War buffs know it as an area where many battles occurred because of its location on the Rappahannock River and the railroad that passed through the town. The Battle of Brandy Station, June 1863, was the largest cavalry battle of the war. Earthworks used by the Union and Confederate armies, ruins of bridges, mills, and other structures that suffered from the war's effects, are still visible.

Today's residents and visitors enjoy the bike trails (marked for 3-, 6-, and 12-mile rides), canoe the Rappahannock, shop at the seasonal Friday afternoon farmers' market on Main Street (open from 3 to 7 p.m.), watch (or participate in) historical demonstrations, or just enjoy the self-guided walking tour. A brochure is available from the town hall. (540) 439-3220; www.remingtonva.org.

Where to Stay in Northern Virginia

ALEXANDRIA

Hotel Monaco Alexandria
480 King St.
(703) 549-6080
www.monaco-alexandria
.com

Morrison House
116 S. Alfred St.
(703) 838-8000 or
(866) 834-6628
www.morrisonhouse.com

Westin Alexandria
400 Courthouse Sq.
(703) 253-8600
www.westin.com

ARLINGTON

Hotel Palomar Arlington at Waterview
1121 N. 19th St.
(703) 351-9170 or
(866) 505-1001
www.hotelpalomar-
arlington.com

Westin Arlington Gateway
801 N. Glebe Rd.
(703) 717-6200
www.westin.com

FREDERICKSBURG

Kenmore Inn
1200 Princess Anne St.
(540) 371-7622
www.kenmoreinn.com

Richard Johnston Inn
711 Caroline St.
(540) 899-7606 or
(877) 557-0770
www.therichardjohnstoninn
.com

LEESBURG

Lansdowne Resort
44050 Woodridge Pkwy.
(703) 729-8400 or
(877) 509-8400
www.lansdowneresort.com

MANASSAS

Bennett House Bed and Breakfast
9252 Bennett Dr.
(800) 354-7060
www.virginia-bennetthouse
.com

MINERAL

Littlepage Inn
15701 Monrovia Rd.
(540) 854-9861 or
(800) 248-1803
www.littlepage.com

UPPERVILLE

Blackthorne Inn and Restaurant
10087 John S. Mosby Hwy.
(540) 592-3848
www.blackthorne-inn.com

Where to Eat in Northern Virginia

ALEXANDRIA

Dandy Restaurant Cruise Ships
Zero Prince St.
(703) 683-6076
www.dandydinnerboat.com

Rocklands Barbeque and Grilling (also Arlington)
25 S. Quaker Lane
(703) 778-9663
www.rocklands.com

ARLINGTON

Athena Pallas
556 22nd St. South
(703) 521-3870
www.athenapallas.com

Jaleo
2250A Crystal Dr.
(703) 413-8181
www.jaleo.com

Tandoori Nights
2800 Clarendon Blvd.
(703) 248-8333
http://indaez.com/
tandoori-nights-clarendon

FAIRFAX

Artie's
3260 Old Lee Hwy.
(703) 273-7600
www.greatamerican
restaurants.com/Arties/
general_info.php

Coyote Grille and Cantina
10266 Main St.
(703) 591-0006
www.coyotegrille.com

Dolce Vita
10824 Fairfax Hwy.
(703) 385-1530
www.dolcevitafairfax.com

FALLS CHURCH

Flavors Soul Food
3420 Carlyn Hill Dr.
(703) 379-4411
www.flavorssoulfood.com

FREDERICKSBURG

Bistro Bethem
309 William St.
(540) 371-9999
www.bistrobethem.com

LEESBURG

Wine Kitchen
7 S. King St.
(703) 777-9463
http://thewinekitchen.com

MANASSAS

Carmello's
9108 Center St.
(703) 368-5522
www.carmellos.com

Okra's Louisiana Bistro
9110 Center St.
(703) 330-2729
www.okras.com

RESTON

Clyde's of Reston
11905 Market St.
(703) 787-6601
www.clydes.com

TYSONS CORNER

Clyde's of Tysons Corner
8332 Leesburg Pike
(703) 734-1901
www.clydes.com

EASTERN VIRGINIA

The eastern section of Virginia includes the **Northern Neck** (along the southern reaches of the Potomac River), the area called **Hampton Roads** where the James River meets the Chesapeake Bay, and the southern part of what is known as the **DelMarVa** (Delaware, Maryland, Virginia) Peninsula, which is across Chesapeake Bay from the rest of the state.

Habitation in the area dates from prehistoric times, when Native Americans settled here. The European presence in America was born with the 1607 settlement of Jamestown. Shipping, vital to our continuance, came through these ports. Our reliance on the Virginia waterfront—for recreation and commerce—is just as strong today. Goods have to be shipped in and out, and they need harbors to do that. Foods are harvested from the waters.

Much has changed throughout Virginia, but the biggest changes seem to be happening or getting ready to happen on the Eastern Shore. Cape Charles was a bustling place until the Chesapeake Bay Bridge Tunnel opened. Then it became the place where they "have all those Sears Catalog mail-order houses." Maybe there was one traffic light.

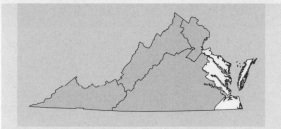

King George

3

301

Rappahannock R.

MARYLAND
VIRGINIA

17

Potomac R.

MARYLAND
VIRGINIA

Chincoteague

360

Tappahannock

Accomac

360

13

Saluda

New Kent

33

17

Gloucester

Eastville

York R.

64

Williamsburg

C H E S A P E A K E   B A Y

N

James R.

Hampton

Cape Charles

Newport
News

CHESAPEAKE BAY
BRIDGE-TUNNEL

0   20 mi
0   20 km

Norfolk

Portsmouth

64

Virginia
Beach

58

Suffolk

Chesapeake

17

168

VIRGINIA
NORTH CAROLINA

AUTHOR'S FAVORITES IN EASTERN VIRGINIA

Annual Pony Swim and Auction
July, Chincoteague
(757) 336-6161
www.chincoteaguechamber.com/ev-july
.html

Chrysler Museum
Norfolk
(757) 664-6200
www.chrysler.org

Hampton University Museum
Hampton
(757) 727-5308
www.hamptonu.edu/museum

Mariners' Museum
Newport News
(757) 596-2222
www.mariner.org

Nauticus the National Maritime Center
Norfolk
(757) 664-1000
www.nauticus.org

Norfolk Botanical Gardens
Norfolk
(757) 441-5830
www.nbgs.org

***Victory Rover* Naval Base cruise**
Norfolk
(757) 627-7406
www.navalbasecruises.com

Virginia Air & Space Center
Hampton
(757) 727-0900
www.vasc.org

Boy, is that changing. Cape Charles and the other "sleepy" towns have become a mecca of ecotourism, artistic and creative ventures, and high-price gated communities with golf course and marina and tony boutiques. It's a nice mix.

You can experience it all—from Native American settlements to colonial life to modern technology.

Middlesex County

We'll start our tour by leaving Washington, DC, and heading down the ***Northern Neck.*** Here you'll find miles of shoreline, forest lands, historic explorations from colonial days forward, quaint towns, good eats, and friendly people.

Urbanna, one of America's original harbor towns (established in 1673), enjoys a marvelously picturesque setting and is the home of the ***Urbanna Oyster Festival.*** Thousands (perhaps 75,000) come to the little harbor on Urbanna Creek the first weekend in November to enjoy the harvest of the famous oyster beds on the Rappahannock River. During the festival there are 125 craft and food booths where you can find oysters fried, stewed, on the half shell, roasted, ready to shuck yourself, or in chowder. During oyster season, oysters are sold by the bushel, processed, packed, frozen, and shipped all over. (804) 758-0368; www.urbannaoysterfestival.com.

If you're traveling in a recreational vehicle and looking for a base of operations, you need look no farther than **Bethpage Camp-Resort** in Urbanna. In fact, you may enjoy Connie McGuire's hospitality so much that you decide to spend all your days there. Rating five stars from *Woodall's,* top ratings from *Trailer Life,* and National Park of the Year for 2005–06 by the National Association of RV Parks and Campgrounds let you know their amenities and recreational opportunities are exceptional. Set along the southern reach of the Rappahannock River, there are plenty of water activities, including a swimming lake with sandy beach, water park, boat ramp, fresh- and saltwater fishing, crabbing, charter boat fishing, and swimming pools with lifeguards. Once you've caught your day's limit, you can take it in to one of the fish cleaning stations so you don't have to do the "messy stuff."

There's a lake pier with a band gazebo, 2 recreation centers (2,000 square feet and 12,000 square feet), catering facilities, camp store, laundry rooms, basketball and tennis courts, horseshoe pits, children's playground, activities, and game room. The 700-plus sites are level and either in the open or in the naturally wooded and beautifully landscaped setting with water, electric (30 and 50 amp service), and sewage hookup.

The season, from April 1 through mid-November, offers plenty of organized activities, from a Cinco de Mayo weekend with Mexican crafts and piñatas through Halloween and the expected costume contest.

Daily, weekly, and monthly rates are available, starting at $39.95 a night and climbing as you get into prime camping time, for 4 people (2 adults and 2 children, with full hookup). Box 178, Urbanna 23175; (804) 758-4349; www .bethpagecamp.com. They've added another facility, Greys Point Camp, Topping. (804) 758-2485; www.greyspointcamp.com.

Down the road from Urbanna is **Deltaville,** "the Boatbuilding Capital of the Chesapeake." At one time there were more than 20 boatbuilders in this area, many of them second and third generation, creating craft that still are used today. Some of the finest houses along the Northern Neck can be found in this area.

The **Deltaville Maritime Museum & Holly Point Nature Park** is located on 30 acres of property donated to Middlesex County by Ms. Pette Clark and includes 2 houses, numerous outbuildings, 3 docks, and a small boat launching area. Within the museum you may see an exhibit about the area's involvement in the Civil War, the museum's part in the John Smith Historic Water Trail (America's first national park on the water), or the changing of the town's name from Sandy Bottom to Deltaville. You may stroll the grounds, which include a Living Shoreline, Woodland, Lindsey Camelia, everlasting Immortals, Willis Wilson, and Community gardens. There's also a Wildflower Meadow and a Children's Garden. Call for operating hours and admission fees. 287 Jackson Creek Rd., Deltaville 23043; (804) 776-7200; www.deltavilleva .com/museumpark/museum.aspx.

King George County

The *King George County Museum and Research Center* is located on Route 3 in *King George.* It opened in September 1997 and is located in the old jail on the east end of the courthouse. Although the county dates from 1721, the Historical Society formed only in the late 1980s. Such items as a pocket pistol from 1863, Civil War relics, Indian projectile points that are about 10,000 years old, photographs, letters, and other articles have been assembled chronologically. A gift shop sells ornaments, coffee mugs, tote bags, books, and other items. Check out the area recipe book, including instructions on how to cook rabbit and squirrel, and the two volumes of *Cemeteries of King George County* books with listings through 1999. The center is open Thurs and Sat from 10 a.m. to 2 p.m. Mar through Oct and Sat from 10 a.m. to 2 p.m. Nov through Feb and by appointment. 9483 King's Hwy., King George 22485; (540) 775-9477; www.kghistory.org.

Westmoreland County

Wandering through the rest of the Northern Neck is more or less whether you feel like turning right or left. There are plenty of historic museums, beaches, famous birthplaces, Westmoreland State Park, great restaurants, and interesting shops, mostly featuring antiques.

Westmoreland State Park (camping, boating, fishing, swimming) was built in 1936 by the Civilian Conservation Corps, one of the original six in the state system. Call (800) 933-PARK for camping or cabin reservations.

Fossil hunters have the opportunity to find items that could be millions of years old. Thousands of fossils of Miocene-era sharks, whales, porpoises, clams, shells, coral, and plants are contained in these rocks, but check with the ranger about where you're allowed, and not allowed, to look for them. You can find remnants of rays, fish, birds, and other animals, with sharks' teeth the most common fossil found in the area. You might, though, find the remains of the scallop *Chesapecten jeffersonius,* the state's fossil, which could date back 5 million years. At the edge of the Potomac River, the soft shale and sandstone *Horsehead Cliffs* rise about 200 feet above the water and stretch 300 to 400 feet along the shore. The formations occurred 5 million to 15 million years ago, when a shallow subtropical sea stretched all the way to the fall line. A ranger-guided fossil walk is available. State Park Road and Kings Highway; (804) 493-8821; www.dcr.virginia.gov/state_parks/wes.shtml.

funfacts

George Washington and Robert E. Lee were both born in Westmoreland County.

Kinsale, a quaint maritime village founded in 1706 on the Yeocomico River, is still considered one of the best deepwater ports in the lower Potomac. It thrived until the early 20th century when steamboat traffic died. The **Kinsale Museum On-the-Green,** in a restored 18th-century pub, chronicles this period with changing exhibits and artifacts of those times. A walking tour of the historic village is available at the museum. It's open Fri and Sat from 10 a.m. to 5 p.m. 449 Kinsale Rd., Kinsale 22488; (804) 472-3001; www.kinsale foundation.org.

Lancaster County

The **Mary Ball Washington Museum** in **Lancaster** has a marvelous collection of local memorabilia, Civil War artifacts (including two battle flags used by troops from Lancaster County), and displays on Northern Neck Indians and life on the water. The genealogical library, said to be one of the best on the East Coast, includes Southern Maryland and Virginia and the migratory paths taken through Virginia into Kentucky. There's also a historical lending library, programs, workshops, and films. Organized to honor the Lancaster County–born mother of George Washington, it's located in the **Lancaster House** (ca. 1800), which was lovingly restored by the Lancaster Women's Club. The museum is open Wed through Fri 10 a.m. to 4 p.m., and the library is open Tues and Thurs 10 a.m. to 4 p.m. and by appointment. Admission is $3 for the museum house and grounds and $5 to work at the library. 8346 Mary Ball Rd., Lancaster 22503; (804) 462-7280; www.mbwm.org.

Merry Point Ferry, one of four remaining free state-run historic river ferries in Virginia (in operation since 1668), crosses the western branch of the Corrotoman River. For years the *Arminta* had plied these waters, carrying three small cars or two regular-size cars and taking about 10 or 15 minutes to cross, but the *Lancaster,* an all-in-one steel boat and scow, is now in service. The *Lancaster* carried 16,378 vehicles and 26,097 passengers in the hurricane-shortened summer of 2003. Taking the ferry from Corrotoman to Ottoman will land you in the town of Lively. The ferry runs "on demand" Tues through Fri from 7 a.m. to 5:30 p.m. and Sat from 9 a.m. to 5:30 p.m. In other words, no service on Sun and Mon and it probably won't be running at times of extreme tides or adverse weather. Take Route 604 off either Route 3 or Route 354 to Ottoman Ferry and Merry Point Roads, Merry Point; (800) 453-6167 or (804) 333-3696; www.virginiadot.org/travel/ferry.asp.

For those who like old churches, there's a dandy one in Irvington. The **Historic Christ Church** was finished about 1735 and is an excellent example of a colonial American church that has been practically unchanged since that time. Built in cruciform design, the church has 3-foot-deep walls. A marvelous three-decker pulpit lets you know immediately where your attention should be focused (whether you were there for services or serenity). The individually enclosed high-backed pews seem to offer privacy for your spiritual thoughts. Stop at the reception center for a slide presentation about the church and then browse through the museum. Services are held on Sun at 8 a.m. from Memorial Day to Labor Day.

antebellumtime

The antebellum manor house that's now the *Inn at Levelfields* was built for Thomas Sandford Dunaway in 1857–58 and is one of the last antebellum mansions constructed in the commonwealth. John Dunn and Charlotte Hollings are the innkeepers. 10155 Mary Ball Rd., Lancaster 22503; (800) 238-5578 or (804) 435-6887; www .innatlevelfields.com.

The church grounds are open daily. The church building is open Mon through Fri 8:30 a.m. to 4:30 p.m. all year. From Apr through Nov, it is also open on Sat 10 a.m. to 4 p.m. and Sun 2 to 5 p.m. They ask a suggested donation of $5 a person. 420 Christ Church Rd., Irvington 22480; (804) 438-6855; www.christchurch1735.org.

Essex County

Drive across the Rappahannock River to the small town of **Tappahannock** that was founded in 1680, the same year as the founding of Philadelphia, and had seen several name changes before settling on this Indian name meaning "rise and fall of water." Thirteen buildings are on the National Register of Historic Places, and you can walk the streets (which still carry their original names) to view the buildings, including the **Old Debtors' Prison** on Prince Street between Church and Cross Streets. The Confederate soldier statue on Prince Street in Tappahannock, a common memorial in many Virginia cities, lists all the local men who fought in the war. Look for a booklet entitled *Essex County Virginia—Its Historic Homes, Landmarks and Traditions* at the **Essex County Museum.** The museum is open daily from 10 a.m. to 3 p.m., except Wed and Sun when it is closed. 218 Water Lane, Tappahannock 22560; (804) 443-4690; www.essexmuseum.org.

Gloucester County

Gloucester County is the home of the annual **Daffodil Festival,** held the last weekend in March or the first weekend in April. Enjoy the parade, entertainment, 5-K race, and a pet show (bring your own) when the fields are abloom with these gorgeous messengers of spring. 6467 Main St., Gloucester 23061; (804) 693-2355; www.gloucesterva.info.

When Hurricane Isabel "visited" the area in late 2003, it damaged the upriver landing of the **Gloucester Point Beach Park** so badly it had to be closed. It reopened in May 2006, and now you can enjoy the Point Walk, picnic areas, swimming, volleyball, a sandy beach, and a wheelchair accessible Beach House that is open seasonally. When it comes time for fishing, just drop a line from the fishing pier (buy your license at the N-Out Convenience store). 1255 Greate Rd., Gloucester 23061; (804) 693 0014; www.gloucesterva.info.

funfacts

The site of James Monroe's birthplace, Monrovia, has been swallowed up by the modern but old-time resort town of Colonial Beach. This land was first settled by James Monroe's great-great-grandfather, Andrew, a Scot, in 1647.

Gloucester is the birthplace of **Dr. Walter Reed** (1851-1902), and his home at the intersection of Routes 616 and 614 is one of the buildings maintained by the Association for the Preservation of Virginia Antiquities. The grounds are open to visitors daily, and the building is open on special occasions or by appointment. (804) 693-3663.

Mathews County

For a delightful escape, head over to **Gwynn's Island,** a 2-by-1.5-mile piece of land off the coast of Mathews County where the Piankatank River flows into the Chesapeake Bay, named after Hugh Gwynn. The island was given to him by Chief Powhatan as a reward for saving Pocahontas's life. Gwynn's Island was the site of one of the first Revolutionary War battles, when in 1776 Lord Dunmore, the last colonial governor of Virginia, was bombarded by Continental forces at Cricket Hill.

Stop by the local museum that's dedicated to preserving the history of Gwynn's Island and Mathews County and to honoring men lost at sea and all who served their country. Housed in a 100-year-old building that was an Odd Fellows Lodge and then the island's first public school, a general store, and a barbershop, it contains school memorabilia, prehistoric fossils, a humpback whale skull, Indian and colonial artifacts, and other displays from the Civil War to the present in its two floors of exhibits.

It's open Fri, Sat, and Sun from 1 to 5 p.m. from Apr through Oct or by appointment; P.O. Box 109, Gwynn's Island 23066; (804) 725-7949; www .qsl.net.

King William County

Back toward Richmond is the **Pamunkey Indian Museum,** which has several nice displays and a videotape about the Pamunkey people and their way of life, from the Ice Age to the present. These people were members of the tribe under the leadership of Chief Powhatan (the name he told the settlers), who was the father of Pocahontas. Some of the items in the 15 display windows are original; some are as it's assumed they were. Of special interest is Pamunkey pottery: a new form, which is glazed and burned, as well as the older coil method. If you time your visit right, you might see a demonstration.

The museum is open Fri and Sat 10 a.m. to 4 p.m. and Sun 1 to 5 p.m. (closed on major holidays). The museum may not open exactly on time, but stay around a few minutes and someone will come by. Admission is $2.50 for adults, $1.25 for children 6 to 13, and $1.75 for seniors. Picnic tables are available. It's located about 10 miles off Route 30 (off I-95) on Route 633 and then Route 673, past the Lanesville cemetery and over the railroad tracks. The road turns, but the signs are easy to follow. For more information call (804) 843-4792; www.baylink.org/Pamunkey.

Not far away, in **West Point,** is the **Mattaponi Museum,** with historical presentations, a fish hatchery, a church, a museum, and a nature trail. Webster "Little Eagle" Custalow is the chief, and Carl "Lone Eagle" Custalow is the assistant chief of this tribe that has had this reservation since 1658. The reservation is approximately 150 acres, with much of it being dedicated to wetlands and approximately 60 of the 450 Mattaponi Indians living on this property.

When you visit both reservations, you'll notice that the Pamunkey property is mostly agricultural, with lots of cornfields and homes scattered throughout the land. The Mattaponi have houses in clusters, with most of their efforts spent on shad fishing. A hatchery and marine science facility feature such programs as fish tagging, water quality monitoring, and the development of educational materials for schools and communities about protecting water resources. (804) 769-3854; www.uppermattaponi.org.

Northumberland County

According to the Northern Neck Tourism Commission (www.northernneck .org), *Reedville* is a small town of 400, with "no restaurants, bars, alcohol, traffic lights, or police," but they do have a "post office the size of your thumb . . . four churches, Victorian-style homes, and the Reedville Fishermen's Museum." Reedville prospered from the menhaden fishing industry, and the plethora of Victorian mansions lining Main Street indicates that it may well have been the richest town per capita in the United States at the turn of the 20th century. The oldest house now standing is part of the *Reedville Fishermen's Museum,* located on the banks of Cockrell's Creek. Still one of the most active fishing ports in the country, the town was established by Captain Elijah Reed in 1867. The museum contains artifacts and historical items relating to the menhaden fishing industry. Here you'll see unique models of boats and tools used in constructing and maintaining the fleet, and information about oystering, crabbers, and pound fishermen. Rotating exhibits and educational programs are scheduled regularly. From May through December the boats still head out for menhaden, and you can view Cockrell's Creek and the boats from a deck at the museum.

Part of the museum is the *William Walker House,* built in 1875. It has been refurbished and refurnished and represents a waterman's home at the turn of the 20th century.

The museum is open daily 10:30 a.m. to 4:30 p.m. May through Oct, and weekends from 10:30 a.m. to 4:30 p.m. the rest of the year. Depending on available staff, you may find it open other days. It is open by appointment at other times. Admission is $5 for adults, $4 for groups, and $3 for seniors; for museum members and children under 12, it's free. 504 Main St., Reedville 22539; (804) 453-6529; www.rfmuseum.org.

Drive off Route 17, following the signs for the *Virginia Institute of Marine Science* (VIMS), but for just a moment keep on driving down to the water. *Gloucester Point* is a great place for a view of the *Yorktown River Bridge* (have your camera ready). At VIMS, part of the *College of William and Mary,* is a free aquarium with more than 50 species of marine organisms from throughout Virginia's waters. There are 8 tanks, containing from 50 to

funfacts

The American social novelist, and a major figure in post–World War I literature, *John Dos Passos* (b. Chicago, January 14, 1896, d. September 28, 1970) is buried in the Yeocomico Church graveyard, near Hague. He and his wife, Elizabeth Dos Passos, retired to Westmoreland County.

3,000 gallons of water, and a special 200-gallon touch tank, so you may, as they say, get up close and personal. VIMS is open Mon through Fri from 9 a.m. to 4:30 p.m. Be sure to ask for a complete set of some great seafood recipe brochures, at no charge.

A 1-acre *Teaching Marsh,* an area restored both for practical and educational purposes, provides a demonstration area for regulated wetland plant species (the educational side) and to naturally remove contaminants from the Coleman Bridge storm water runoff, thus improving the water quality in the York River (the practical side). The VIMS Waterman's Hall is open daily from 9 a.m. to 4:30 p.m. Ninety-minute public walking tours (best suited for adults and older children) are available and can include the Teaching Marsh. They are offered on Fri from late May through Aug and require reservations. Tours start in the Watermen's Hall. Other activities, including a monthly after-hours lecture series, provide other information about our environment. There's a gift shop on the premises, too. Route 1208 Grete Road, Gloucester Point 23062; (804) 684-7846; www.vims.edu.

The *Sunnybank Ferry* crosses the Little Wicomico River on Route 644 between Kayan and Sunnybank, just as it has done since 1903. Well, it started as a hand-pulled cable and it's now a motorized one, transporting cars, bicycles, and pedestrians. The boat, the *Northumberland,* was built in nearby Deltaville in 2010. It is free, operated by Virginia Department of Transportation (VDOT), and generally runs on demand Mon through Fri from 8 a.m. to 4:30 p.m. and Sat from 8 a.m. to noon except during inclement weather and unusual water levels (either too high or too low).

Newport News

Now, it's across the York River and into Hampton Roads. We'll head east and south and then come back to tour the historical triangle area of Williamsburg, Jamestown, and Yorktown.

Underhanded?

At the entrance to the Christopher Newport University, at J. Clyde Morris and Warwick Boulevards, stands a 24-foot **bronze statue of Captain Christopher Newport,** created by sculptor Jon Hair. His statue is heroic and shows the strength, determination, and courage of the man who was responsible for the success and survival of the English Settlement at Jamestown. It also shows him with two hands even though he lost his right arm in battle many years before arriving in Virginia.

OTHER PLACES WORTH SEEING

FORT EUSTIS

US Army Transportation Museum
(757) 878-1115
www.transchool.lee.army.mil

NORFOLK

Bea Arthur Dog Park
(757) 622-7382

Norfolk Tides Baseball Club
(757) 622-2222
www.norfolktides.com

OAK GROVE

Ingleside Plantation Vineyards and
Winery
(804) 224-8687
www.inglesidevineyards.com

VIRGINIA BEACH

Military Aviation Museum
(757) 721-7767
www.militaryaviationmuseum.org

WILLIAMSBURG

Busch Gardens Williamsburg
(800) 343-7946
www.buschgardens.com

Water Country USA
(800) 343-7946
www.watercountryusa.com

Set on the grounds of *Christopher Newport University,* the *Ferguson Center for the Arts* is a 1,700-seat concert hall where the Russian National Ballet, Sir James Galway, Ralph Stanley and the Clinch Mountain Boys, and Bill Cosby were among the performers during its 2006 inaugural season. In 2011, they had *Monty Python's Spamalot, Rain,* Bill Engvall, *Forever Plaid,* the totally irreverent and completely hysterical Capitol Steps, Tim Conway and Friends, and the Virginia Symphony Orchestra. That's a schedule to give you enough reason to move to Newport News. The concert hall joined a 440-seat music and theater hall, a 200-seat studio theater, and rehearsal space. The firm of Pei Cobb Freed and Partners (of I. M. Pei fame) designed the $54 million complex (incorporating part of the old Ferguson High School) with perfect acoustics and sight lines. William R. Biddle serves as executive director. 1 University Place, Newport News 23606; (757) 594-7448; www.cnu.edu/fergusoncenter.

When people say you can discover some of the best craftsmanship on Earth at the *Mariners' Museum,* believe them. Founded in 1930 by Archer M. Huntington, the museum contains one of the world's finest collections of figureheads and perhaps the largest figurehead of all time: the *Lancaster Eagle.*

Opened in March 2007, the *USS Monitor Center,* a $30 million, 63,500-square-foot facility, is filled with recovered artifacts, original documents, paintings, personal accounts, and interactive experiences that paint a dazzling

Raising the *Monitor*

During the summer of 2001, after 28 days of around-the-clock work, and after years of planning, the 30-ton steam engine of the shipwrecked Civil War ironclad **Monitor** was raised from its watery bed 240 feet below the surface, off the shore of Cape Hatteras, North Carolina. It was taken to the Newport News Shipbuilding yard on July 18 and then the **Mariners' Museum** in Newport News started taking it through a multi-year conservation process. In the intervening years, the engine and the turret that was rescued have been the subject of extensive studies and restoration and the projected completion date keeps moving onward and onward. The amount of concretion (the combination of sand, sediment, marine life, iron oxide—rust—that had bonded to the surface of the artifacts continues to amaze them. A blog lets you follow their progress.

portrait of the USS *Monitor* and the CSS *Virginia*. You can walk the deck of a full-scale replica of the USS *Monitor,* try your hand at maneuvering a sailing frigate in battle, visit the officers' living quarters, and go inside an archaeological re-creation of the *Monitor's* revolutionary gun turret. You can be transported back in time to the famous Battle of Hampton Roads (March 8 and 9, 1862), and to the night of December 31, 1862, when the *Monitor,* the US Navy's first ironclad warship, sank 16 miles off the coast of Cape Hatteras, North Carolina. Sound and imagery combine to leave you amazed, entertained, and educated.

August F. Crabtree's collection of 16 miniature ships (at a scale of about a quarter-inch to the foot) follows the evolution of the sailing ship. Born in 1905 in Oregon, Crabtree was the grandson of a Glasgow shipbuilder. It took Crabtree and his wife, Winnifred (they met when he was building model ships for Hollywood movies and she was painting them), more than 27 years to complete this world-famous collection. The ships are enclosed in glass cases with mirrors underneath so that you can see completely around them. Some boards are not in place so that you can see inside, and there's a magnifying glass on some so that you can appreciate the exacting detail work. This display is worth the visit, all by itself.

funfacts

A Fresnel lens, used at the Cape Charles, Virginia, lighthouse from 1895 until 1963, produced a concentrated beam of light that was visible up to 20 miles at sea. It now greets visitors to the Mariners' Museum's Chesapeake Bay Gallery.

Guided tours are available, during which you might hear how Admiral Lord Nelson was shipped home in a wine casket or learn some other interesting military information.

There are 12 galleries featuring decorative arts, ship models, small crafts from workboats to pleasure craft, with 100 fascinating full-size boats from around the world, ships' carvings, and seapower, as well as a gallery for changing exhibits.

Guarded by the 10-foot 4 inch statue (and it seems much taller) of Leif Eriksson, the *Age of Exploration Gallery* display shows how scientific and technological developments in shipbuilding, ocean navigation, and cartography led to the explorations of the 15th and early 16th centuries. Exhibited in the gallery, which opened in conjunction with the quincentenary celebration of Columbus's voyage to the New World, are ship models, rare books, illustrations, maps, navigational instruments, shipbuilding tools, and other maritime artifacts. Fifteen short videos that bring the Age of Exploration to life feature footage filmed in Spain, India, and other countries. The hands-on Discovery Library features reproductions of navigational instruments and facsimiles of charts and books used by early mariners. Do you have an explorer growing up in your family? It's all sensational and can be found here.

funfacts

The **Lancaster Eagle** at the Mariners' Museum is a hand-carved, 3,000-pound gilt eagle figurehead from the frigate USS *Lancaster,* 1881 to 1921. It has an 18½-foot wingspan.

Be sure to stop by the museum shop, which contains a large selection of maritime books, educational toys, gifts, and prints.

The Mariners' Museum is open Wed through Sat 10 a.m. to 5 p.m., Sun noon to 5 p.m. It is closed on Thanksgiving and December 25. Admission is $12 for adults; $11 for seniors, military, and students; and $7 for children ages 6 through 17. 100 Museum Dr., Newport News 23606; (757) 596-2222; www.mariner.org.

The *Virginia Living Museum* combines the best and most enjoyable elements of a native wildlife park, science museum, botanical garden, aquarium, and planetarium. They are all in one inspiring, beautiful setting. Hundreds of native American eastern coastal creatures—including mammals, birds, marine life, reptiles, and insects—go about their daily routines as you discover the secrets of life in the wild. C'mon have you ever seen pine voles, ghost crabs, or moon jellyfish? You can here. Indoors, you will find a 60-foot living panorama of the James River, beginning with life in a mountain stream and ending in the amazing depths of the Atlantic.

There's an ever-popular touch tank for a safe approach to the up-close feel. Outdoors you can stroll amid the natural beauty of the lakeside forest as a picturesque boardwalk leads you on an up-close safari into the lives of native water animals. The walk is less than ⅗ of a mile, and there are benches along the way. You are asked to stay on the paths and not to touch the animals, enclosures, or electric fences.

An amphitheater overlooking Deer Park Lake opened in spring 2008 for animal programs and special events.

If you've ever wondered how things work (I'm not sure I've ever seen this information on those TV shows about how things work), then take the museum's Behind the Scenes Tours. You'll learn how the animals and fish are acquired, how their diets are prepared, how the water matches the oceans and rivers, what happens when critters get sick or injured, and then learn what a herpetologist and an aquarist do. You can even watch trout being fed and see where coyotes sleep at night. The list could be endless. I've not counted.

The museum is open daily 9 a.m. to 5 p.m. from Memorial Day through Labor Day. Winter hours are Mon through Sat 9 a.m. to 5 p.m. and Sun noon to 5 p.m. Combination tickets (for museum/observatory and planetarium) are $21 for adults ($17 for museum only) and $17 for children from 3 through 12. Behind the Scenes and Animal Confidential ticket is $10 plus the general admission. They do not participate in the AZA reciprocal admission program. 524 J. Clyde Morris Blvd., Newport News 23601; (757) 595-1900; www.thevlm.org.

My first visit to the *Downing Gross Cultural Arts Center* was a serious WOW! This is the building that held the 1918 Walter Reed Elementary School that my mother and some of her siblings attended. Now, it's a performing and visual arts center with the Ella Fitzgerald Theater, a permanent exhibit of folk artist Anderson Johnson, mirror-lined dance rooms, meeting facilities, and so much more. 2410 Wickham Ave., Newport News 23607; (757) 247-8950; www .downinggross.org.

Hampton

When most Americans think of our space program, they think of the centers at Houston and Cape Canaveral. The original seven Mercury astronauts, however, trained right here, thus the street name *Mercury Boulevard* (formerly Military Boulevard).

You can also find Commander Shepard Boulevard (named for Alan B. Shepard) and bridges named for M. Scott Carpenter, L. Gordon Cooper, John H. Glenn, Virgil I. Grissom, Walter M. Schirra, and Donald K. Slayton. One of these days when you have nothing better to do, spend some time wandering around *Hampton* or poring over a map to find these historic spots. When you give up, try the *Hampton Visitors Center,* at 710 Settler's Landing Rd. They compiled a list for me and promised to keep it handy for you.

The *Virginia Air and Space Center/Hampton Roads History Center* is a blast (off?). It isn't as large as the Smithsonian's Air and Space Museum in Washington, DC, but it isn't nearly as crowded either. Shaped like a huge wing ready for takeoff, it features walls of windows and light and space that set your creative mind in motion and your quest for adventure throbbing. Taking the Hampton city theme "From the sea to the stars," the displays are informative, interactive, touch-me, and unusual.

Imagine standing face-to-face with aviators from the past. There are 30 life-size mannequins of such people as Christopher Newport (as in Newport News), Samuel P. Langley, Orville Wright, Alan Shepard, and a generic female pilot. It's fun to check your size and stature against these giants of aviation. You can pretend you're an astronaut for a moment by projecting your face into a replica of an official NASA space suit. It makes you feel as though you're floating above it all. Little ones can pop their heads through a moon landscape like lunar gophers. For a moon relic take a look at the 3-billion-year-old moon rock. Check out the 10 air- and spacecraft suspended from the center's 94-foot ceiling, and take a serious gander at the *Apollo 12* command capsule, which journeyed to the moon and back, in the middle of the gallery's floor. Take your time as you walk the gantry and pretend you're going on the next shuttle launch.

Within the center are more than 100 history, aeronautic, and space exhibits. Each end of the building is a glass wall that lets light cascade in and through the structure. The solid walls are painted a neutral color that seems to make them disappear into the horizon, so you feel as though you're standing in and among all the planes that are suspended above and around you.

You'll also want to save some time for the IMAX movie, which has included such features as *The Old Man and the Sea, Galapagos ED, Bears, Harry Potter and the Goblet of Fire,* and *Extreme.*

The Air and Space Center is open Mon through Wed 10 a.m. to 5 p.m. and Thurs through Sun 10 a.m. to 7 p.m. from Memorial Day through Labor Day. Shorter hours are in effect the rest of the year, and the center is open some evenings for special programs and IMAX films. Admission prices for the museum only are $11.50 for adults, $10.50 for seniors (65 and older) and military/NASA/Riverside employees, and $9 for students 3 through 18. Combination tickets for the Center and IMAX film are available. 600 Settlers Landing Rd., Hampton 23669; (757) 727-0900; www.vasc.org.

funfacts

Booker T. Washington received his degree from Hampton Institute (now Hampton University) in 1875.

To bring yourself gently down to Earth, walk out onto the plaza or **Carousel Park** to see the marvelously restored 1920 **Hampton Carousel,** taken from Buckroe Beach. Take the 4-minute ride Mon through Wed noon to 5:30 p.m. and Thurs through Sun noon to 7:30 p.m. Memorial Day through Labor Day, Mon through Thurs noon to 3 p.m., and Fri through Sun noon to 5:30 p.m. the rest of Sept, and Fri through Sun noon to 5:30 p.m. from Oct through Nov. Tickets are $2 per person. 602 Settlers Landing Rd., Hampton 23669; (757) 727-0900.

After your ride, walk a block over to Queen's Way on a Saturday from 9 a.m. to 1 p.m. from the end of May through early August and then all October for the Downtown Hampton Market Place to check out the fresh produce, herbs, cut flowers, soaps, jellies, seafood, and more. (757) 727-0800 ext. 705.

Aviation buffs should also catch the **Air Power Park,** with its awesome outdoor exhibit of missiles, rockets, and military aircraft from the country's various service branches, including a Nike surface-to-air missile, an F-105D Thunderchief, and an F-100D Super Sabre, the first Air Force fighter with supersonic performance. There's also a model airplane collection and a wind tunnel exhibit. The park is open daily from 9 a.m. to 4:30 p.m. There is no admission fee. 413 W. Mercury Blvd., Hampton 23669; www.hampton.va.us/parks/parks_and_trails.html.

The **Hampton University Museum** is the oldest African-American museum in the country. The world-renowned American Indian Collection consists of more than 1,600 pieces from 93 tribes. The collection was established in 1878 when the US government began sending young Indians from western reservations to be educated at Hampton Institute. Now located in the recently renovated Beaux Arts–style Huntington Building, the museum's galleries include the Native American Gallery, the Asian and Pacific Gallery, and the Hampton (Institute/University) Gallery.

A Little Chapel

The **Little England Chapel,** built around 1879 to introduce religion to post–Civil War blacks in Virginia, is the state's only known African-American missionary chapel. It contains a permanent exhibit explaining the religious lives of post–Civil War blacks in Virginia. There are handwritten Sunday school lessons, photographs, 19th-century religious books, and a 12-minute video. The chapel has been designated a State and National Historic Landmark. 4100 Kecoughtan Rd., Hampton 23669; (757) 728-1710.

From Little Acorns

In 1863 the members of the Virginia Peninsula's black community gathered around an oak tree on the grounds of what is now Hampton University to hear the first reading of President Lincoln's Emancipation Proclamation. Mrs. Mary Peake, daughter of a free black woman and a Frenchman, conducted the first lessons taught under that tree on the university's campus. The National Geographic Society designated the *Emancipation Oak* as one of the 10 Great Trees of the World.

The Hampton Museum is open Mon through Fri 8 a.m. to 5 p.m., Sat noon to 4 p.m. There is no admission fee. 11 Frissell Ave., Huntington Building, Hampton 23668; (757) 727-5308; http://museum.hamptonu.edu.

The *Casemate Museum,* set in an impressive location—a cavern of rooms built within the thick walls of *Fort Monroe*—relates the battles of Hampton Roads, particularly during the Civil War.

The story of the *Monitor* and *Merrimac* battle is told here, and you can see the area where Confederate president Jefferson Davis was imprisoned after the war. When construction of Fort Monroe was completed in 1834, it was referred to as the "Gibraltar of the Chesapeake" because of the strength of its fortifications. You can walk through the fort, the third oldest in America, and take a look at the *Old Point Comfort Lighthouse* built in 1802 and in continuous use since then. Fort Algernourne was on this site from 1609 to 1667. Fort George was built in 1727 and destroyed by a hurricane in 1749. Weakened coastal defenses during the War of 1812 allowed the British to sack Hampton and attack and burn Washington by sailing up Chesapeake Bay.

Discussions about the future of the Fort created a battle that lasted longer than the Civil War. In May 2011, the US Army announced it was going to vacate the Fort in late 2011, deeding the property to Virginia. Part of the land will become a National Park, some buildings will be used by the State, and some low-intensity development will be allowed.

Fort Monroe was America's only active-duty fort that was completely surrounded by a moat and remains the largest stone fort ever constructed on this continent. A walking tour is available—note Quarters Number One, stop nine on the tour. The oldest building at the fort, it was built between 1819, shortly after the fort's construction began, and 1823 and has been in use ever since.

The museum is open daily from 10:30 a.m. to 4:30 p.m. There is no admission charge. 20 Bernard Rd., Fort Monroe 23651; (757) 727-3391; www.monroe.army.mil.

Virginia Beach

Okay, it's time to zip across the Hampton Roads Bridge-Tunnel and head toward *Virginia Beach,* where residents and vacationers have a lot of options for their leisure time, with Mount Trashmore, catching rays, or traveling back and forth across the Chesapeake Bay Bridge-Tunnel, that 17-mile-long route connecting Cape Charles on the DelMarVa Peninsula to the western shore.

I've never seen a study about this, but it seems odd to me that so many theme parks are in areas where you could find something different to do almost every day of the year and, yet, we choose to pay for thrills and entertainment. Having said that, the 19-acre *Ocean Breeze Waterpark* has expanded its attractions. In addition to water slides, million-gallon Runaway Bay wave pool (now, there is an advantage over the ocean—no jellyfish), the new owners, Kieran Burke and Gary Story, have built even more things to do. Although some of the rides have a minimum height of 42" and 48", there is a children's area that includes a pint-sized inner tube Lazy River ride, a pirate ship (you must be under 48" for this one), and a silly slide.

Open daily from Memorial Day through Labor Day, various hours depending on day of the week and month. Admission fees vary. 849 General Booth Blvd., Virginia Beach 23451; (757) 422-4444 or (800) 678-9453; www.ocean breezewaterpark.com.

The *Norwegian Lady Statue* is a 9-foot bronze replica of the wooden figurehead of the Norwegian barque *Dictator* that sank on March 28, 1891. The figurehead had washed ashore and then stood as a memorial on the oceanfront for 60 years. The residents of Moss, Norway, commissioned this statue and gave it to Virginia Beach in 1962 with a duplicate erected in Moss to link the sister cities. 25th Street and Oceanfront, Virginia Beach 23451; www.vabeach.com.

The Old Coast Guard Station, housed in the former Life Saving Station (which became the Coast Guard) is the only station in Virginia that's open to the public. It was built in 1903, when the men who risked their lives to save others worked for little more than a dollar a day. It was decommissioned in 1969. There's now a gift shop inside as well as the historical memorabilia of shipwrecks and lives saved. The Old Coast Guard Station museum is open Mon through Sat 10 a.m. to 5 p.m. and Sun noon to 5 p.m. It is closed on Mon from October 1 to Memorial Day. Admission to the station is $4 for adults, $3 for senior and military, and $2 for children 6 through 18. There's no charge to go into the museum store, though. 24th Street and Atlantic Avenue, Virginia Beach 23451; (757) 422-1587; www.oldcoastguardstation.com.

Two-thirds of the 9,250-plus acres of the *Back Bay National Wildlife Refuge* are marshlands while the rest is beach, dunes, woodland, and farm fields. The refuge is home to waterfowl, loggerhead sea turtles, and ghost crabs. Some 10,000 snow geese and a large variety of ducks stop by the refuge during December, the peak of the fall migration. You can take a self-guided walking or biking tour, or enjoy fishing to your heart's content. The outdoor areas are open daily from dawn to dusk. Stop by the Visitor Contact Station for information and a bird list. Pets are not allowed on the refuge and swimming, sunbathing, surfing and "other non-wildlife-dependent activities are prohibited." What you can do is hike, photograph, fish, observe, and educate or be educated. Please stay on the trails and roadways and do not enter the dunes.

It's open weekdays from 8 a.m. to 4 p.m. and weekends 9 a.m. to 4 p.m. from Apr through Nov; it is closed on Sat the rest of the year. Fees vary by when you visit and whether you enter by foot or vehicle, although from Nov through Mar there is no admission charge. 1324 Sandbridge Rd., Virginia Beach 23456; (757) 301-7329; www.fws.gov/backbay.

Virginia Beach is noted for **Mt. Trashmore,** which solved two major problems in this community. First, it provided a place for a solid-waste landfill. Instead of filling shallow holes (impossible because of the high water table), the city built a mountain. Second, it provided a large recreational facility. Mt. Trashmore, measuring 165 acres and 60 feet in height and more than 800 feet long, was the first overground landfill created especially as a municipal park.

Kite flying is a trip in the spring, and on a brisk March day the air is filled with colorful boxes and other flights of fancy. You can also enjoy picnic shelters, playgrounds, volleyball courts, a 7-foot deep bowl, 13.5-foot vertical ramp, and a 1.45 mile walking trail. On the not-so-active side, the Water Wise demonstration garden displays xeriscaping and you can learn how to create your own garden with minimal water use.

Virginia Beach Trivia

The **Virginia Beach Boardwalk** (actually concrete) is 40 blocks long and open for in-line skating, jogging, or strolling. A bikes-only strip of asphalt with lane markings runs next to the boardwalk.

No, you're not suddenly transported to La-La Land, but you are seeing plaques honoring such famous Virginians as Arthur Ashe, Patsy Cline, Katie Couric, Thomas Jefferson, Pocahontas, and Edgar Allan Poe along the **Virginia Legends Walk** at Virginia Beach's 13th Street Park. Thirty-six such notables have been honored so far and others are sure to be added. 1300 Atlantic Ave.; (757) 463-4500; www.va-legends.com.

TOP ANNUAL EVENTS

MARCH

Williamsburg Film Festival
Williamsburg
(919) 957-0222 or (757) 482-2490
www.williamsburgfilmfestival.org

MARCH-APRIL

Easter Decoy and Art Festival
Chincoteague
(757) 336-6161
www.chincoteaguechamber.com

APRIL

Flounder Fishing Tournament
Wachapreague
(757) 789-3222
www.wachapreague.com/tournies

Virginia International Tattoo
Norfolk
(757) 282-2800
www.vafest.org

Historic Garden Week
Statewide
(757) 428-2285 or (800) 822-3224
www.vagardenweek.org

APRIL-MAY

International Azalea Festival
Norfolk
(804) 644-7776
www.azaleafestival.org

MAY

Annual International Migratory Bird Celebration
Chincoteague
(757) 336-6161
www.chincoteaguechamber.com

Dominion Riverrock
Richmond
(804) 285-9495
www.dominionriverrock.com

JUNE

Afrikan–American Festival
Hampton
(757) 727-8311 or (757) 728-5173
www.hampton.gov/calendar.html

Annual Newport News Greek Festival
Newport News
(757) 596-5599
www.newportnewsgreekfestival.org

Blackbeard Pirate Festival
Hampton
(757) 727-0900
www.blackbeardpiratefestival.com

Without fear of contradiction I will say that Mt. Trashmore was an inspiration for dozens of other cities in this country and in other countries as a solution for solid waste and recreational problems. The park is open daily from 7:30 a.m. to sunset. 310 Edwin Dr., Virginia Beach 23462; (757) 473–5237; www.vbgov.com/parks.

A notable eating place is the *Lynnhaven Fish House Restaurant.* Opened in 1981, the restaurant offers indoor and outdoor dining (in season). They have fresh oysters and clams, steamed shrimp, and, as they say, the largest selection of the freshest fish in all of Hampton Roads. Included with each dinner are

Hampton Jazz Festival
(800) 800-2202
www.hamptonjazzfestival.com

Harborfest
Norfolk
(757) 441-2345
www.festevents.org

JULY

Volunteer Fireman's Carnival and Annual Pony Penning and Auction
Chincoteague
(757) 336-6161
www.chincoteaguechamber.com

AUGUST

Annual AT&T Latino Music Festival
Norfolk
(757) 441-2345
www.festevents.org/mini-site/latino-music-festival

SEPTEMBER

Neptune Festival Boardwalk Weekend
Virginia Beach
(757) 498-0215
www.neptunefestival.com

Irvington Stomp
Irvington
(804) 438-5559
www.irvingtonstomp.com

OCTOBER

Eastern Shore of Virginia Harvest Festival
Kiptopeke
(757) 787-2460
www.esvachamber.org

NOVEMBER

100 Miles of Lights
Hampton, Newport News, Norfolk, Portsmouth, Virginia Beach, and Williamsburg
(888) 493-7386, ext. 100
www.100milesoflights.com

Urbanna Oyster Festival
Urbanna
(804) 758-0368
www.urbannaoysterfestival.com

fresh-baked Lynnhaven Bread, hush puppies, and melted marshmallows if you order the sweet potato as a side dish. The restaurant expanded its wine selection to include key vintages from all over the world, and the fully trained staff is available to assist you in making just the right choice for your dining pleasure. Look for your favorites, or establish a favorite from the selection of blush, cabernet sauvignon, chardonnay, dessert wine, merlot, pinot noir, sauvignon blanc (and other white wine), sparkling wine, and various blends and other reds.

The support staff has been with the restaurant for years, meaning you're sure to find the service is friendly and efficient. If that's not enough, the view is "second to none." 2350 Starfish Rd., Virginia Beach 23451; (757) 481-0003; www.lynnhavenfishhouse.net.

"Is there gold in seawater?" "How do waves change our coastline?" "What is it like beneath the surface of Chesapeake Bay?" The answers to these questions and more are waiting to be discovered at the *Virginia Aquarium and Marine Science Center.*

Now that a major renovation of the center's galleries is complete, you will be taken on two journeys: a journey across water that focuses on the diverse natural habitats across Virginia today and a journey through the habitats of Virginia's past in a new 12,000-square-foot gallery titled Restless Planet: A Journey Across the Planet that Brings You Closer to Home. Immersive habitats will look, feel, sound, and smell like a Malaysian peat swamp, a coastal desert, the Red Sea, and an active volcano.

This is one of the most visited museums in the state and one of the most popular science museums and aquariums in the country. It's an enjoyable, hands-on educational operation from just about the moment you walk in.

The aquarium is open daily 9 a.m. to 5 p.m. and closed on Thanksgiving and December 25. Aquarium admission is $17 for adults, $16 for seniors (62-plus), and $12 for children (ages 3 through 11). IMAX admission is $8.50 for adults, $8 for seniors, and $7.50 for children. Combination tickets start at $23, $22, and $18. Group rates are available with prior reservations. 717 General Booth Blvd. Virginia Beach 23451; (757) 385-0300; www.virginiaaquarium.com.

The *Old Cape Henry Lighthouse* is special because from here you can see the lighthouse that replaced it in 1881 offering you the option of taking a photo of a lighthouse from a lighthouse or taking a picture of two lighthouses in one shot.

This lighthouse was authorized and funded by America's first Congress, was built in 1791 and was the first public building authorized by that body. This lighthouse, near the entrance to the Chesapeake Bay, was used for almost 90 years, until 1881. The stones were mined in the Aquia Quarries, which also provided stone for the US Capitol, the White House, and Mount Vernon. It's open daily 10 a.m. to 5 p.m. mid-March to November 1, and 10 a.m. to 4 p.m. the rest of the year. It is closed on Thanksgiving, December 24, 25, and 31, January 1, and during some events such as the Shamrock Marathon. The last visitors are admitted 15 minutes prior to closing. *Note:* The lighthouse is located on the grounds of Fort Story military base, so you must clear security and everyone 16 and over must have photo identification. Admission fees are $5 for adults (13 and over), $3 for children 3 through 12, and free for younger children and APVA members. A combo ticket for the tower and walking tour is $8 for adults and $6 for children. There is a height requirement of 42 inches to enter the lighthouse. Enter through the Fort Story gate, off Route 60; 583 Atlantic Ave., Fort Story 23459; (757) 422-9421; www.apva.org/capehenry.

It was off Cape Henry that the ships of Admiral François Joseph Paul Comte de Grasse—while the land side was blocked by the Franco-American armies of Washington, Rochambeau, and Lafayette—prevented action by General Lord Cornwallis and led to his surrender to Washington on October 19, 1781. This little-mentioned skirmish apparently had no victor, but it allowed the Americans time to bring up their heavy siege guns, which marked the beginning of the end of the Revolutionary War. A statue of Admiral de Grasse, a gift from France, is located at Fort Story in Virginia Beach, within sight of the Old Cape Henry Lighthouse.

Norfolk

Travel west from Virginia Beach and you'll arrive in *Norfolk,* where the appeal starts at its international airport. In other airports you're almost held captive between flights. At Norfolk you can take a 15-minute walk and arrive at the enchanting paradise of the *Norfolk Botanical Gardens,* with its 155 acres of azaleas, camellias, dogwoods, roses, and other flora nestled among tall pines and placid waters, where something always is in bloom. The garden was started in 1938, with 200 African-American women and 20 men planting 4,000 azaleas as a WPA project. It now boasts one of the largest collections of azaleas, camellias, roses, and rhododendrons on the East Coast. Norfolk's unique climate allows the coexistence of botanical species that are usually found widely separated geographically. The presence of California redwoods in the garden's collections is a perfect example. Start in the Baker Hall visitor center with its state-of-the-art audiovisual program that will help orient you to the garden's

Mermaids on Parade

Yes, Virginia has mermaids. An innovative public art project idea was introduced by Norfolk attorney Pete Decker at a November 1999 business breakfast meeting who credited his wife, Bess, with the idea, borrowed from Chicago's Cows on Parade. The subject would be based on the mermaid logo adopted by Norfolk in 1998. You should be able to find more than a dozen of them downtown while others are tucked away in not-so-public places. The symbolic choice of the mermaid has gone beyond the original goal of raising money for the arts in Norfolk. The project has captured the spirit of the destination and given visitors a means to map and commemorate a Norfolk travel experience. Visitors can view Mermaids on Parade sculptures via several self-guided trails. (757) 664-4000; www.mermaidsonparade.com.

lush landscapes. A changing educational exhibit area will have programs on plant groups and other horticultural topics. Thirty-minute narrated tours are offered; they are provided on trackless train and canal boats.

Now open at the garden is the exclusive exhibit *World of Wonders (WOW),* designed especially for children. The WOW, set in 3 acres, aims to foster a connection between children and environment by encouraging them to utilize their natural curiosity to explore the garden. The WOW is open daily from 9:30 a.m. to 6:30 p.m.

In the 2 acres of the *Bristow Butterfly Garden* are butterflies and moths, from swallowtail to monarchs, in various stages of their life cycle. Come by to see what you need in your garden to attract and support their visits.

Bike Nights (Apr through mid-Oct) are a great way for families to explore the beautiful landscape and authentic gravel paths surrounding the garden. From April to September, guests are invited to grab their bikes and head to the garden for three hours (Mon, Wed, and Thurs only) of bike riding bliss! Families will also be thrilled by the Family Overnight package, where sleeping under the stars inside the garden proves to be the experience of a lifetime.

If flowers aren't your primary interest, you can spend your between-flight time—or other time—joining others as they do their daily walking and jogging exercises along 12 miles of meandering pathways surrounded by more than 20 theme gardens, including the Renaissance, Japanese, camellia, and holly gardens.

When you're through with the viewing or the exercising, stop by the gift shop for garden books, tools, and gifts, or visit the teahouse for lunch, snacks, and refreshments.

The grounds are the site of more than 100 weddings a year and the annual *April International Azalea Festival.*

Get on the NET

Getting around downtown Norfolk is easier than ever with the free *Norfolk Electric Transit (NET).* These bright blue electric buses run from the Tides baseball home at Harbor Park through the middle of town and connect to the renovated shopping and restaurant district. The weekday route is 2.2 miles with 15 stops in the downtown area while the weekend route makes 9 stops between Nauticus to the Chrysler Museum and back again. Mon through Fri, the buses run from 6:30 a.m. to 11 p.m., from noon to midnight on Sat, and noon to 8 p.m. on Sun. (757) 664-4000; www .norfolk.gov/visitors/net.asp.

The gardens are open daily 9 a.m. to 7 p.m. Apr through mid-Oct and 9 a.m. to 5 p.m. the rest of the year. Adult entry fee is $9, seniors and military $8, and children (3 through 18) $7. Canal boat tours are $5 for adults, Look for the sign at the airport, or follow the road signs from I-64 to 6700 Azalea Garden Rd., Norfolk 23518; (757) 441-5830; www.norfolkbotanical garden.org.

Beautifully landscaped MacArthur Square in downtown Norfolk is the site of the four buildings that make up the *Douglas MacArthur Memorial,* honoring the life of Gen. Douglas MacArthur.

Inside the memorial is a theater with a continuously running 24-minute film on the life and times of the general, one of the most colorful and controversial men in American history. The *Jean MacArthur Research Center* (named after the general's late wife) houses the library and archives, an education wing, and the administrative offices for the MacArthur Memorial and the General Douglas MacArthur Foundation. The gift shop displays General MacArthur's 1950 Chrysler Imperial limousine, which he used from 1950 to the end of his life. Nine galleries on two floors circle the rotunda, where the general and his wife are buried.

There is no admission fee to the memorial, which is open Tues through Sat 10 a.m. to 5 p.m. and Sun 11 a.m. to 5 p.m. MacArthur Square, Norfolk 23510; (757) 441-2965; www.macarthurmemorial.org.

Early Jewish immigrants played an important part in Norfolk history, and their traditions are interpreted at the *Moses Myers House.* The original part of the house was constructed in 1792, then expanded in 1797 to include a commodious dining room for entertaining, and two bedrooms for the nine children Moses and Eliza Myers had. Five generations of descendants of the Myers family lived in this home until it was sold to a preservation group in 1931. In the early 1950s the City of Norfolk bought the residence, and the property is administered by the Chrysler Museum of Art. Nearly 70 percent of the furnishings are original.

You know the famed Gilbert Stuart painting of George Washington; well, there's a matched set of portraits of the senior Myers by Stuart hanging in the drawing room. Other noted American artists are also represented.

The house is open Fri through Sun noon to 4 p.m., Sun 1 to 4 p.m. Tours are given hourly through 3 p.m. 323 E. Freemason St., Norfolk 23510; (757) 333-1087; www.chrysler.org/Myers_house.asp.

The *Chrysler Museum of Art* was named for Walter Chrysler Jr. in 1970, when Norfolk offered to add a wing and rename its museum for him if he would move his art collection from Provincetown, Massachusetts, to Norfolk. The city also named a concert hall at Scope Arena for him.

Naval Station Norfolk

Due to reorganization and consolidation within the US Navy, the world's largest naval station is now officially known as *Naval Station Norfolk.* It occupies about 8,000 acres in the Hampton Roads area and includes the naval base, port services, and air operations. It's home to more than 78 ships from the Atlantic Fleet. Check the website for the 45-minute guided bus tour to see aircraft carriers, destroyers, frigates, historic homes, and more. The fee is $10 for adults and $5 for children 3 through 11 and seniors. A photo ID is required for everyone 16 and older. Buses are not wheelchair accessible. 9079 Hampton Blvd., Norfolk 23505, next to gate 5; (757) 444-7955; https://cnic.navy.mil.

Long considered one of the finest galleries in the country, the Chrysler suffered a potentially severe setback when Chrysler, the museum's chief bene-factor, died and left 751 of his works to a nephew. They had been on loan to the museum, and the loss could have been devastating. The museum, however, retains more than 15,000 works (all gifts of Chrysler) in the permanent collec-tion, valued at more than $100 million. After a $13.5 million renovation and new wing project that increased the museum's space by half, the gallery had a reopening. They also eliminated the admission fee, although contributions are always welcome.

Also unveiled at that time was the James H. Ricau collection of American neoclassical sculpture, considered the most splendid of its kind.

The museum is open Wed 10 a.m. to 9 p.m., Thurs through Sat 10 a.m. to 5 p.m., and Sun noon to 5 p.m. 245 W. Olney Rd., Norfolk 23510; (757) 664-6200; www.chrysler.org.

Anyone who's spent any time in Norfolk is sure to mention *Doumar's Drive-in.* Abe Doumar created the ice-cream cone at the 1904 St. Louis Exposi-tion. He originally called his rolled-up wafer that contained ice cream the "ice-cream cornucopia." After that he opened a concession at Coney Island in 1905 and visited state fairs (President Teddy Roosevelt had a cone at Raleigh, North Carolina). In 1907 a shop was opened in Ocean View, Virginia, where in 1925 his brother George and crew sold 22,600 cones in a single day. After the 1933 hurricane destroyed much of Ocean View Park, George opened the Doumar Drive-in at 19th and Monticello Streets in Norfolk. It was the first and is now one of the last curbside restaurants in Virginia.

Although many people claim the credit for making the first ice-cream cone, Doumar's story stands up the best. The Smithsonian Institution has collected some of his pictures and memorabilia to add to an exhibit in the Museum of

American History in Washington, DC. Barbecue is the main menu item, after the interest in the cones. As they will take the machine out for demonstrations, call to determine whether it will be operational on the day and at the time you want to visit.

Oh, yes, Guy Fieri did visit and feature Doumar's on his Food Network show *Diners, Drive-Ins & Dives* in 2008.

Doumar's is open Mon through Thurs 8 a.m. to 11 p.m., Fri and Sat 8 a.m. to 12:30 a.m. 1919 Monticello Ave., Norfolk 23517; (757) 627-4163; www .doumars.com.

In 1912 a grand lady, the **Wells Theatre,** now the **Virginia Stage Company at the Wells Theatre,** opened to a capacity house with the musical *The Merry Countess.* The theater was converted into a movie house in 1935 after such stars as Billie Burke, Douglas Fairbanks, Fred and Adele Astaire, Will Rogers, and others had trod her boards. As at other theaters of the time, the '60s brought the garish light of X-rated flicks, and a bar was built where the stage had been. The fair damsel was saved from such distress when the Virginia Stage Company took over in October 1979 and the bar was removed. The thrust stage was built, and the lobby was returned to its approximate original size. The interior and exterior were scrubbed clean, paint was applied, seats were reupholstered, new carpet was laid, and productions once again were mounted.

The Virginia Stage Company presents a handful of plays each year, usually worth seeing, but the amazing artistry that went into this steel-reinforced concrete structure of the pre–Beaux Arts period is a command performance. 108–114 E. Tazewell St., Norfolk 23510; (757) 627-6988 (administration) or (757) 627-1234 (box office); www.vastage.com.

The 53-acre **Virginia Zoological Park** has been established to accurately reflect an entire habitat for its more than 350 animals and birds, so when you visit you will find plants in the animal exhibits and animals in the plant exhibits. With the monkeys are vines and assorted habitat plants; with the cats are jungle flora. This is such an important part of the operation that visitors receive a *Botanical Conservatory Guide* to help you through the zoo.

Cannonball Run

Well, actually it's the **Cannonball Trail** winding its way along historic sites in downtown Norfolk. The walk-it-yourself tour is a storytelling stage for interpreting 400 years of Norfolk's history with 40 stops along the way. Begin your sojourn at the Freemason Street Reception Center, 401 E. Freemason St., Norfolk 23510; (757) 664-6620 or (800) 368–3097; www.norfolkcvb.com.

The conservatory was built in 1907. Also there are more than 3,000 blooming annuals and 150 hanging baskets. The rose garden has beds of floribunda, hybrid tea, and climbing varieties.

There was plenty of excitement in 2007 with several new arrivals, including Yin, a 1-year-old red panda from the San Diego Zoo; prairie dog pups who can be seen tumbling around their exhibit and learning prairie dog social skills from their parents; new eastern gray kangaroos in their freshly renovated exhibit; a squirrel monkey named George; and a dromedary camel named Hercules.

The zoo is open daily 10 a.m. to 5 p.m. except on major winter holidays. Admission is $11 for adults, $10 for seniors 62 and older, and $9 for children 2 through 11. Zoo members and rug rats are free. The zoo train schedule depends on the season and definitely only runs on days when the temperature is 50 degrees Fahrenheit or above. Train tickets are $2 each. 3500 Granby St., Norfolk 23504; (757) 441-2374; www.virginiazoo.org.

The **d'ART Center** (Dockside Art Review of Tidewater) resides in the heart of downtown's historic **Selden Arcade.** The complex features 1930s art deco–style architecture and houses 50 artists (sculptors, painters, jewelers, potters, etc.) who create, display, and sell their works. Free studio tours are available, and children's and adult classes and workshops are offered. Five galleries hold changing exhibits of local, regional, and national artists.

Open Tues through Sat 10 a.m. to 5 p.m. and Sun 1 to 5 p.m., there's no admission charge so you should be able to afford a wonderful souvenir that you wouldn't find anywhere else. 208 E. Main St., Selden Arcade, Norfolk 23510; (757) 625-4211; www.d-artcenter.org.

We all "know" that milk comes from stores, not cows. And unless your children have watched or helped you put up jams and jellies, one can only assume that the little ones think these things come from stores, too.

Take your school-age children to **Rowena's** to watch them make jams and jellies, pound cakes, cooking sauces, and other items. Carrot jam is a Rowena's specialty. The kitchen boasts two extra-large mixers that used to be on the USS *United States*. Rowena Fullinwider started this operation in 1983 and now is doing a million-dollar business shipping food to such exotic places as Guam and Finland. Take the paper tour hat, try some samples, and receive a place mat children can color. Tours are available from mid-January through mid-October, $2 each and reservations are required. Allow 30 minutes, plus time in the gift shop where you can buy cakes, sauces, foods produced for Colonial Williamsburg, recipes, and children's story cookbooks *The Adventures of Rowena and the Wonderful Jam and Jelly Factory,* and *The Adventures of Rowena and Carrot Jam the Rabbit*. Remember, the factory can get very warm during the summer months. The store is open Tues through Sat 9 a.m. to 5 p.m.

Home Porting

Home porting is the phrase used by the cruise industry as cruise ships are based in various ports around the country, eliminating the need for travelers to fly to somewhere to get somewhere.

Carnival's *Glory* departs periodically from Norfolk's $36 million ship terminal, called **Half Moone Cruise and Celebration Center.** It's an 80,000-square-foot, 2-story terminal, located between Nauticus and Town Point Park. It's made of corrugated steel and glass that gives it a smooth, nautical look. It was the first cruise terminal in the nation to fully comply with Homeland Security standards. Norfolk certainly knows its starboard from its port. (757) 664-1000; www.cruisenorfolk.org.

all year, and a catalog is available. The tearoom is open Fri and Sat 11 a.m. to 4 p.m. 758 W. 22nd St., Norfolk 23517; (800) 627-8699 or (757) 627-8699; www .rowenas.com.

Not everything is old in Virginia, although it may cover historic material. **Nauticus, the National Maritime Center** is a hands-on entertainment and education center with scores of interesting exhibits about the exploration of the world's oceans. This is a wonderful place to learn how vast the influences of water are on our lives, for it encompasses marine biology and oceanography, commercial shipping, naval technology, shipbuilding, and energy exploration. Whether your fascination is with science, technology, commerce, or the siren call of the deep, you'll see how the sea connects to our existence—and it's fun.

What does all this mean? Simply that you can sit in the captain's chair in the Navy pilothouse and observe the harbor from the bridge. You can plot ships in the harbor on the live Nauticus radar. How would you like to land your plane (F14 or prop) on an aircraft carrier (video game) or be a weatherman and conduct your own television show? One of my favorites in any marine exhibit is the touch pool, where you can feel the creatures of the sea, and Nauticus has one. Kids of various ages love periscopes, so they can check this one out and target in on a ship in the harbor.

This $52 million project is set on three levels at Norfolk's Waterside complex, at the west end of the waterfront, adjacent to Town Point Park. There's docking space on the water for research ships and active Navy ships, which you may visit.

Exhibits have been assembled with the assistance of the Coast Guard, Navy, Old Dominion University, Norfolk State University, the College of William and Mary's Institute of Marine Science, and the National Oceanic and Atmospheric Administration.

As part of the US Navy's 225th anniversary in late fall 2000, the battleship *USS* **Wisconsin** was located adjacent to Nauticus. Launched December 7, 1943, the warship—at 888 feet one of the longest ever built—was one of the last four battleships built by the United States for service in World War II. It also saw action during the Korean conflict and the Persian Gulf action. Norfolk was the home port of the *Wisconsin* during most of its active-duty career. Included in locating the ship here was the building of a berth and a connecting walkway to the museum. The ship is open daily 10 a.m. to 5 p.m. from Memorial Day through Labor Day; Tues through Sat 10 a.m. to 5 p.m., and Sun noon to 5 p.m. the rest of the year. www.nauticus.org/exhibits/battleship-wisconsin.

In addition, the **Hampton Roads Naval Museum** has been relocated to this spot (perhaps the only naval museum not on a Navy installation). Nauticus is open daily 10 a.m. to 5 p.m. Memorial Day through Labor Day, Tues through Sat 10 a.m. to 5 p.m. and Sun noon to 5 p.m. the rest of the year. Admission, which includes the USS *Wisconsin,* is $11.95 for adults and $9.50 for children from 4 to 12. Discounts are available for seniors and members of AAA and the military. A package Nauticus and 2-hour boat tour aboard the *Victory Rover* ticket is also available. 1 Waterside Dr., Norfolk 23510; (757) 664-1000; www.nauticus.org.

Portsmouth

By water or highway, it's south of Norfolk to the town of Portsmouth.

When Herb Simpson started the **Virginia Sports Hall of Fame and Museum,** he said, "Virginia has an outstanding record of producing great athletes." After a look at the Texas Sports Hall of Fame in Dallas, he thought Virginia should honor its talent, too, so he helped organize the Hall of Fame in 1966, and in March 1972 the first induction banquet was held in Portsmouth. It opened in Olde Towne on April 3, 1977. A 35,000-square-foot facility opened in April 2005, and it has a digital theater with a 16-foot high-definition project screen to show Virginia's sports traditions and televised games. Displays show uniforms, trophies, and other memorabilia highlighting the careers and records of Cy Young, Sam Snead, Arthur Ashe, Norman Snead, Shelly Mann, and more than 200 Virginia athletes representing 20 sports. Recipients must have been

ferrymeback tooldvirginny

The first ferry service in America was established in 1636 on the Elizabeth River between Portsmouth and Norfolk. The *Gosport,* the first steam-powered ferry, was christened in 1832 and crossed the Elizabeth River in 5 minutes.

born in Virginia or have made significant contributions to their sport(s) in Virginia.

You can dribble a basketball, toss a football, pitch a baseball, or take a virtual treadmill hike through the Shenandoah. The museum has something for everyone, from the Redskins room to the NASCAR racing area!

The architectural team, van Dijk Pace Westlake, is known for its work with both the cultural arts and nonprofit organizations across the country.

The Hall is open from Mon through Sat 10 a.m. to 5 p.m., and Sun 1 to 6 p.m. Memorial Day through Labor Day; Tues through Sat 10 a.m. to 2 p.m., and Sun 1 to 5 p.m. the rest of the year. Admission is $7 per person, $6 for seniors and military personnel. Children 2 and under are free. 206 High St., Portsmouth 23705; (757) 393-8031; www.vshfm.com.

The ***Children's Museum of Virginia*** is more than 74,000 square feet of foot-stomping, bubble-blowing, music-making, educational fun. Located in Olde Towne Portsmouth, the museum is based on the philosophy that children learn by doing. With more than 90 interactive exhibits (making it the largest interactive children's museum in Virginia) dedicated to enhancing the cultural, educational, and recreational development of children, the museum encourages a lifelong love of learning.

See the stars in the planetarium. Find out how much power it takes to run household appliances. Learn how sound travels in waves. Blow some bubbles. Make music. Climb a rock wall. Discover that bits, bytes, and chips aren't just in chocolate chip cookies. And be sure to marvel at the $1 million Lancaster Antique Toy and Model Train Collection, an amazing collection of antique toys and one of the most incredible train collections in the world!

Huge expansion plans caused the museum to be closed for a while, but as of May 25, 2011, the doors were reopened to many more years of educational fun. Yes, the bubble machine, the antique toy and train collection, and the planetarium will be retained. 221 High St., Portsmouth 23704; (757) 393-5238; www.childrensmuseumva.com.

While you're in Portsmouth's Olde Towne, take the long (1-hour) or short (15-minute) walking tour along the brick sidewalks through this oldest portion of Portsmouth. Land patents were granted as early as 1659. Look for Historic Portsmouth markers on the streetlamps, which indicate stopping points.

Along the way you'll see the ***Cassell House,*** with its hand-carved arched doorway and stone lintels and sills at the windows; the Old Courthouse, built in 1846; Trinity Church, the oldest church in Portsmouth, dating back to 1761; and numerous other buildings that represent a variety of architectural styles and influences including Dutch colonial, English basement, Gothic Revival, Victorian, Federal, and Romanesque Revival.

Additional information about Portsmouth's architecture is available for a slight charge at the Office of City Planning, 1 High St.

Isle of Wight

Smithfield is the self-proclaimed "Ham Capital of the World." P. D. Gwaltney Sr. started his curing process in 1870, and the Smithfield curing process is protected by law. Only a ham cured within the Smithfield town limits can bear the name. You can smell the delicious aroma for miles around. The *Isle of Wight County Museum* offers a display about ham history and exhibits on the Civil War and Indian artifacts. There's also a reproduction of an old country store. The museum is open Mon through Sat from 10 a.m. to 4 p.m. and Sun from 1 to 5 p.m. 103 Main St., Smithfield 23430; (757) 357-7459; www.smithfield-virginia.com.

Pick up the brochure for the scenic Smithfield *Historic Old Town Walking Tour* and proceed past buildings dating from the mid- and late-1750s (the completely restored Old Courthouse—which is one of the state's oldest operating courthouses—and Clerk's Office at 130 Main St. and Pollard House at 108 Cary, the Old Jail at 106 N. Mason, the Eason-Whitley House at 220 S. Church, and others) up to pre–Civil War times. The mix of housing styles is almost eclectic. Early residents either tore down or updated their homes to make way for the newest styles (keeping up with the Smiths rather than the Joneses, if you will). Therefore, as you stroll around, you'll see Colonial, Federal, and Victorian styles. Fifteen homes and four buildings, 14 of which predate the Revolutionary War, are authentically 18th century. You can also view the four identical Victorian houses on Main Street and the Gingerbread Cottage on Grace Street. You can spend at least 90 minutes on this walk and expand it to three hours. For information call (757) 357-5182 or (800) 365-9339.

Guided walking tours are offered by the Tourism Bureau and iPod tours (iPods provided) are available at the Isle of Wight County Museum. Group tours should be scheduled in advance. Agricultural tours also are available at *Darden's Country Store and Smokehouse,* in season, to see peanuts from seeds to shelling and grading and cotton from plants to ginning and the Darden

funfacts

When you stop by the *Isle of Wight County Museum,* take a look at the interactive exhibit of a one-ton-plus ham biscuit. A Guinness World Record was awarded for this super-size edible created in honor of Smithfield's 250th anniversary. You can also see Smithfield Ham's oldest ham—more than 100 years old—protected in a glass case.

family's popular smokehouse tour. The hours are Mon through Sat 7 a.m. to 6 p.m. 16249 Bowling Green Rd., Smithfield 23430; (757) 357-6791.

The **Schoolhouse Museum** is an African-American History Museum of Public Education. The two-room building was constructed in 1932 and features period desks and books. Oral histories have been given by those who attended the school. 516 Main St., Smithfield 23431; (757) 365-4789; www.theschool housemuseum.com.

Gracious lodging is available at the **Smithfield Inn and Tavern Bed and Breakfast,** said to be one of the town's most enduring landmarks. It's been providing lodging in its 5 rooms (some with fireplaces) and serving meals since 1752, with slight interruptions when it was used as a rectory for the Christ Episcopal Church and for a period after the Civil War when it was uninhabitable. 112 Main St., Smithfield 23430; (757) 357-1752; www.smithfieldinn.com.

Fort Huger, the "gateway to the Confederate capital" is the newest old attraction in the area. From here you can see the ghost fleet on the James River, take a walk through the trails, and see cannon mounted along the edges of the fort. The fort is open daily from 8 a.m. to dusk. 5080 Talcott Terrace, Smithfield 23430; (757) 357-5182; www.visitsmithfieldisleofwight.com.

Those who love to wander the waters around the James River and find their way to Pagan River have been delighted with **Smithfield Station Waterfront Inn and Marina,** at the junction of the two creeks that form the river. Run by Ron and Tina Pack, it's a carefree place dedicated to those who want to pull up to a dock, be greeted by the owners, and not have to worry about "dressing" for dinner. The specialties at the restaurant are, naturally enough, seafood and pork, including Smithfield "Lean Generation Pork." Entertainment and special events are held on the boardwalk adjacent to the restaurant. Newlyweds and anniversary celebrants might enjoy the Cape Chesapeake Bay–style lighthouse building with honeymoon suites.

Stay a day or two and rent a bicycle or canoe to really "sit back" and relax. Then head out and go crabbing or look for osprey and eagles, deer, and muskrat. 415 S. Church St., Smithfield 23430; (757) 357-7700; www.smithfield station.com.

Just across the street from the Station is the new **Windsor Castle Park,** a 209-acre riverside facility in the heart of downtown Smithfield. From here you have 4 miles of wooded walking trails, a dog park, state-of-the-art canoe/kayak launch, fruit orchards, fishing pier, scenic overlooks, picnic areas, and the Windsor Castle Historic Site. It's open daily from dawn until dusk and there's no admission charge. 301 Jericho Rd., Smithfield 23430; (757) 356-9939.

About 2 miles south of Smithfield on Route 10 is historic **St. Luke's Church (or St. Luke's Shrine),** known also as the "Old Brick Church," the nation's oldest original Gothic church. The construction date is pegged at 1632, although the style is perhaps that of 75 years earlier. On the other hand, the earliest Anglican records date several decades after the 1630s. One theory says that the church was built by members of the Lost Colony of Roanoke Island, even before the settlement of Jamestown. At the entrance you'll find a wicket door within a larger door. Inside are a mid-17th-century communion table and chairs, a 17th-century silver baptismal basin, original Gothic tracery windows, and a 1665 English organ.

The church is open daily from 9:30 a.m. to 5 p.m. and Sun 1 to 5 p.m. from Apr through Oct with the property gates opening at 8 a.m. and closing at 7 p.m. During the winter, it is open Tues through Sat 9:30 a.m. to 4 p.m. and Sun 1 to 4 p.m. The gates close at 5:30 p.m. Admission is $5 for adults, $4 for seniors (62 and older), and $3 for students. Children 12 and under are admitted with no charge. 14477 Benn's Church Blvd., Smithfield 23430; (757) 357-3367; www.historicstlukes.org.

Fort Boykin Historic Park, on the high cliffs over the James River (which is navigable to Richmond), has been around since 1623 and has been involved in every military campaign fought on American soil. It first protected the colonists against the "Spaniards by sea and the Indians by land" and then was refortified during the Revolutionary War. It is named in honor of Major Francis Boykin, a member of General George Washington's staff. Its current seven-pointed star shape was created during the War of 1812, but much of the property was destroyed by a Union landing party. While the American poet Sidney Lanier was stationed here during the Civil War, he wrote "Hoe Cakes" and "Beautiful Ladies" and started his novel *Tiger Lilies*. The property had pretty much returned to nature until 1908, when Mr. and Mrs. Herbert Greer bought it and started landscaping the grounds. Picnickers are welcome and the grounds are open daily from 8 a.m. to dusk. 7410 Ft. Boykin Trail, Smithfield 23430; (757) 357-0115; www.co.isle-of-wight.va.us.

Suffolk City

Just the name of the ***Great Dismal Swamp National Wildlife Refuge*** sounds depressing, but nature lovers should jump for joy. Wander along the 140 miles of hiking and biking trails in this 111,000-acre swamp and you'll see bald cypress, shady creeks, and maybe barred owls, otters, bats, raccoons, and bears. Canoe and kayak access to Lake Drummond is via the feeder ditch near Chesapeake. There are no entrance fees.

The headquarters is open Mon through Fri from 7:30 a.m. to 4 p.m. 3100 Desert Rd., Suffolk 23434; (757) 986-3705; http://greatdismalswamp.fws.gov.

The **Prentis House** (circa 1800), one of the oldest standing homes in Suffolk, has undergone an extensive restoration and is now the Suffolk Visitor Center and Division of Tourism office. The center is open daily from 9 a.m. to 5 p.m.

Narrated bus tours of the Great Dismal Swamp National Wildlife Refuge depart from the center. 321 N. Main St., Suffolk 23434; (866) SEE-SUFK or (757) 923-3880; www.suffolk-fun.com/welcome.html.

In 1837 Mills Riddick built an impressive Greek Revival house, a style fairly common in the Midwest but rarely seen this far south, and it was immediately labeled **Riddick's Folly.** As with most follies that still stand, he was proven right over the years. The carved cypress woodwork survives, as do the decorative medallions that crown the 14-foot ceilings.

The rooms that housed five generations of his descendants are now home to gallery space for changing and semipermanent exhibits, lectures, and art workshops; a gift shop where local artists and crafters sell their work; and the archives of the Suffolk Nansemond Historical Society.

Riddick's Folly is open Thurs through Fri 10 a.m. to 5 p.m., Sat 10 a.m. to 4 p.m., and Sun 1 to 5 p.m. Ninety-minute guided tours are available. Admission is $4 for adults, $3 for seniors and active military, and $2 for children. It is partially wheelchair accessible. 510 N. Main St., Suffolk 23439; (757) 934-0822; www.riddicksfolly.org.

Surry County

A visit to the **Surry House Restaurant** is required for so many people visiting this area, particularly on a sunny Sunday after church. In operation since 1954, the Surrey House specializes in ham, seafood, pork, and poultry dishes as well as other regional fare—it's Southern cooking at its best! I recommend that you begin your meal with peanut soup, a creamy delicacy full of chunky bits of world-famous Virginia peanuts. As a main dish, the Surrey House Surf and Turf is typically Virginian, featuring a combination of ham and crab cakes. Other regional dishes include delicious hamhocks, great Southern fried chicken, and house-made desserts. For the latter, if you haven't had enough of the peanuts yet, try the peanut raisin pie, a proudly served local variation on the South's ubiquitous pecan pie. It's delicious. This restaurant has a waiting list on weekends and holidays, so reservations are recommended. 11865 Rolfe Hwy., Surry 23883; (757) 294-3389; www.surreyhouserestaurant.com.

The free **Scotland-Jamestown Ferry,** or the Jamestown-Scotland Ferry (clearance 12 feet, 6 inches), connects Route 31 over the James River and is the only 24-hour state-run ferry operation in Virginia. Four ferries (*Virginia,*

Williamsburg, Surry, and *Pocahontas*) can carry from 28 to 70 cars. Highway 31; (800) VA-FERRY; www.virginiadot.org/travel/ferry-jamestown.asp.

Historic Triangle

Now it's time to head east-northeast, and then west-northwest, traveling along Route 58 as the most direct route. Then pick up I-664 to take the Monitor-Merrimac Memorial Bridge Tunnel and go toward the historic triangle of *Jamestown, Yorktown,* and *Colonial Williamsburg.*

These areas are not exactly off the beaten path, but there is some confusion about Historic Jamestowne and Jamestown Settlement, and neither they nor Yorktown are visited by as many people as stop in Williamsburg.

As a child, my visits to *Jamestown Settlement,* previously Jamestown Festival Park, were at least an annual treat. It's amazing how much things have changed over the years as historians have learned more about what happened here and how people lived here centuries ago.

Stockades used to be a feature; they aren't now because historians determined that stockades weren't used in Colonial Jamestown.

Costumed guides no longer talk in first person because they found it off-putting for some people who didn't know how to ask questions and difficult to stay in character when confronted with a question about cameras, for example. The guides still wear what was worn, to some extent, but you'll also find guys with earrings, and one would suspect that the early settlers didn't do that.

Obviously, history buffs love this area and at *Historic Jamestowne* you can see the first permanent English settlement in North America. Of particular interest is the Nathalie P. and Alan M. Voorhees Archaearium where objects belonging to the colonists 400 years ago and unearthed from the James Fort site are on display. The objects display a new understanding of the settlers and their relationship with the Virginia Indians. Learn how the archaeologists found the fort and see arms and armor, medical instruments, and much more. Yes, dead men do tell tales, and you can see the remains believed to be of Captain Bartholomew Gosnold, a Jamestown founding father.

Historic Jamestowne is open daily from 8:30 a.m. to 4:30 p.m., although once admitted, you may stay until dusk. It is closed on major winter holidays. Tickets are $10 for adults and free for children 15 and under. They're good for 7 consecutive days. Combination tickets for Historic Jamestowne, Jamestown Settlement, Yorktown Battlefield, and the Yorktown Victory Center are available at $29.25 for adults, $19.25 for youth 13 through 15, and $9.25 for children 6 through 12. Jamestown Visitor Center, Colonial Parkway; (757) 856-1200; www.historicjamestowne.org.

It's a New World

The New World, an epic film written and directed by Terrence Malick and starring Colin Farrell as John Smith, Christian Bale as John Rolfe, Christopher Plummer as Christopher Newport, August Schellenberg as Chief Powhatan, and Q'orianka Kilcher as Pocahontas, opened in movie theaters in January 2006 and portrays the adventure of the first encounter of European and Virginia Indian cultures during the founding of Jamestown settlement in 1607. *The New World* shot for six months in Charles City and James City Counties, in Richmond, and at the Chicohominy Wildlife Management Area.

The Jamestown Settlement is located adjacent to the entrance of Historic Jamestowne. The Settlement area features Powhatan Village, a Riverfront Discovery Area, and the life of the settlers through film, gallery exhibits, and living history. You can see and board replicas of the three ships—the *Susan Constant, Godspeed,* and *Discovery*—that sailed from England in 1607. Guided tours of the museum's living-history areas are offered several times daily. The Settlement is open daily from 9 a.m. to 5 p.m., and until 6 p.m. from mid-June through mid-Aug.

Basic Jamestown Settlement tickets are $15.50 for adults and $7.25 for children 6 through 12. However, they have more combinations, Web specials, and more ticket options than you can shake a stick at, so check the site to see what's available when you want to visit. (757) 253-4838; www.historyisfun.org/ Jamestown-Settlement.htm.

At the ***Yorktown Victory Center,*** you'll see the history of the October 19, 1781, decisive military campaign of the American Revolution. The Siege of Yorktown ended the 6-year struggle for American independence. Today you can see the evolution from colonial status to nationhood with film, exhibits, and outdoor living history. The indoor exhibits follow 10 ordinary men and women who experienced the Siege. A re-created Continental Army encampment is outdoors, and you can learn about the daily lives of American soldiers at the end of the war. There's even a 1780s farm with a house, kitchen, tobacco barn, crop fields, and herb and vegetable gardens.

Yorktown Victory Center is open daily from 9 a.m. to 5 p.m., and until 6 p.m. from mid-June to mid-August. Admission to the center is $9.50 for adults and $5.25 for children 6 through 12. See the prices for the Jamestown Settlement for combination prices. (757) 253-4838 or (888) 593-4682; www.historyis fun.org/Yorktown-Victory-Center.htm.

You can also visit the Yorktown Battlefield and the Yorktown Visitor Center, the Nelson House (open spring through fall), Moore House (open spring through fall as staffing permits), and more. The area is open daily from 9 a.m. to 5 p.m. Admission is $10 for 7 days and includes Historic Jamestowne. Colonial Parkway; (757) 898-2410; www.nps.gov/york.

It's said the Williamsburg Pottery (outlet center) has more visitors than **Colonial Williamsburg** does, perhaps because history is history, but a good bargain is hard to beat. Nevertheless, I promote repeat visits to Colonial Williamsburg because displays change, seasons change, and your perspective changes.

moorepeace, please

The **Moore House,** part of the Colonial National Historical Park, at Yorktown, is the site where the terms of surrender for the British army were negotiated on October 17, 1781. The house is restored and decorated with 18th-century–style furnishings. It is open as staffing permits, so contact the office for current hours: (757) 898-2410.

Some differences are more subtle than others. During winter some furniture may wear slipcovers or some pieces may be displayed that wouldn't be displayed in the summer heat. During fall you can watch or even participate in grape stomping, something you won't find in spring or summer.

In recent years more emphasis has been placed on making the colonial experience accessible to those with hearing, vision, or maneuverability limitations. Some places are accessible, some places have portable wheelchair ramps available, and slide programs about inaccessible areas of some of the buildings are being created.

On the other hand, there are few curbs in the restored city, and automobiles are not permitted on the main streets during the day. An escorted walking tour is available for the visually impaired, and a special tour of the Powell-Waller House can be arranged. Free publications for the hearing impaired are available, as are discount tickets for some programs. For a copy of the *Colonial Williamsburg Guide for the Handicapped,* write to P.O. Box C, Williamsburg 23187, or call (757) 229-1000.

The Governor's Palace has undergone a remarkable makeover to show the lifestyle of Lord Dunmore, the last royal governor of Virginia, and his family. The Lord issued a proclamation in 1775 calling for all able-bodied men to assist him in defense of the British colony, including slaves who were promised their freedom in exchange for service in the King's Army. This was very controversial at the time, especially among slaveholders, who feared a mass slave rebellion. But the proclamation proved successful and within a month Dunmore had more than 800 soldiers.

Other changes over the years include exhibits and tours featuring "The Other Half" of the population, for during the 18th century half the population

Sign on the Dotted Line . . .

The **Nelson House,** on Main Street in Yorktown, was the home of Thomas Nelson Jr., a signer of the Declaration of Independence, a governor of Virginia, and commander of the Virginia Militia during the Siege of Yorktown. The Georgian mansion has been restored, and you can tour it depending on staffing availability. (757) 898-2410; www.nps.gov/york.htm.

of Williamsburg was black. Some of these African Americans, both slave and free, were cooks, maids, footmen, and drivers; others were skilled carpenters, blacksmiths, coopers, wheelwrights, and spinners. Take the Other Half tour, or pick up a brochure to learn how they influenced life in Colonial Williamsburg.

As a marker of time passing, when this book was first published, the **DeWitt Wallace Decorative Art Museum** had just opened. It's now been around long enough that it's been redone and once again is open for your enjoyment and astonishment at the beautiful things housed there. You'll find finely crafted 17th- to 19th-century household items here. The **Abby Aldrich Rockefeller Folk Art Museum,** in its expanded facility, features America's premier collection of works created by unschooled American artists, so this is the place to visit if you like rough-hewn toys, weather vanes, and painted furniture.

Evening programs have expanded, so you don't have to stay in your hotel room watching the television as if you weren't even on vacation. Family tours, shows, and concerts explore Colonial Williamsburg at night, and topics might include what frightened people out of their breeches and how they explained the unexplainable.

There are a handful of ticketing options for Colonial Williamsburg, including a hotel guest pass, Historic Area, Art Museums of Colonial Williamsburg, Programs and Tours, and Memorable Family Experiences. Go through the options to see which is best for you. Williamsburg Visitor Center; (800) HISTORY; www.colonialwilliamsburg.com.

Charles City County

A short drive west of Williamsburg (or east of Richmond), in Charles City County, is **Piney Grove at Southall's Plantation** that offers bed-and-breakfast style lodging and keeps you in a historic mood while you're visiting the nearby colonial sights. Depending on the season, your visit begins with mint juleps on the front porch or hot toddies by a roaring fire. Another option is a bottle of Virginia wine or cider from the Piney Grove wine cellar selection, including vintages from the Williamsburg Winery.

In the 1857 Ladysmith House, the guest rooms are furnished with antiques and modern conveniences. Outside, there's a pool, gazebo, nature trail, and lawn games for those times when you just can't spend one more minute in a shop or tour another historic site. Animals occupy the barnyard.

You might not want to think about sleeping in, though, for the farm bell announces your plantation candlelight breakfast in the 1790 log room.

House and garden tours are available, either on a separate ticket or as a package with other local plantations. 16920 Southall Plantation Lane, Charles City 23030; (804) 829-2480 or (804) 829-2196; www.pineygrove.com.

All that sightseeing and shopping can make one hungry, but not everyone wants to stop for food. Helen and Ike Sisane, the proprietors of the **Williamsburg Sampler Bed & Breakfast,** help solve that problem with Ike's "Skip Lunch" breakfast. It started when a former Penn State football player stayed over, and Ike decided the guy needed a little extra food for breakfast. The former football player described it as a "skip lunch meal" and the name stuck. A typical meal includes orange juice, fruit platter, eggs, meat and potatoes, muffins, and beverage.

The home is a stately 3-story, 18th-century plantation-style building with 6 bedrooms, including a 2-room suite. 922 Jamestown Road, Williamsburg 23185; (757) 253-0398 or (800) 722-1169; www.williamsburgsampler.com.

funfacts

John Tyler was the first vice president to ascend to the presidency when he assumed the office after the death of William Henry Harrison, ninth president of the United States.

You've no doubt heard that Virginia is the mother of presidents, and John Tyler, 10th president of the United States, lived from 1842 until his death in 1862 at **Sherwood Forest Plantation.** This classic example of Virginia Tidewater design has been elegantly restored and furnished with Tyler's possessions and shows the lifestyle of this mid-19th-century family. The home is situated on 25 acres of terraced gardens and lawns, woods, and landscape and surrounded by six original outbuildings. The home is still owned by the Tyler family, and his great-grandson, who still resides at the plantation with his wife, oversaw the important restoration in the mid-1970s.

At more than 300 feet long, this is reported to be the longest frame house in America. President Tyler added a 68-foot ballroom in 1845 to accommodate the popular dance of his time, the Virginia Reel.

The house and grounds are open for self-guided tours for $10 per adults with children 15 and under admitted free. The house tour is available by appointment, for $35 per person. 14501 John Tyler Hwy., Charles City 23030; (804) 829-5377; www.sherwoodforest.org.

DelMarVa

The most logical way to cross the Chesapeake Bay, unless you have a boat, is to use the **Chesapeake Bay Bridge-Tunnel,** officially called the Lucius J. Kelkew Jr. Bridge-Tunnel, to get from the main part of Virginia to the Eastern Shore, the southern part of the DelMarVa (Delaware, Maryland, Virginia) Peninsula.

Trains still use a ferry service provided by the Bay Coast Railroad Car Barge between Norfolk/Virginia Beach (Little Creek) and the Eastern Shore. This service provides essential service from one of the busiest ports in the country and reduces truck traffic that otherwise would have to take I-64 and I-95 north and east or transfer cargo to trucks to go across the bridge-tunnel. The 26 miles of water route is said to be the longest water route in the country. A similar barge service, "64 Express," connects Hampton Roads to the Port of Richmond that takes lots of trucks off I-64. 202 Mason Ave., Cape Charles; (737) 331-1094, ext. 13.

The bridge-tunnel, at 20 miles, is the world's longest bridge-tunnel complex. There are 2 mile-long tunnels, more than 12 miles of trestled railway, 2 bridges, nearly 2 miles of causeway, 4 man-made islands, and 5.5 miles of approach roads.

At **One Island** (the one closest to Virginia Beach, 3.5 miles), you can eat at the **Chesapeake Grill** restaurant, which is owned by Christopher and Kellson Savvides, the owners of Black Angus Restaurant and Catering in Virginia Beach. It is open 7 a.m. to 6 p.m. mid-Sept through mid-May and 6 a.m. to 10 p.m. mid-May through mid-Sept. Additionally, **Virginia Originals** store offers things that are good about the Commonwealth.

Take a minute or two to watch the ships coming into and going out of the harbor; drown a line for bluefish, trout, croaker, flounder, shark, and other species from the 625-foot fishing pier (bait and tackle are available). Leo Olivarez, a utility contractor company supervisor, gave proof to the bounty of the sea when he was fishing around the rocks of the third island on June 22, 2008. Although he was fishing for small bluefish to use for flounder bait, he ended up with a world-record setting 9 pound, 13 ounce spadefish (on 6-pound test line), which earned him an award from the Virginia Saltwater Fishing Tournament.

Whether you stop to visit or go from one side to the other, it's sure a marvelous way to see the magnificent confluence of the Chesapeake Bay and the Atlantic Ocean. A 45-minute film about the bridge-tunnel is available for viewing by appointment.

The toll is $12 (for automobiles) each way with a $5 charge if you return within 24 hours and show your receipt; if, however, you tell the toll taker that you're going out to the island and will be returning without going all the way across the bay, you will be charged only once. If you don't do this ahead of time, you will be charged a second $12 toll for coming back the other direction. E-ZPass is now an acceptable payment. (757) 331-1-2960; www.cbbt.com.

Just before you travel the bridge-tunnel (or in case you really don't want to travel it), the western tunnel entrance is great for watching the bay shipping traffic navigate the waterways. You might see a submarine come booming out of the water (they can't traverse the bay submerged) or an aircraft carrier, but you're almost certain to see something interesting. So, grab a cup of coffee and sit a few minutes; perhaps you'll have a tale to tell your friends and family for years to come.

As mentioned in the introduction, two Virginia counties are located on the Eastern Shore of the DelMarVa Peninsula. Normally, thousands of people just drive north or south on US 13 and never bother to see what's on either side of them. Fortunately, for those who like to get off that beaten path, there's a lot happening here.

Jim Rapp is the director of the ***DelMarVa Low Impact Tourism*** (DLITE), a group of businesses, conservation organizations, and other partners from the peninsula who, since 2001, have worked and continue to work to encourage nature- and heritage-based tourism and conservation on the Peninsula. They promote such activities as birding, biking, kayaking, and stand-up paddling. They teach park and museum employees the joys of the local stories and low-impact travel. Their website has lists of events, activities, wildlife, camping, destinations, museums, resources, and so much more so you can be part of the "Leave No Trace" movement. P.O. Box 669, Salisbury, Maryland 21803; (443) 944-8097; www.dliteonline.net.

Some of the "happenings" are very today and tomorrow. Sometimes the FedEx pickup and delivery depends on the winds across the Bridge Tunnel and if they're too stiff, then trucks aren't allowed across the bridge. Some things tell their old tales. For instance, the two counties have the oldest consecutive court records in the entire United States of America.

For those who participate in the annual Christmas bird count, you'll gladly have your pinfeathers pulled when you learn that more than 150 species have been spotted. That's one of the highest counts north of Florida. Monarch butterflies migrate through here, and birders have been known to band every-thing from bald eagles to hummingbirds.

Could any place be more idyllic?

Oh, you say, birds and butterflies don't mean anything to you. You want to fish! Be one on one with nature and the deep. Okay, this is the place for you: You can try your luck catching—are you ready?—amberjack; Atlantic, Spanish, and king mackerel; black and red drum; blue and white marlin; bluefin and yellowfin tuna; bluefish; croaker; dolphin; flounder; gray trout; sea bass; spot; striped bass; tautog; and wahoo.

Northampton

The two Virginia counties on the Eastern Shore are Accomac and Northampton. The dozens of hamlets in these two counties are known for their surf and deep-water fishing, seafood, crafters, sweet potatoes, chicken, and a grand welcome to those who are "come-heres" (families who have been in Virginia for less than three generations).

Almost all directions are given as "off Route 13," for that is the main high-way through this area. There are several "searoads," which basically parallel the highway, such as Route 316 on the bay (Chesapeake) side and Routes 600 and 604 on the sea (Atlantic Ocean) side. It's along these roads that you'll find some of the unique Eastern Shore architecture, including homes with four different roof levels referred to as "big house, little house, colonnade, and kitchen."

If you've been here and delighted in the quaint drawbridge over the Chincoteague Channel, a swing bridge that started service in 1940, it's gone. It was demolished in January 2011 and, yet, it won't be forgotten. The town requested a few relics from the bridge including the control cab, the bridge tender's house, and the slide gates. A bridge fender will be used as a fishing and observation pier in the downtown area. Oh, you still can travel to Marsh Island via a new causeway that was recently completed.

Many people come for the most popular draw, or at least the best known, the pony roundup and penning at Chincoteague. Others want sun and sand or the antiques and the duck decoys. They're all available here. My advice on buying decoys is to look at quite a few first so that you can compare them and then decide what you want. There are decorative decoys (they look pretty) and working decoys (those that were hollowed out and had weights placed on the bottom for balance in the water and were used to lure ducks to the blinds). Some are brand-new and machine turned (you can even assemble and paint them yourself), some have intricately carved feather structures, and some are old and drab looking. You can expect to pay from $50 to $700 or more.

Birding from the Bridge

Fishing, dining, and traveling between the eastern and western shores of Virginia are not the only uses for the Chesapeake Bay Bridge-Tunnel. Birders flock here to see black-tailed gulls, harlequin ducks, king eiders, loons, marbled godwits, oystercatchers, purple sandpipers, red-breasted mergansers, and tricolored herons. Some of these birds are attracted to the small fish and mollusks that gather around the man-made islands; others are migratory fowl traveling between arctic Canada and Greenland and points south. It's one of the top birding spots on the East Coast. A fee is charged and you must arrange a fixed time and date for your visit, so check in with the Bridge-Tunnel office (32386 Lankford Hwy., Box 111, Cape Charles 23310; 757-331-2960) and avoid the extra toll. www.cbbt.com/birding.

We'll start our tour at the southern end of the peninsula, and then head north.

At the southern tip of the DelMarVa Peninsula is the ***Eastern Shore of Virginia National Wildlife Refuge.*** It features a variety of habitats ideal for millions of migrant birds including warblers, tree swallows, and other songbirds and thousands of raptors as they travel on their journey south, starting in late August and peaking around mid-November. Before that, the monarch butterfly migration goes through October. They come to stage (gather in large groups) until the winds and weather are favorable for an easy flight over the Bay.

According to the US Fish and Wildlife Service, this land was known as Fort John Custis, and during World War II there were radar towers and large bunkers housing 16-inch guns to protect the naval bases and shipyards of Virginia Beach and Norfolk.

Within the 1,123 acres of maritime forest, myrtle and bayberry thickets, grasslands, croplands, and fresh and brackish ponds, there's even a place for you—there are trails and a photo blind. On Saturday afternoons from October through March, the service offers free tours (4-mile walking tour) to Fisherman Island, an area otherwise closed to the public. No entrance fee. Stop by the welcome station for detailed information. The Wise Point Boat Ramp is now open with passes to launch and/or park at the ramp set at $10 for a one-day pass and $120 for an annual pass. The ramp is open daily from 5 a.m. to 10 p.m. Oct through Jan. Overnight use is not permitted. 5003 Hallett Circle, Cape Charles 23310; (757) 331-2760; http://easternshore.fws.gov.

Wander around ***Cape Charles*** and see one of the largest concentrations of late-Victorian and turn-of-the-century buildings on the East Coast. The homes were built for the expanding merchant class and the executives of the Pennsylvania Railroad, for Cape Charles was established as the railroad's southern terminus, from which steamships carried passengers and freight to Norfolk. The town received Historic District designation in 1989 and was placed on the National Register of Historic Places in 1991.

The town took a huge hit when the ferry to Norfolk stopped running. Businesses shuttered and, well, you know how some small towns just get smaller and smaller. Now it's changing and businesses are opening with nary a chain store in sight. Yet.

Coffee has been filling the air since the opening of the **Cape Charles Coffee Company,** located in a 1910 bank building. Paneled wood walls and chandeliers are the setting for espressos, lattes, and the signature Cafe Cape Charles (coffee, hazelnut, caramel, and melted chocolate). Food's available. The cafe is open daily from 8 a.m. to 5 p.m. 241 Mason Ave., Cape Charles 23310; (757) 331-1880; www.capecharlescoffeehouse.com.

Many years ago, my family and about a half-dozen other families went camping at **Cherrystone Family Camping Resort,** just north of Cape Charles, on the Chesapeake Bay, for a week. We raked oysters off the campground coastline and went to Oyster (on the Atlantic side of the peninsula) to get clams. We found a guy there who was really, seriously upset because his crab trap was filled with blowfish (probably the one creature that really scares crabs), so we took them off his hands and carefully filleted them and understood why they're called the "chicken of the sea." My Uncle Joe Smith had a boat in Hampton Roads and Sunday morning was "guy day," so he took all the guys out fishing and they came back with a bunch of palm-size spot that were perfect for breakfast cooked over the fire. One of the guys had brought some venison, so we did have a little variety in our meals, but basically, except for some prepackaged cereal to keep the children happy, we lived off the land for the entire week. Of course, the mosquitoes lived off us, so maybe that was Mother Nature's way of evening the score.

Should you not want to feed off the land by your own hands, rest assured the campground has plenty of activities with a craft shop, horseshoes, minigolf, arcade, splash park, swimming pools, and much more. They have cottages, camping cabins, and rental trailers in case you don't care to bring your own accommodations. 1511 Townfield Dr., Cape Charles 23310; (757) 331-3063; www.cherrystoneva.com.

Bay Creek Golf and Marina Resort may be in a still-sleepy area, but it's sure getting a lot of buzz. The 2,000-acre year-round planned community offers a marina, shopping, restaurants, water sports, tennis, pools, a replica of a 19th-century lighthouse, a beach, and two 18-hole intersecting golf courses designed by Arnold Palmer and Jack Nicklaus. Foxes and sea birds nest along the courses that are lined with old growth woods, magnolias, roses, and native

Elvis Ate Here, Sorta

The **Exmore Diner,** originally in New Jersey, has been in Exmore since P. C. Kellam had it trucked to town in 1953. In the trucking business, he'd gone to see a Yankees game in New York, stopped by the diner for a bite to eat, and saw the FOR SALE sign. He realized he had a hundred truckers a day coming to his place, and there was no restaurant in town. He had his wife wire the $5,000 to him, and he owned a diner.

According to waitress Ann Adams, Elvis Presley ate in the diner when it was in New Jersey, but she doesn't know where he sat or what he ordered.

A bright neon clock highlights the stainless steel exterior; the interior has 4 tables and 24 stools. Historians and historic preservationists think it's one of the most delicious-looking diners in the state. According to Evelyn Pruitt, who was working here as a waitress for 10 years before she took over the business in 1991, the patrons go for the chicken and dumplings, chipped beef, butterfly shrimp, and hamburger steak. And if family operations are your favorite, you'll be pleased to know that "employees" Sean Pruitt, Allen Packett, and Bonnie Packett are all relatives.

The diner is open Mon through Sat 5 a.m. to 8 p.m., Sun 6 a.m. to noon. 4264 Main St., Exmore 23350; (757) 442-2313; www.exmorediner.com.

beach grasses. The resort stretches along 3-plus miles of the Bay on one side and the Old Plantation Creek on the other.

Boaters can stay aboard their boats in Bay Creek's marina, which can accommodate boats up to 150 feet long (7-foot-deep low tide channel) with access to the Intracoastal Waterway, the Bay, and the Atlantic Ocean. Boat and kayak rentals are available.

Homes range from long- and short-term condominiums (you can rent for a week), and privately owned, single-family home rentals. 3335 Stone Rd., Cape Charles 23310; (757) 331-8742; www.bay-creek.com.

North of Cape Charles is **Eastville,** the Northampton County seat where a time capsule was buried with a legend on it that says EASTVILLE COURT RECORDS TIME CAPSULE COMMEMORATING 365 YEARS OF THE OLDEST CONTINUOUS COURT RECORDS IN THE UNITED STATES. DEDICATED SEPTEMBER 20, 1997. TO BE OPENED EVERY 25 YEARS. So mark your calendar for a return visit in 2022.

The town has a population of about 200 people, depending on the season and who's counting. Take time to stroll around the town, see the old courthouse (1731), the new courthouse, the prison (1814), Christ Episcopal Church (1741), and the attractive homes that line the streets of this quiet town.

On my last visit to Eastville, I stopped by **The Gallery at Eastville,** owned by award-winning designers Mary Miller and David Bruce Handschur.

If I had my druthers, I'd probably still be wandering through the selection of 100 percent hand-loomed earthdesign® sweaters, one-of-a-kind jewelry pieces, wooden fish (for desk or tabletop, mantel, or windowsill), paintings, block prints, fused art glass, posters, and more. The Gallery is located in a restored 1908 Sears house (Queen Anne Victorian style) in the historic Courthouse District.

The Gallery is often open Fri through Mon from 11 a.m. to 5 p.m. However, you should call to confirm the hours. 16319 Courthouse Rd., Eastville 23347; (757) 678-7532; www.thegalleryateastville.com.

Accomac County

Traveling north off US 13 and then Route 605, you'll find Wachapreague, which bills itself as *The Little City by the Sea.* This fishing resort is said to have the state's largest charter boat marina, with all the wonderful fishing tournaments that accompany so many people involved in such a delightful sport. Call the town hall, 6 Main St., Wachapreague 23480; (757) 787-7117 for details; www .wachapreague.org.

The really big buzz as this was being written is that Chef Charles Thann, a graduate with honors of the prestigious Johnson & Wales University, who had been chef at the Eastville Inn for 8 years, was moving to the *Island House Restaurant.* The restaurant overlooks the Wachapreague harbor and specializes in fresh seafood, as one would hope and expect. Besides great views and good food, you can climb the spiral staircase for a view of the barrier islands from the lookout tower. 17 Atlantic Ave., Wachapreague 23480; (757) 787-4242; www.wachapreague.com.

The picturesque harbor town of Onancock, on Chesapeake Bay 2 miles west of US 13 via Highway 179, is delightfully typical of Eastern Shore towns. A short walking tour of more than a dozen historical homes and churches begins

Kiptopeke State Park

At the very southern tip of the DelMarVa Peninsula is *Kiptopeke State Park;* its 536 acres offer a variety of outdoor recreational and conservation activities. There's a charge, but this is a great area for camping, boating, swimming, picnicking, and fishing. Kiptopeke is a Native American word for "big water." The site was named in honor of the younger brother of a king of the Accawmack Indians who befriended early settlers in the area. 3540 Kiptopeke Dr., Cape Charles 23310; (757) 331-2267; www.dcr.state.va.us/parks/kiptopek.htm.

at *Kerr Place,* the 1799 home of the Eastern Shore Historical Society. Be impressed with an exhibit of how an ancient boat-carving technique changed five large logs into a boat used for oystering, crabbing, and fishing. It's open Tues through Sat 10 a.m. to 4 p.m. Mar through Dec and by appointment. Admission is $5 for adults, $4 for AAA members, and $2 for children under 17. Kerr Place is closed Jan and Feb except for special events. 69 Market St., Onancock 23417; (757) 787-8012; www.kerrplace.org.

If you can't find tasty fried chicken on the Peninsula, you may as well give up the search. *Tammy & Johnny's* is one place that should please you. Somehow owner Ronnie Edward (the diner's named after his children) puts all the right ingredients together and you're sure to be licking those fingers. Word has it, this place is the reason two chicken chain operations tucked tail and left town. Be sure to order some hush puppies. Oh, and yes, you can get scrumptious burgers, made to order, and seafood. 27352 Lankford Hwy., Melfa 23410; (757) 787-1122.

It's said that *Accomac* is the second-largest restored town next to Williamsburg—or maybe it's the second-largest colonial-period city after Annapolis. In any case it certainly shouldn't be mistaken for the tourist attraction that either Williamsburg or Annapolis has become. It does, however, have a lot of colonial-period buildings. The chamber of commerce (now in Melfa) used to occupy the Customs House (ca. 1816), a historic landmark; (757) 787-8012.

Another historic landmark in Accomac, on Route 764, is the *Debtors' Prison* (ca. 1783), a 2-story-and-loft building with a high pitched roof and Flemish Bond pattern to the brickwork. The west chimney is an inside unit to conserve heat. Make an appointment for a tour, or stop by the county clerk's office across the street to pick up the key.

Even if the building isn't open, you can peek in the windows to see the two rooms on the first floor. One room has been furnished as it might have been when John Snead, the resident jailer, and his family lived there between 1806 and 1815. The other will recall days when the building was a prison for debtors. After the General Assembly prohibited the jailing of debtors, the building was used for a variety of purposes including storage, a public library (1911–27), scout headquarters, and WPA workroom, until 1953, when the Drummondtown Branch of the Association for the Preservation of Virginia Antiquities received custody of the building and repaired and restored it as a museum. It's open by appointment. Front Street (Business Route 13), Accomac 23301; (757) 789-3247; www.apva.org/debtorsprison.

Parksley's Railroad Depot was acquired in 1988 from Nancy Shield of Accomac. Now it's the *Eastern Shore Railway Museum.* The original depot was here in the late '60s and was a little larger than this 60-foot version, but the town is grateful because it is in such good condition.

Dozens of citizens donated their time to clean the site and paint and electrify the station; they also donated a potbellied stove, a railroad safe, a spike hammer, railroad lanterns, a railroad jack, a depot ceiling fan, and more than $20,000 for the museum. A 1943 caboose was donated by the Norfolk Southern Corporation, and the Tidewater chapter of the National Historical Railway Society promised a railway baggage car. All of this celebrates the history of the train on the Eastern Shore when that was the principal form of transportation and the only way to ship things in and out of the area. The museum is open Mon through Sat 10 a.m. to 4 p.m. Admission is $2 per adult for a guided tour. 18468 Dunne Ave., Parksley 23421; (757) 665-RAIL; www.parksley.com/seeus.shtml.

There's also the ***Accomack-Northampton Antique Car Museum*** to complement the Railway Museum. Started by the late Melvin Shreves, the museum has received numerous items from local families, including neon car dealership signs and other memorabilia from old Hudson, Studebaker, Nash, and Durant auto dealers. There are gas station signs, pedal cars, antique toy cars, and a rotating supply of old cars. Stop by and you might see a 1935 Auburn Cabriolet, a 1922 Durant Touring car, a 1964 Plymouth, and that classic, a 1956 Thunderbird convertible. The museum is open Wed through Sun from noon to 4 p.m. If you have any items you would like to donate or display in the museum, or if you have any questions or need directions to the museum, please contact Frank Russell at (757) 665-6161; www.parksley.com/seeus.shtml.

Wallops Island is occupied by the ***National Aeronautics and Space Administration's (NASA) Visitor Center.*** This was the nation's first rocket-firing and testing station, and 19 satellites have been launched from Wallops Island, 16 of which remain in orbit. It's possible that the flight center could be used for commercial satellite launches in the future. The site is geared toward small launchings, making it less expensive and easier for private firms to use than the Kennedy Space Center in Florida. Patented to John Wallop in 1672, Wallops Island became a National Advisory Committee for Aeronautics (NACA) site for aerodynamic research, while part of it was leased to the Navy for aviation ordnance testing. The NACA eventually became NASA, which took over the site when the nearby Chincoteague Naval Air Station closed at the end of World War II.

funfacts

Wallops Island is named after John Wallop, a 17-century surveyor and original owner of the island.

You're invited inside the NASA museum for a self-guided tour that can last from 15 minutes to several hours. (Groups of more than 20 are asked to make advance reservations.) There's an *Apollo 17* moon-rock sample collected by astronaut Jack Schmitt from near the landing site in the Taurus–Littrow Valley region of the moon. Films, one on the 40-year history of Wallops Island and one on space highlights, are shown on a regular basis. Unlike at some other space and government areas, cameras are encouraged at this facility. The gift shop sells postcards, plates, cups, mugs, books, T-shirts, patches, and other space flight souvenirs. There are 100 to 150 space launches a year from Wallops, but there's little to no advance schedule; you have to stay several miles away, and some of them go up so fast they're off the ground and out of sight before you've blinked your eyes. Call (757) 824-2050 for launch information. Model rocket launches are held the first Saturday of every month.

To get to Wallops Island, Chincoteague, and Assateague Island, turn east off US 13 at T's Corner, onto Route 175.

The visitor center is open daily from July 4 through Labor Day, Thurs through Mon 10 a.m. to 4 p.m. There is no charge. NASA Wallops Visitor Center, Building J-17, Wallops Island 23337; (757) 824-2298 or (757) 824-1344; http://sites.wff.nasa.gov/vc/.

After your NASA visit, you're ready to drive the last few miles to *Chincoteague* ("beautiful land across the water") and nearby *Assateague Island.* Once in Chincoteague you'll find lots of places to shop and eat and do a variety of other activities, including a decoy festival, *Second Saturdays Art Strolls* (www.chincoteagueculturalalliance.org), concerts, blessing of the fleet, and other events, but the main attractions are the *Chincoteague National Wildlife Refuge* and *Assateague Island National Seashore.*

Is there a soul alive who has not read the book, seen the movie, or in some way heard about Misty, Marguerite Henry's famed horse from Chincoteague? Yes, the miniature horses still exist, and every year since 1925, there's an *Annual Pony Swim and Auction* held to sell off some of the horses to keep the herd at a manageable size. Thousands attend this event at the carnival grounds, held the last Wednesday and Thursday of July.

No Tokens Needed

In July or August 2008, 84 subway cars were added to the *Blackfish Banks Artificial Reef,* located less than 10 miles from Chincoteague Inlet. They join 100 New York City subway cars that were "dumped" there in late 2002. No, they didn't come by rail, but by barges from the 207th Street Overhaul Shop on the banks of the Harlem River. Yes, they were stripped of all toxins and somehow made alluring to such fish as small sea bass, flounder, trout, amberjacks, jack crevelle, and some sharks. www.daybreakfishing.com/blackfish-reef.html.

The wild ponies, which are assumed to be descended from mustangs that swam ashore from a wrecked Spanish ship in the 16th century, are auctioned by members of the volunteer fire department on Chincoteague. The members dress up in cowboy garb and corral the ponies, then carefully supervise them as the horses swim to Chincoteague, where they can sell for more than $2,000 each. How nice to be able to visit Misty's relatives and stroll alongside them as they munch the grass of this seashore wildlife refuge that is their home. Be warned: As many as 40,000 people come to see ponies swim for about 3 minutes. It is generally hot and humid and there are no restrooms nearby. Unless you really want to see the auction, come another day. Chamber of Commerce, P.O. Box 258, Chincoteague Island 23336; (757) 336-6161; www.assateague.com.

Throughout the refuge you can take hikes, ride bikes, sit in the sun, and enjoy yourself. There's a 3½-mile bicycle/hiking loop open dawn to dusk for pedestrians and bikes (no mopeds allowed) and on which autos are allowed from 3 p.m. to dusk. Some 250 different birds fly by, and snow geese can be seen most of fall and winter. The refuge is a major resting and feeding area for the endangered peregrine falcon. Forest underbrush has been cleared in some areas, and nesting boxes have been constructed for the endangered DelMarVa fox squirrel. Scattered throughout the refuge are the sika (an oriental elk), Virginia white-tailed deer, and, of course, small bands of wild ponies.

The *Assateague Lighthouse* was built in 1833 and rebuilt in 1867. It's 22 feet above mean high water and stands 142 feet high, and the 800,000 candle power light can be seen for 19 nautical miles. You can tour the lighthouse and climb its 198 steps Fri through Sun 9 a.m. to 3 p.m., April 1 through May 29 and November 1 through November 28; daily from 9 a.m. to 3 p.m. from June 1 through October 31. The lighthouse is being restored, so there may be times when it's closed. Adults are $5 and children are $3 (ages 2 through 12). (757) 336-3696; www.piping-plover.org/lighthouse.html.

The *Museum of Chincoteague Island* started life in 1965 as the Oyster Museum and was renovated in 2011 with a change to its name to more accurately reflect what's inside. Walk around and you'll see exhibits reflecting life on the islands from pre-historical to more recent times. The first order Fresnel lens (made in Paris in 1866) that was used in the Assateague Lighthouse greets you at the entrance. The museum is open Apr through Thanksgiving. 7125 Maddox Blvd., Chincoteague 23336; (757) 336-6519; www.chincoteaguemuseum.com.

There may not be a better combination than getting away to someplace "remote" and finding it has almost all the conveniences of home, particularly if you're on a business trip. That's what you can find at the *Island Motor Inn,* which has all waterfront guest bedrooms, an indoor pool, exercise rooms, and a conference room with large windows overhanging and overlooking the waterfront. Oh, and add Ann Stubbs as a most gracious hostess. 4391 Main St., Chincoteague 23336; (757) 336-3141; www.islandmotorinnresort.com.

The *Locustville Academy Museum,* on Route 605 in the Academy Building, Locustville, is the only remaining school of higher learning of about a dozen that existed on the Eastern Shore during the 1800s, and the weatherboarding, brick foundations, and interior are intact. The school provided advanced studies for college-bound students or those entering business at a far lower cost than boarding schools. Advanced courses included Latin, Greek, and French, and in 1862 tuition did not exceed $20 for a semester. The school operated from the fall in 1859 until 1879 (except for brief periods during the Civil War) and apparently looks much as it did when it was in operation, although the original entrance road has been closed. Inside are an old teacher's desk and student's desk, old textbooks, photographs, documents, and historical artifacts from the area. It's open by appointment. (757) 787-2460; www.easternshoretowns.com/locustvl/locustvl.shtml.

Where to Stay in Eastern Virginia

BELLE HAVEN

Bay View Waterfront
35350 Copes Dr.
(757) 442-6963 or
(800) 442-6966
www.bayviewwaterfrontbed
andbreakfast.com

CAPE CHARLES

**Cape Charles House
Bed-and-Breakfast**
645 Tazewell Ave.
(757) 331-4920
www.capecharleshouse
.com

CHINCOTEAGUE

Channel Bass Inn
6228 Church St.
(757) 336-6148 or
(800) 249-0818
www.channelbassinn.com

1848 Island Manor House
4160 Main St.
(757) 336-5436 or
(800) 852-1505
www.islandmanor.com

Miss Molly's Inn
4141 Main St.
(757) 336-6686 or
(800) 221-5620
http://missmolleys-inn.com

Refuge Inn
7058 Maddox Blvd.
(757) 336-5511 or
(888) 257-0038
www.refugeinn.com

CHURCH VIEW

Dragon Run Inn
35 Wares Bridge Rd.
(804) 758-5719
www.dragon-run-inn.com

GLOUCESTER

Inn at Warner Hall
4750 Warner Hall Rd.
(804) 695-9565 or
(800) 331-2720
www.warnerhall.com

HAMPTON

Crowne Plaza
700 Settlers Landing Rd.
(757) 727-8915 or
(866) 727-9990
www.hamptonmarinahotel
.com

**Magnolia House Bed and
Breakfast**
232 S. Armistead Ave.
(757) 722-2888
www.maghousehampton
.com

MATHEWS

Buckley Hall Inn
11293 Buckley Hall Rd.
(888) 450-9145
www.buckleyhall.com

NORFOLK

**Bed and Breakfast at the
Page House Inn**
323 Fairfax Ave.
(757) 625-5033 or
(800) 599-7659
www.pagehouseinn.com

Marriott, Norfolk Waterside
235 E. Main St.
(757) 627-4200 or
(800) 228-9290
www.marriott.com/hotels/
travel/orfws-norfolk-
waterside-marriott

ONANCOCK

Charlotte Hotel & Restaurant
7 North St.
(757) 787-7400
www.thecharlottehotel.com

PORTSMOUTH

Patriot Inn Bed and Breakfast
201 North St.
(757) 391-0157
www.bbonline.com/va/
patriot

Glencoe Inn
222 North St.
(757) 397-8128
www.glencoeinn.com

REEDVILLE

Fleeton Fields Bed and Breakfast
2783 Fleeton Rd.
(804) 453-5014 or
(800) 497-8215
www.fleetonfields.com

TAPPAHANNOCK

Essex Inn Bed and Breakfast
203 Duke St.
(804) 443-9900 or
(866) 377-3982
www.essexinnva.com

VIRGINIA BEACH

There are more than 100 accommodations in the Virginia Beach area, from camping to bed-and-breakfast to condo to resort. They're in the town center, Bayside, Little Neck, Hilltop, Lynnhaven, Great Neck, Sandbridge, Kempsville, the Chesapeake Bay Area, and the Resort Area. Here are a few options or you can check the Virginia Beach website to select the options that are perfect for you, www.vbfun.com/visitors/accommodations.asp.

Angie's Guest Cottage
302 24th St.
(757) 491-1830
www.angiescottage.com

Barclay Cottage
400 16th St.
(757) 422-1066 or
(866) INN-1895
www.barclaycottage.com

Schooner Inn
215 Atlantic Ave.
(757) 425-5222 or
(800) 283-7263
www.vbhotels.com/
schooner

WILLIAMSBURG

Fife & Drum Inn
441 Prince George St.
(888) 838-1783
www.fifeanddruminn.com

Great Wolf Lodge
549 E. Rochambeau Dr.
(800) 551-9653
www.greatwolf.com/
williamsburg/waterpark

Newport House
710 S. Henry St.
(757) 229-1775 or
(877) 565-1775
www.newporthousebb.com

Where to Eat in Eastern Virginia

CAPE CHARLES

Bay Creek Railway
202 Mason Ave.
(757) 331-8770
www.baycreekrailway.com

Chesapeake
307 Mason Ave.
(757) 331-3123

CHINCOTEAGUE

Don's Seafood Market & Restaurant
4113 Main St.
(757) 336-5715
www.donsseafood.com

Island Creamery
6243 Maddox Blvd.
(757) 336-6236
www.islandcreamery.net

Sea Shell Cafe
7085 Maddox Blvd.
(757) 336-6005
www.theseashellcafe.com

COLONIAL BEACH

Dockside Restaurant and Blue Heron Pub
1787 Castlewood Dr.
(804) 224-7230
www.docksiderestaurant
andblueheronpub.com

JAMESTOWN

Jamestown Settlement Cafe
1760 Jamestown Rd.
(757) 253-2571
www.jamestowncafe.com

HAMPTON

Grey Goose
101-A W. Queens Way
(757) 723-7978
www.greygooserestaurant
.com

NASCAR Sports Grille
1996 Power Plant Pkwy.
(757) 224-5802
www.nascarsportsgrille
hampton.com

NASSAWADOX

Great Machipongo Clam Shack
13037 Lankford Hwy.
(757) 442-3800
www.greatclams.com

NEWPORT NEWS

Crab Shack on the James
7601 River Rd.
(757) 245-2722
www.crabshackonthe
james.com

99 Main Restaurant
99 Main St.
(757) 599-9885
www.99mainrestaurant.com

NORFOLK

Schlotzky's Deli
246 E. Main St.
(757) 627-2867
www.schlotzskys.com

219 American Bistro
219 Granby St.
(757) 416-6219
www.219bistro.com

ONANCOCK

Bizzotto's Gallery
41 Market St.
(757) 787-3103
http://bizzottos.esva.net

Blarney Stone Pub & Restaurant
10 North St.
(757) 302-0300
www.blarneystonepub
onancock.com

PORTSMOUTH

Bier Garden
438 High St.
(757) 393-6022
www.biergarden.com

Lobscouser
337 High St.
(757) 397-2728
http://lobscouser.com

Starboards
101 High St.
(757) 478-0056
www.starboards.biz

REEDVILLE

Crazy Crab
902 Main St.
(804) 453-6789

WACHAPREAGUE

Island House
17 Atlantic Ave.
(757) 787-4242
www.wachapreague.com

WILLIAMSBURG

BackFin Seafood
3701 Strawberry Plains Rd.
(757) 565-5430
www.backfinrestaurant
.com

Captain George's (Other locations)
5363 Richmond Rd.
(757) 565-2323
www.captaingeorges.com

Christiana Campbell's Tavern
101 S. Waller St.
(757) 229-2141
www.colonialwilliamsburg
.com

Fireside Chophouse Bar & Grill
1995 Richmond Rd.
(757) 229-3310
www.firesidechophouse
.com

Shields Tavern
422 E. Duke of Gloucester St.
(757) 229-2141
www.history.org/visit/
diningExperience/shields/

CENTRAL VIRGINIA

The central portion of Virginia is a huge mix of the cosmopolitan Richmond-Petersburg area and an almost 19-century feeling of people still practicing rural folk ways. This is the proverbial breadbasket of the state, the source of tobacco, cantaloupe, grains, forage, and tomatoes. You'll also see beef and dairy products. Here you'll travel through miles and miles of moderately rolling piedmont dotted with gracious plantations. The area is flanked by the **Blue Ridge Mountains** on the west and northwest and the **Tidewater** area on the east. A look at a topographical map makes you think this is the palm of someone's hand that is protecting the people and their interests.

This is where you'll find Tiffany windows, museums, peanuts, fishing, boating, fine restaurants, good shopping, and what advertisers and marketing specialists call a great quality of life. This area is home to nationally renowned amusement theme parks and county fairs.

Traversing the central area can be done via several interstate highways, including I-95, I-85, both running north and south, and I-64, running east and west. There are several scenic routes, including US 29, 15, 160, and 360/58.

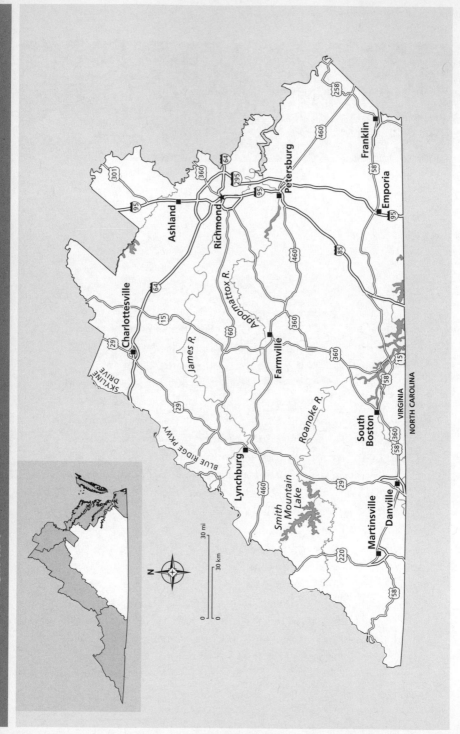

CENTRAL VIRGINIA

Richmond

Richmond is a good place to start and a good place for a home base while exploring other parts of the state. Many of the suggested stops can be made in a day's drive. You can see how central and significant the city was for transportation when you look at the railroad structure at Fifteenth and Dock Streets. Three main railroads crossed here, the Seaboard Air Line, the Southern, and the Chesapeake and Ohio. Reportedly, this is the only three-level train crossing in the world.

"The River City," as it's sometimes called, is filled with monuments and a ***Monument Avenue***—the only street in the nation to be designated a National Historic Landmark—with statues of Confederate leaders and Arthur Ashe.

In 2007 a 38.5-foot-long ***Virginia Wall of Honor*** was unveiled that pays tribute to 141 Virginians killed in the Global War on Terrorism. Look for it, with a brief biography and a photo about each person who lost his or her life in the effort, in the Main Street lobby (900 E. Main) of the Office of the Attorney General.

Start your day with a hearty "buy-the-farm" breakfast at the ***Dairy Bar*** (formerly known as Curles Neck Dairy Bar), said to have the best milkshakes in town. A cow mascot adorns the building and invites you inside and encourages young diners to color the mascot and have their art displayed on the walls. The diner is open Mon through Sat 7 a.m. to 3 p.m. and Sun 9 a.m. to 2 p.m. 1602 Roseneath Rd., Richmond 23230; (804) 355-1937; www.dairybar restaurant.com.

AUTHOR'S FAVORITES IN CENTRAL VIRGINIA

Historic Garden Week
April, statewide
(804) 643-7141
www.vagardenweek.org

Lewis Ginter Botanical Gardens
Richmond
(804) 262-9887
www.lewisginter.org

Montpelier
Montpelier Station
(504) 672-2728, ext. 100
www.montpelier.org

Old Blandford Church and Cemetery
Petersburg
(804) 733-2396
www.petersburg-va.org/tourism/
blandford.htm

Science Museum of Virginia
Richmond
(804) 864-1400
www.smv.org

Once you've finished some sightseeing, stop by **Buz & Ned's Real Barbecue** for a serving of slow-roasted pork barbecue that comes from a 150-year-old recipe. Look for the billboard with the big red arrow pointing to the restaurant.

Buz and Ned's is open Mon through Thurs 11 a.m. to 9 p.m., Fri and Sat 11 a.m. to 10:30 p.m., Sun 11 a.m. to 9 p.m. 1119 North Blvd., Richmond 23230; (804) 355-6055; www.buzandneds.com.

Artemis Gallery offers a unique selection of handcrafted arts and crafts, including Bob Rioux kaleidoscopes, frozen motion glass, ceramics, fusion sculpture, acrylic clocks, paintings, steel fabrications, and glassworks. 1601 W. Main St., Richmond 23220; (804) 254-1755; www.metallic-art-graphics.com/artemis.html.

A lot of the Civil War was fought in Virginia, and a look at a map shows what a strategic part it played in the war. Richmond, the capital of the Confederacy, was under frequent attack from 1861 to 1865. The **Richmond National Battlefield Park** commemorates 11 sites involved in three battles that came within miles of the city. These include skirmishes at Gaines' Mill, Malvern Hill, and Cold Harbor. Stop by the park visitor center on E. Broad Street; park rangers will provide maps so that you can tour the battlefield.

Within Gaines Mill, Cold Harbor, Malvern Hill, Fort Harrison, and Drewry's Bluff, there are interpretive walking trails, with ranger-guided tours, scheduled talks, living history programs, and summer season youth programs (also at other times by request). Cold Harbor and Fort Harrison have tour roads, and their visitor centers have exhibits about the battles. In May, June, July, and September, there are activities that coincide with the anniversary of one of the park's major battles.

Within the Chimborazo Visitor Center are a scale model of the Chimborazo hospital (the Confederacy's largest) and Civil War artifacts. A 22-minute motion

New-and-Improved Virginia Museum of Fine Arts

In May 2010, the newly expanded **Virginia Museum of Fine Arts** reopened to the public with more special exhibition space, public areas, an amazing-looking atrium, and a sculpture garden—a mere $150 million project. Within 10 months, the VMFA brought in an exhibit of 176 works by Pablo Picasso for a 3-month visit. It was the only museum on the East Coast and only one of three in the United States, and one of seven in the entire world to be the exhibit's host. 200 North Blvd., Richmond 23220; (804) 340-1400; www.wmfa.state.va.us.

Lights, Camera, Action

Richmond is in constant demand for movie shoots with the pilot for the short-lived TV show *Commander in Chief,* starring Geena Davis, using the University of Richmond and New Millennium Studios in Petersburg.

Virginia Film Tours and Crowne Plaza hotel offer film-related getaways, whether it's a Red Hatter's Movie Delight, Girl Friends Movie Getaway, or the Ultimate Movie Lover's Escape Weekend. The tours provide an insider's look at the many sites used for Hollywood movies and TV shows made in Richmond. Or you can sign up for an interactive weekend tour that includes makeup and a screen debut for your 15 minutes of fame (take the video home to show your friends and family). There's also a one-day Civil War movie tour. 401 N. 3rd St., Richmond 23219; (804) 744-1718; www.virginiafilmtours.com.

picture depicts the battles that took place near the city. Some research facilities are available.

The contact station at Chimborazo Park is open all year, but the ones at Cold Harbor, Glendale Cemetery, and Fort Harrison are open subject to staff availability.

To find out which is open when and where to find them, and to pick up a cassette tape that explains the defense of Richmond for your self-guided driving tour, stop by the visitor center first. It is open 9 a.m. to 5 p.m. daily, and the parks are wheelchair accessible. There's no admission fee, but donations are accepted, and there's a bookstore at the visitor center. 3215 E. Broad St., Richmond 23223; (804) 226-1981, ext. 23; www.nps.gov/rich.

The ***American Civil War Center at Historic Tredegar*** is the first museum in the nation to tell the Civil War story from the perspectives of Union, Confederate, and African-American men, women, and children whose lives were forever changed by this powerful event. This 10,000-square-foot center incorporates artifacts, media, and interactive features so you'll be engaged and enlightened. The tour starts with the causes for the war, moves into the war years, and then finishes with the legacies it left.

Scouts (including Brownies, Daisies, Cubs, Junior Girls, etc.) can earn a patch, specially designed for them,

seacreatures

Embedded in the black limestone squares of the checkerboard-patterned floors around the rotunda and halls of the capitol in Richmond, you can see snails (including a giant marine snail shell from the Ordovician period), nautiloid, shell, sea lily, coral, and algae fossils.

by completing a scavenger hunt booklet covering the campus. There are two workbooks, one for kindergarten through fifth and one for fifth through 12th (parents and teachers are encouraged to enjoy the fun and learning process, too). The program fee is $5, including the workbook, patch, and admission. Opportunities to satisfy several other requirements for merit badges, belt loops, pins, or patches are offered, covering such themes as heritage, culture, archaeology, and nature.

The center, 500 Tredegar St., is open daily 9 a.m. to 5 p.m. (closed on Thanksgiving, December 25, and January 1). Admission is $8 for adults, $6 for students and seniors (age 65 and up), and $2 for children (6 and up). Children under 6 are free. Visit on Monday when most museums in Richmond are closed. It might be a little more crowded because of this, but it's a great way to spend a day. (804) 788-1865; www.tredegar.org.

For pure architectural and historical enjoyment of a structured nature, visit *Richmond's Fan District,* bordered by Monroe Park, the Boulevard, and Monument Avenue on the north and Cary Street on the south. The Fan District, with about 2,000 town houses, is said to be the largest intact Victorian neighborhood in the United States. The aptly named Monument Avenue has monuments to Confederate generals Robert E. Lee, Thomas "Stonewall" Jackson, and J. E. B. Stuart; Confederate president Jefferson Davis; Commodore Matthew Fontaine Maury, "Pathfinder of the Seas"; and tennis legend Arthur Ashe. A suburb of this bustling town back in the 1890s, the Fan District is now incorporated into the city of Richmond.

The Fan, a mile-square, tree-lined district of streets radiates, or fans out, and a map of the district slightly resembles the fashionable accessory Southern ladies are so noted for. The town houses carry Victorian, Greek Revival, Italianate, Tudor, and Georgian touches. They're joined by party walls or separated by narrow walkways. For walking and driving tour maps, you can contact the Fan District Association, 208 Strawberry St., Richmond 23220; http://fandistrict.org.

A visit and tour of the 1790 *Capitol* is a special treat, particularly the hidden dome, which Thomas Jefferson designed, in the Italian-architecture–inspired building. Beneath that dome is the only statue of George Washington that was modeled from life. Sculptor Jean Antoine Houdon visited Washington at Mount Vernon to mold his head in a gooey plaster mix and measured his body as accurately as a tailor would. Such details as the vein in his thumb and the stitching in the cloak facing are included. This Washington does not look like the Washington of the ubiquitous Gilbert Stuart painting, and most likely it's a much more accurate interpretation of his appearance.

The Capitol has undergone a $74 million renovation that includes an underground visitor center on the south side (Bank Street, near 10th Street) of the building. The Capitol is open Mon through Sat 8:30 a.m. to 5 p.m., Sun 1 to 5 p.m. Guided one-hour and self-guided tour options are available. (804) 698-1788; www.virginiacapitol.gov.

The large equestrian statue of George Washington in the northwest corner of the square was constructed to be his final resting place, before his body was buried at Mount Vernon. If you're interested and can find an agreeable guard, you can climb up the inside of the statue.

Of course, there is the option of doing nothing, or almost nothing, and a great place to do that is at the *Lewis Ginter Botanical Garden.* Ginter made his first fortune in dry goods, his second in the stock market, his third in tobacco (he sold the rights to his cigarette-paper rolling invention to Duke, figuring it would never fly), and his fourth fortune in real estate development. The obvious and correct implication here is that he lost his fortunes in between earning them. It was through the real estate fortune that he most directly affected Richmond. Among other things he built the Jefferson Hotel, Ginter Park (Richmond's first suburb), and a number of buildings that are part of Virginia Commonwealth University.

This world-class botanical garden contains the 3.5-acre *Henry M. Flagler Perennial Garden,* one of the largest on the East Coast. The Ginter garden people aren't aware of any connection between Flagler and Ginter; although surely Ginter would have known of Flagler, they aren't sure if Flagler knew of Ginter. Nevertheless, the Flagler people donated this garden. It is the largest single display, with some 12,000 plants and with 4,000 species planted within bordered walkways and meandering streams. New is a program called A Million Blooms. It started with orchids that created what is thought to be the largest collection of orchids on public display in the mid-Atlantic area. The garden changes just about daily and is appealing even into the deepest of winter

It's a Grave Matter

Richmond's *Hollywood Cemetery* was designed by John Notman, who pioneered romantically landscaped cemeteries. A Gothic Revival chapel marks the entrance, and outstanding examples of Victorian monuments and ornamental ironwork can be found almost everywhere. A 90-foot pyramid honors the 18,000 Confederate soldiers buried on the property. US presidents James Monroe and John Tyler and Confederate president Jefferson Davis are also buried here. Walking tours are offered Mon through Sat at 10 a.m. (call 804-649-0711, ext. 334). Oh, and the name Hollywood is for the large holly trees that grace the ground; not that city out in California, Florida, or Southern Maryland. 412 S. Cherry St., Richmond 23220; (804) 648-8501; www .hollywoodcemetery.org.

because there is either something blooming all the time or because of the interesting foliage. Check the website to see what's blooming the day of your visit.

Groups of children (not necessarily school groups, but at least 15) are encouraged to come through the Children's Garden, where they can learn that flowers come from the ground, not from the florist shop or the street corner vendors. The programs are participatory, and the children are allowed to dig in the garden, harvest flowers and vegetables, and learn about the ecology of the garden and animals found there. Call (804) 262-9887 for reservations.

The Lucy Payne Minor Garden features daffodils, daylilies, and true lilies, so you can see the different varieties next to one another. The Martha and Reed West Island Garden displays a variety of native plants that thrive in wetlands and as you stroll across the bridges to the three islands, you can catch sight of carnivorous pitcher plants, Japanese goldfish, Great Blue Heron, and native birds and plants. A 20-year master plan includes an azalea garden and walk, production greenhouses, and an education facility and library. Geoffrey Raush, of Environmental Planning and Design in Pittsburgh, created the overall design of the garden. (The firm also is responsible for beautiful work in Chicago and St. Louis.) There's also a Japanese teahouse.

The 23,000-square-foot E. Claiborne Robins Visitor Center is a classic, Georgian-style building and features an exhibit hall, garden shop, meeting and banquet room, and cafe.

Spring highlights include tulip week, beginning about April 16 or a week before Virginia's Garden Week. The Ginter garden sponsors a plant sale in the last full week of April and a Mother's Day concert in early May, complete with food.

The garden is open daily 9 a.m. to 5 p.m. (check for details about the other attractions within the garden), with Tues and Thurs evening hours until 9 p.m. from June through Aug. Admission is $10 for adults, $9 for seniors (55-plus), and $6 for children. 1800 Lakeside Ave., Richmond 23228; (804) 262-9887, ext. 345; www.lewisginter.org.

If you haven't been to Richmond in a while, and you love nature, the ***Robbins Nature and Visitor Center at Maymont*** is for you. This 100-acre park was the country home of Richmond financier James H. Dooley and his wife. They had no heirs, so they willed the land to the city in 1926. The 33-room Victorian mansion has been restored to its glory days, and there are formal Italian and Japanese gardens, an arboretum, a children's farm, and a petting zoo. All attractions are open to the public and free, although there is a $4 suggested donation.

Within the center is a state-of-the-art complex that houses 13 aquaria that follow the life and ecosystems of the James River, including shallow pools,

OTHER PLACES WORTH SEEING

BEAVERDAM

Scotchtown, Home of Patrick Henry
(804) 227-3500
www.apva.org/scotchtown

CHARLOTTESVILLE

Monticello
(434) 984-9822
www.monticello.org

Virginia Discovery Museum
(434) 977-1025
www.vadm.org

DANVILLE

Danville Museum of Fine Arts &
History
(434) 793-5644
www.danvillemuseum.org

DOSWELL

Paramount's Kings Dominion
(804) 876-5000
www.kingsdominion.com

RICHMOND

Richmond Braves
(804) 241-0833
www.richmondbraves.net

Richmond CenterStage
(804) 592-3330
www.richmondcenterstage.com

Valentine Richmond History Center
(804) 649-0711
www.richmondhistorycenter.com

open water, backwaters, a turtle pool, estuaries, and channel runs. Along with lots of fish, there are snapping turtles (in the turtle pool, of course) and even two otters, the center's mascots, in an indoor-outdoor tank.

Children 8 and up can explore the natural world with microscopes and other lab equipment. A discovery room is available for younger children, and there's an area that explores nightlife, not of discos and bars, but of such nocturnal animals as owls, meadow voles, and white-footed mice. There's also a gift shop with science-related items and a cafe for a brief bite to eat.

The visitor center, the grounds, wildlife exhibits, and gardens are open daily from 10 a.m. to 5 p.m. The Maymount House Museum, nature center exhibits, children's farm barn, and carriage collection are open Tues through Sun noon to 5 p.m. Carriage rides are offered on Sun from noon to 4 p.m., Apr through Oct. Tram rides run a loop Tues through Sun noon to 5 p.m. Fees are charged or a donation is requested, depending on what you do. 2201 Shields Lake Dr. (visitor center), Richmond 23220; (804) 358-7166; www.maymont.org.

A superb overlook of the city is off E. Broad Street, west up 23rd Street, with a right turn on Grace Street until it dead-ends, where you can view downtown Richmond. It is particularly beautiful on a clear night.

For the Kids

The *Children's Museum of Richmond* is designed for children 12 and younger. The museum provides exhibits, programs, performances, and demonstrations. In its 42,000 square feet of exhibit space, children can climb trees, explore an eagle's nest, and discover how food travels through the human body. A stage, art studio, and "how-it-works" area allow families to work and create together. A branch has opened in West Broad Village with exhibits, programs, and more.

The museum is open Tues through Sun 9:30 a.m. to 5 p.m. from Memorial Day through Labor Day and reduced hours the rest of the year. Admission is $8 for children and adults (1 to 59), $7 for seniors, and reduced rates for groups. 2626 W. Broad St., Richmond; (804) 474-7000; www.c-mor.org.

The *Science Museum of Virginia* features, among many things, the Ethyl IMAX Dome, a tilted hemispherical projection dome, 23 meters in diameter and almost 5 stories tall.

Within the dome is an Omnimax projection system manufactured by the Imax Corporation of Canada. This 280-seat auditorium has a hemispheric 76-foot-diameter screen that visually envelops you with its projections.

The dome also houses a Digistar 2 planetarium system. This system, from the Evans & Sutherland Corporation, uses a Sun computer and Evans & Sutherland graphics system to project the stars, planets, and moons of our solar system. The Digistar 2 system was installed in January 1997 to replace the original Digistar system; the world's first permanently installed such system.

The dome's 6-channel audio system has 34 three-way speaker systems and 6 subwoofers driven by 54 BGW amplifiers capable of a combined output power of more than 13,000 watts.

Shows are presented daily (except Thanksgiving and Christmas Day and during changeover periods). Occasional lectures, concerts, and laser light shows are also presented. Call (804) 367-6552 or (800) 659-1727 for current information on program offerings and schedule. There's also an aquarium displaying the various fish of the James River.

This is definitely a hands-on museum, and you're invited to discover and explore the scientific world in language and displays that reach all levels. Other attractions at the museum are the computer works sections, where you can pick up the basics or go one-on-one against the superbrains. After you've played mind games, head for the visual perception area and play games with your eyesight with mirrors and other optical illusions. Five crystal-shaped structures

fill the rotunda floor, and these crystals house a complete display on the formation of crystals and their importance.

The science museum is located in the historic former Broad Street Railroad Station. Originally opened in 1919, the building was designed by John Russell Pope.

The exhibits are open Mon through Sat 9:30 a.m. to 5 p.m. and Sun 11:30 a.m. to 5 p.m. The Planetarium and Space Theater are open Mon through Thurs 11 a.m. to 5 p.m., Fri and Sat 11 a.m. to 9 p.m., and Sun noon to 5 p.m. Admission prices to the exhibits are $11 for adults, $10 for seniors (60 and over), and

TOP ANNUAL EVENTS

JANUARY
Charlottesville Restaurant Week
(434) 295-8700, ext. 227
http://cvilleyum.com

APRIL
Historic Garden Week
Statewide
(804) 653-7141

Richmond Restaurant Week
Richmond
www.richmondrestaurantweek.com

JUNE
Summer Solstice Wine Festival at James River Cellars
Glen Allen
(804) 550-7516
www.jamesrivercellars.com

JULY
Hanover Tomato Festival
Mechanicsville
(804) 365-4695
www.hanovertomatofestival.com

Horse & Hound Wine Festival
Bedford
(877) 447-3257
www.bedfordwine.com

Virginia Cantaloupe Festival
South Boston
(804) 572-3085

Mineral Bluegrass Festival
Mineral
(540) 894-9811
www.mineralbluegrass.com

AUGUST
Powhatan County Fair
Powhatan
(804) 598-2924
www.powhatanfair.org

SEPTEMBER
State Fair of Virginia
Richmond
(804) 569-3200
www.statefairva.org

Taste of the Mountains Main Street Festival
Madison
(540) 948-4455
www.madison-va.com

Virginia Peanut Festival
Emporia
(434) 348-4219
www.thevirginiapeanutfestival.com

OCTOBER
Blues Festival at Mountain Vineyards
Lovingston
(434) 299-5080
www.mountaincovevineyards.com

children (4 through 12) and active military. An exhibit/IMAX ticket is $16 and $15. Exhibit admission is always free for members. Children 3 and younger and museum members are admitted free.

The museum is at 2500 W. Broad St., Richmond 23220; (804) 864-1400 or (800) 659-1727; for information about the planetarium, call (804) 25-STARS; www.smv.org.

Planted firmly in mid-tap at Leigh and Adams Streets is the **statue of Bill "Bojangles" Robinson,** noted tap dancer and entertainer, by Ashland sculptor Jack Witt. Robinson was born at 915 N. 3rd St. in Richmond's Jackson Ward neighborhood. He gave money for a traffic signal at this corner to help the neighborhood children safely cross the street and to a variety of other charitable causes, and in 1973 the city of Richmond erected this statue in his honor. He's portrayed as we all remember him, tap dancing down (or up) a flight of stairs.

The 1895 *Jefferson Hotel,* a massive, white-brick hotel blending Louis XVI and Colonial Renaissance styles, was once the finest hostelry in the South. It burned in 1901 and again in 1944.

Live alligators lived in the two reflecting pools in the Palm Court lobby from the early 1900s until 1948, with "Old Poppy" being one of particular note. Several of the bellhops of that period told stories of finding the alligators crawling on the upholstered chairs in the lobby and having to chase them back into their pools.

The alligators are now enshrined in bronze, permanently situated at the foot of the Thomas Jefferson statue; however, when the Ringling Brothers, Barnum and Bailey Circus came to town a few years ago, they brought a real alligator to the Jefferson for some publicity photographs. You never know what you'll find here. Just be sure when you put your feet up on a footstool that it doesn't walk away.

The grand staircase, which legend says was the model for the staircase in *Gone with the Wind,* is back. Film buffs might recognize the hotel from the film *My Dinner with André,* which was shot at this location. History seems to invade your very pores at the *Jefferson Hotel* and the new Lemaire restaurant will take you back to living off the land with their farm-to-table cuisine.

The hotel is at 101 W. Franklin St., Richmond 23220. Call (804) 788-8000 or (800) 424-8014 for more information; or visit www.jeffersonhotel.com.

The *Virginia Holocaust Museum* is a tribute to Richmond Holocaust survivors and a unique hands-on children's museum specifically geared for students in the 8th through 10th grades. The first five exhibit rooms cover Kristallnacht (the Night of Broken Glass), life in the Jewish ghetto, and other significant elements from the history of the Holocaust. A time line features the story of Jay Ipson (executive director of the museum) and his parents, Richmond residents since 1947. During the Holocaust the family lived in Lithuania in a 9-by-12-by-4-foot area hidden under a potato field. There is no admission fee to the museum. It is open Mon through Fri 9 a.m. to 5 p.m. and Sat through Sun 11 a.m. to 5 p.m. It is closed on January 1, the first day of Rosh Hashanah, Yom Kippur, Thanksgiving, and December 25. 2000 E. Cary Street, Richmond 23223; (804) 257-5400; www.va-holocaust.com.

At the *Virginia Aviation Museum* (a division of the Science Museum of Virginia) by the Richmond International Airport is the Shannon collection of historic airplanes. The exhibit offers you an hour's walk through aviation history. Here you can see Captain Dick Merrill's 1930s open-cockpit mail plane, examine aircraft engines from the pioneering days (aviation pioneering, not Daniel Boone pioneering), take a memorable close look at a World War I SPAD, stroll past exhibits of aviation artifacts, and see the special exhibit dedicated to Virginia's legendary Admiral Richard E. Byrd. A small gift shop is open in the lobby.

The museum is open Tues through Sat 9:30 a.m. to 5 p.m. and Sun noon to 5 p.m. It is open on Mon only when there is a school holiday. Admission prices are $6.50 for adults, $5.50 for seniors (60 and over) and children, and $6 for active military. Children 3 and under are admitted free. 5701 Huntsman Rd., Sandston 23250; (804) 236-3622; www.vam.smv.org.

Hanover County

Traveling north a bit, you come to Hanover, the Hanover County seat, where the historic *Hanover Tavern* was given a license as an ordinary (tavern) in 1733. Patrick Henry, Virginia's first governor, and his wife, Sarah Shelton Henry, lived here, as did George Washington and Lord Cornwallis.

Time, the automobile, Prohibition, and any number of other factors led to the tavern's decline and disuse. It saw a rebirth in 1953 when an acting troupe opened Barksdale Theatre, combining dinner with a show (not at the same time), and then they moved on to other projects.

By 1990, the Hanover Tavern Foundation acquired the property and set about the massive task of restoration. A second phase was completed in 2005, and the tavern now has refinished interior flooring and painting, 2 dining rooms, and a restored theater that seats 156 people. A brick terrace has been laid, with an accessible ramp, and now serves as the new entrance. The space is used for art shows, lectures, and as an educational center promoting Virginia history.

Self-guided tours of the tavern are available Tues through Sun 11 a.m. to 8 p.m. with a requested donation of $2. Guided tours are available by reservation

Hot Tomato

The *Hanover tomato,* hero of the annual *Tomato Festival* and title of the annual football bowl game between Patrick Henry and Lee-Davis, was bred to ripen early enough that people could have ripe, juicy, delicious tomato with their hamburgers when they celebrate July 4 with family cookouts. This was long before hot houses and "place-saver" objects that look like tomatoes but certainly don't taste like them.

on Tues through Sun 10 a.m. to 6 p.m. for $4 for adults and $3 for children under 10. 13181 Hanover Courthouse Rd., Hanover 23069; (804) 537-5050; www.hanovertavern.org.

Hopewell

Travel south on I-95 and branch off on Route 10 to **Hopewell and City Point Historic District,** where you can view the confluence of the Appomattox and James Rivers. This small, bustling town adjacent to Fort Lee had a population of 40,000 during World War I, with an additional 65,000 at the then Camp Lee. The DuPont Nemours plant was known for making guncotton for dynamite. At the end of the war, Hopewell's population returned to 1,369, about the same as after the Civil War. Local historian Mary M. Calos prepared a walking- and driving-tour brochure. There's also a driving tour of the Sears, Roebuck homes that were purchased from the catalog, shipped to the home site, and assembled.

The City Point Early History Museum and Gardens is Hopewell's first museum. It is housed in **St. Dennis Chapel,** and features a time line from 1635 through World War I, when Hopewell became a city. Check the exhibit that tells the story of Hopewell's only china factory, with a display of how china was made there in the 1920s and 1930s. Almost 100 pieces of the china are exhibited.

The museum is located at 609 Brown Ave., Hopewell 23860; and guided tours of the house and grounds are available Mon through Sat 10 a.m. to 4:30 p.m. and Sun 1 to 4:30 p.m. Admission is $3 for adults although there is no charge to visit the grounds. (804) 458-4682; www.historichopewell.org.

If you've been tracing the trail of the **WPA murals** and sculptures through the two dozen post office buildings in Virginia, you've noticed a similarity in style and execution even though the paintings were created by many different artists. Now look at Edmund Archer's painting, *Captain Francis Eppes Making Friends with the Appomattox Indians,* representing a gesture of friendship, at the Hopewell Post Office at 117 W. Pythress St. Reportedly, Captain Eppes arrived on the ship *Hopewell,* which gave the city its name. Archer was born in Richmond, in 1904, and taught at the Corcoran School of Art in Washington, DC, before returning to Richmond in 1968. He was buried in Richmond's Hollywood Cemetery in 1986.

Petersburg

There are two **murals** in the Petersburg Post Office, 29 Franklin St., Petersburg. One, *Riding to Hounds,* by Edwin S. Lewis, is about fox hunting (he also did the mural in the Berryville Post Office), and supposedly his wife is portrayed as the central figure in this painting. The second, on the east wall, is by William Calfee (who did the Tazewell and Phoebus murals as well); it's more pastoral and entitled *Agriculture Scenes in Virginia,* with tobacco on one side and peanuts on the other.

The **Old Blandford Church and Cemetery** is the highest spot in the Petersburg area. Embark on your tour of the church and cemetery at the interpretation center with a free 18-minute slide show that runs about every 30 minutes.

The church, built in 1735 with an inverse ship's hull ceiling design, is a Confederate memorial and one of the art treasures of the country. It's known for its 15 magnificent Louis Comfort Tiffany stained-glass windows, reportedly the only building in the country with every window an original Tiffany production. The original plan called for windows to represent each of the Confederate states, each depicting one of the Apostles, and smaller ones for the states whose sympathies had been divided. The windows took 8 years to complete, and each cost between $100 (for the smaller Maryland window) and $400, including shipping. The Cross of Jewels window was donated by Tiffany. A booklet about the windows is available through the Petersburg Museum gift shop or by calling (804) 733-2396 for $10.40 plus shipping.

If possible, you might want to see the church twice or even three times: the first when there isn't much sun, the second when there's a brilliant sun, and the third at sunset, to see the magnificent beauty of the Cross of Jewels. The windows change almost moment by moment, with a three-dimensional effect coming from the Tiffany talents. Three visits may seem a large demand on your time, but these windows are worth it.

The church was restored in 1901 through the efforts of the Ladies Memorial Association of Petersburg, whose remembrances of the war dead launched our Memorial Day tradition. Reportedly a Union general's wife saw "Miss Nora" Davidson and schoolchildren placing flowers on Confederate graves. The general persuaded Congress to declare a national holiday to honor the war dead.

UVA Library Collections

Included in the University of Virginia library collections are letters written to American novelist **John Dos Passos.** The gift was donated by Elizabeth Dos Passos, widow of the "lost generation" writer. Letters by poets e. e. cummings and Archibald MacLeish, critic Edmund Wilson, and Ernest Hemingway (which include gossip about mutual friends and tell about life in Key West) are also part of the collection. Manuscripts and typescripts of the author's novels, histories, works of journalism, poetry, and most of his short stories also are in the collection. Dos Passos was a writer-in-residence at the university and an admirer of the university's founder, Thomas Jefferson.

The cemetery began before the church building was constructed, and the oldest known grave dates to 1702. Some of the finest examples of cast and wrought iron in the nation are found here. Many locals are buried here, along with 30,000 Confederate soldiers who were brought in from other areas. William Phillips, British general, was buried here secretly—the only British general to have been buried in American soil for many, many years. But the Blandford cemetery is not just for Civil War casualties. Joseph Cotton—actor, Petersburg native, and narrator of the film at the Siege Museum—is interred here.

The church and cemetery are open Mon through Sat 10 a.m. to 4 p.m. and Sun noon to 4 p.m. A donation for touring the church and grounds is $5 for adults and $4 for seniors (60 and over), active military, group members, and children. Residents of Petersburg are admitted free. A block ticket for Old Blandford Church, Siege Museum, and Centre Hill Mansion is available. Old Blandford Church Memorial Day services are held on June 9 each year. The church and cemetery are at 111 Rochelle Lane, Petersburg, 23803. (804) 733-2396; www.petersburg-va.org/tourism/blandford.htm.

Over in Old Towne Petersburg (which was referred to as Old Towne years ago) is the Petersburg tour's second most outstanding attraction, the **Siege Museum,** which tells the tale of life in Petersburg during the 10 months the city was under attack, the longest siege of any city during the Civil War. The museum is in the former Bank of Petersburg, and it, like the other 800 buildings in the city, was under attack for 2 to 3 hours a day. Conditions were terrible, and the museum shows the war's effect on the economy, industry, and the people themselves. View the film first, shown every hour on the hour, and then wander through to learn how the women were the real heroes. Learn how ladies' hoop skirts hid food, supplies, and ammunition for the defenders. You'll see two bullets that met in midair and fused. Also on display is one of only two revolving cannons ever built—the first exploded when it was fired, and the second was never shot. View the photographs, eyewitness descriptions, and artifacts. Admission fees are $5 for adults and $4 for seniors and group members. The museum is open Mon through Sat 10 a.m. to 4 p.m. and Sun noon to 4 p.m., except Thanksgiving Day, December 24 and 25, and New Year's Day. The museum is at 15 W. Bank St., Petersburg 23803; call (804) 733-2404 for information; www.petersburg-va.org/tourism/siege.htm.

Think of Civil War battlefields, and you most likely think of the National Park Service. But just south of Petersburg, between I-95 and I-85, there's a privately owned attraction called *Pamplin Historical Park and the National Museum of the Civil War Soldier.* This is where the "beginning of the end" occurred as Federal troops outnumbered a small brigade of North Carolinians. Within a week, Lee surrendered at Appomattox. In private hands since then, the area was ignored and overgrown.

A highly dramatic-looking museum and interpretive center with an unusual design replicates (interpretively) the shape of the Confederate defensive line. You can see exhibits of Civil War artifacts and relics and learn at the interactive stations. You can follow the breakthrough from April 2, 1865, via maps, a diorama, and a state-of-the-art fiber-optic battle map.

aquadrilateral havingnotwo sidesparallel

Recall your math to define what a trapezium is, or be satisfied to know that Charles O'Hara built his home in 1817 without parallel walls. Legend says his West Indian servant told him evil spirits could not reside in such a building. Or it could be O'Hara just had an unusually shaped lot on which to build. *The Trapezium House* is open during some community events. 425 Cockade Alley, Petersburg 23803; (804) 733-2400; www.virginia.org.

Outside, there are 1.1 miles of walking trails among the trees and original earthworks fortifications (some 12 feet high) built to protect Petersburg. Along the trail is a reconstructed soldiers' hut of the kind used by Confederates in the winter of 1864–65. Park guides provide tours, and special programs explain the life, weapons, and uniforms of the era from spring to fall.

Nearly three million men served in the American Civil War. More than 620,000 of them never returned home. The *National Museum of the Civil War Soldier,* a 25,000-square-foot, $16 million facility, includes an exhibit in the main gallery, Duty Called Me Here, where you select a "soldier comrade" from a group of 13 real Civil War soldiers. Wearing a personal audio device, you become intimately acquainted with your comrade as you tour the gallery, hearing his own words taken from diaries and letters. By the end of the gallery tour, the real-life fate of your comrade is revealed, making the experience of the Civil War soldier a very personal one for you. Children may choose as their comrade 13-year-old drummer boy Delevan Miller, whose story is central to the Discovery Trail, the park's tour designed especially for children. The National Museum of the Civil War Soldier is also home to the Hardtack and Coffee Cafe, providing hearty fare for hungry troops, and the Civil War Store, one of the finest Civil War book and gift shops in the country.

Tudor Hall, on an additional 68 acres, is an 1812 plantation owned by the Boisseau family until 1864, when the opposing armies turned their farm into a battle and camping ground. It was a descendant of this family, Dr. Robert B. Pamplin Jr. (a great-great-nephew), and the Pamplin Foundation that funded the purchase of the property as it was about to be sold for lumbering. The home has been restored and is open for exhibition.

The Pamplin Park Civil War Site is at 6125 Boydton Plank Rd., Petersburg 23803. It's open Mon through Sat 9 a.m. to 5 p.m. in winter and until 6 p.m. June 14 through August 17. The admission fee is $12 for adults and $7 for children 6 through 12. (804) 861-2408 or (877) PAMPLIN; www.pamplinpark.org.

The US Army Quartermaster Corps is the branch of the service that supplies food, clothing, and military equipment to our armed forces. The **US Army Quartermaster Museum** at Fort Lee (formerly Camp Lee) shows life-size exhibits of colorful uniforms, weapons, Pershing's office furniture, General Patton's jeep, and furniture from Eisenhower's and Kennedy's offices. You'll also see a drum used in President Kennedy's funeral cortege and the architect's original model for Arlington National Cemetery's Tomb of the Unknowns.

fun facts

North of Richmond in Glen Allen is the **Hohner, Inc.** harmonica (and other instruments and harmonica-themed jewelry) manufacturer who supplied dozens and dozens of harmonicas to the troops in Operation Desert Shield so that they would feel more "at home." 1000 Technology Park Dr., Glen Allen 23059; (804) 515-1900; www.hohnerusa.com.

There is no admission charge (donations accepted), but you must have a photo ID and proof of vehicle insurance to enter the base. The museum is open Tues through Fri from 10 a.m. to 5 p.m., and Sat, Sun, and holidays from 11 a.m. to 5 p.m. 1201 22nd St., Fort Lee 23801; (804) 734-4203; www.qmmuseum.lee.army.mil.

When Fort McClellan, Alabama, was closed, the Women's Army Corps Museum there was closed, too. Fort Lee, where members of the WAC were trained from 1948 to 1954, was chosen as the new site for the museum because of its historical ties to the WAC. Today hundreds of Army women are trained at Fort Lee.

The renamed *US Army Women's Museum* depicts the day-to-day service and duties of women in the military from Revolutionary days through Desert Storm. There are 40 exhibits, thousands of artifacts and archival materials, and more than 300 videos in the 13,325-square-foot museum. Apparently, the museum receives a lot of requests to identify the first to do this or that or the oldest or youngest. Most likely, they don't have an answer, so don't bother asking. Ergo, the US Army Women's Museum "will not sanction any claim of 'firsts, etc.'"

It is open Tues through Fri from 10 a.m. to 5 p.m. and Sat 11 a.m. to 5 p.m., and by appointment. There is no admission charge, but you must present photo identification to the gate personnel. 2100 A Ave., next to the Quartermaster Museum at Fort Lee, Petersburg 23801; (804) 734-4327; www.awm.lee.army.mil.

Appomattox County

Stop by the *Appomattox Visitor Information Center* to see the original brick, wrought iron, and wood of the old railroad depot. The center, open daily from 9 a.m. to 5 p.m., has displays of local attractions, brochures, a theater, gift shop, and operates as a reservation center. You can pick up a self-guided walking tour brochure that highlights 50 stops that include buildings on the National Register of Historic Places, turn-of-the-(last)-century homes, and markers about the Civil War. 214 Main St., Appomattox 24522; (434) 352-8999; www.tourappomattox.com.

Once you've spent the day absorbing the past, stop by *Baines Books and Coffee* for a cup of refreshment from the Lexington Coffee Roasting Company. All the coffee beans have been roasted within the last two weeks (of your visit). Once you've admired the cup, you can probably meet the staff member who made it or other cups, pitchers, bowls, etc. Then, listen to local and regional performers entertaining with folk, Americana, and Blue Grass music on Fri and Sat evening from 7 to 10 p.m. Or, if you've always wanted to try your skills at an open mic night, stop by on Tues from 8 to 10 p.m. The store is open Mon through Wed 7 a.m. to 9 p.m., Thurs 7 a.m. to 9:30 p.m., Fri 7 a.m. to 10 p.m., Sat 8:30 a.m. to 10 p.m., and Sun 11 a.m. to 5 p.m. 205 Main St., Appomattox 24522; (434) 352-3711; www.bainesbooks.com.

Prince Edward County

You can visit the area history at the *Robert Russa Moton Museum and the Center for the Study of Civil Rights in Education.* In 1951 this was the site of the first nonviolent student demonstration that became part of the 1954

Brown vs. Board of Education case heard before the US Supreme Court. That case led to the mandate of equal education for all Americans, not just separate but equal. It's located in the Moton High School, which is one of the 41 sites in the Civil Rights in Education Heritage Trail. Call for an appointment Mon through Fri 9 a.m. to 5 p.m. 900 Griffin Blvd., Farmville 23901; (434) 315-8775; http://motonmuseum.org.

Green Front Furniture, in Farmville, is known for its bare-bones 750,000 square feet (about 12 football fields) of furnishings in 12 old tobacco ware-houses, mostly located along Main Street, and then along South, Depot, Second, and, well, you get the idea. Check the website to determine what is in which building (e.g., upholstery is in buildings 5, 6, 8, 9, and 10). There are thousands of pieces of furniture. Green Front features traditional furniture, and owner Richard Cralle carries lines from more than 200 manufacturers, alphabetically from Althorp Living History to Zimmerman. There are case goods, authentic English antiques, unique accessories, and more. The Oriental rugs come from India, Afghanistan, Pakistan, Iran, China, and Nepal.

Green Front is open Mon through Thurs 10 a.m. to 5:30 p.m., Fri 10 a.m. to 5:45 p.m., and Sat 9 a.m. to 6:15 p.m. 316 N. Main St., Farmville 23901; (434) 392-5943; www.greenfront.com.

To the northwest of Petersburg is Colonial Heights, home of Violet Bank (the name Violet Bank seems to have come from the profusion of violets growing on the hillside), a spreading cucumber tree (planted in 1833, it's one of the largest in the world and very rare east of the Blue Ridge Mountains), and Lee's headquarters for five months beginning June 8, 1864 (he had to leave when the falling leaves bared his position). The **Violet Bank Museum** here boasts an autographed photograph of "Stonewall" Jackson and other items of interest to Civil War buffs. The Colonial Heights Federated Women's Club is responsible for the restoration of the ornamented ceilings and the 1815 reproduction furniture.

The museum is open Tues through Sat 10 a.m. to 5 p.m. and Sun 1 to 6 p.m. A donation is requested. It's at 303 Virginia Avenue, Colonial Heights 23834. For more information call (804) 520-9395; www.nps.gov/nr/travel/james river/vio.htm.

Sussex County

The first commercial peanut crop grown in Virginia was grown in Sussex County, southeast of Petersburg on US 460, in 1844. Today peanuts represent a multimillion-dollar industry in the state, so it's not surprising that you'll find "peanut this" and "peanut that" all along US 460 and throughout the Southside.

The peanut, filled with protein, is the basis for several recipe booklets, which include recipes for crunchy chicken bits, cookies, glazed peanut bread, peanut-stuffed squash, peanut party biscuits, wine-cheese logs, cream of peanut soup, peanut broccoli salad, peanut spinach balls, Oriental crepes, peachy peanut spread, and, of course, peanut butter pie. Write to Production Promotion, Division of Markets, Virginia Department of Agriculture and Consumer Services, P.O. Box 1163, Richmond 23209, for a copy.

For miles along US 460 before you come to Wakefield, you see billboards announcing how many miles it is to the *Virginia Diner,* noted for its treatment of peanuts. It's an old 125-seat diner that is singularly unimpressive in appearance, but don't let that deceive you. It started life in 1929 as a refurbished 1860 train car and has grown ever since. You'll find Virginia Fancy and Virginia Jumbo peanuts, which are first boiled in water, then roasted in special vegetable oil, causing the peanuts to blister, giving them extra crunch. Remember to visit the diner's gift shop for all those ham and peanut needs. The diner is open daily, except December 25, from 6 a.m. to 9 p.m. in summer and until 8 p.m. in winter. 408 County Dr. North, Wakefield 23888; (800) 339-3463; www .vadiner.com.

Across the street is *Plantation Peanuts,* with a select variety of nuts chosen for their classic style and flavor. Each batch is slightly cooked and hand salted (ask them how they salt peanuts in the shell), and it's all done in the back room, except for the candied or sugared nuts, which are prepared elsewhere. 509 N. County Dr., Wakefield 23888; (757) 899-8407; www.plantation peanuts.com.

Charlottesville

Going northwest out of Richmond along I-64, you can stay in this direction and go to Charlottesville, or you can turn north to Gordonsville.

We'll head for Charlottesville, an independent city within Albemarle County, first, home of Thomas Jefferson's Monticello, the University of Virginia, and so much more.

The National Trust for Historic Preservation named Charlottesville to its 2007 list of America's Dozen Distinctive Destinations. The Trust honored the city because of the "spectacular natural beauty of the region" and its "architectural and cultural heritage."

You can take a walking tour of *Historic Downtown Charlottesville* along the pedestrian mall with 30 restaurants, 120 shops, and flowering fountains, set in and around historic buildings. For your entertainment there are street performers, free concerts in an open-air amphitheater, an ice park, and

What About Bob?

If you're stopping by **Smith Mountain Lake** for fishing, you may realize that this is where the movie *What About Bob?* was shot (with Bill Murray and Richard Dreyfuss). The story goes that the location scout loved the lake but needed a small town next to it. There's no small town next to Smith Mountain Lake, but Virginia Film Commission people took care of that by showing them a nearby town and suggesting that people could drive by on power lawn movers with sail masts attached and bobbing around in the background. The production company bought the idea. So when you next watch the movie, check the shot of Bill Murray with the sail masts "floating" behind him while he's in town.

other diversions. Art exhibitions are held the first Friday of the month (check www.theparamount.net).

I love historic theaters, particularly those built in the golden age of movie palaces, before the multiplex was invented. The **Paramount Theater** in Charlottesville was constructed with a Georgian facade, an elegant lobby, chandeliers, and 18th-century–style scenes painted on silk panels. When constructed in 1931, it was one of the last of these fine theaters. It had remarkable sight lines and astonishing acoustics. It quickly became a landmark that lasted for the next four decades. By mid-1974 it had been shuttered and was threatened with demolition several times.

Fortunately, some community leaders bought the theater in 1992, had it renovated and expanded, so the old 12-foot-deep stage is now 36 feet deep, and there's fly space above the stage for curtains, lighting, and scenery. There are also rehearsal rooms and scene shops. The orchestra pit in front of the stage has a hydraulic lift to raise the theater's Mighty Wurlitzer Theatre Organ to stage level. So, now the Paramount is alive and well and doing what it's supposed to be doing—providing live entertainment, including Yo Yo Ma, Chick Corea and Touchstone, *Swan Lake,* and *The Prisoner of Second Avenue,* and a sing-along to the musical *Grease,* in the center of Charlottesville's Downtown Mall. 215 E. Main St., Charlottesville 22902; (434) 979-1333 (box office) or (434) 979-1922 (administrative office); www.theparamount.net.

The **Boar's Head Inn's** history started with an 1834 waterwheel gristmill that survived the Civil War, ran for 60 years, and then, when John B. Rogan

dmb

The **Dave Matthews Band** travels far and wide and has an extremely loyal following, but perhaps the most loyal are Charlottesville residents. DMB was formed here and gave their first public performance on Earth Day of 1991.

bought it in the early 1960s, was dismantled. Rogan had the pieces numbered and reconstructed on the Boar's Head Inn property. Fieldstones from the mill's original foundation were used in the inn's fireplace and in the arched stone entrance below the ordinary (a public house or tavern). The blue boar's head was a symbol of hospitality in Elizabethan England and is well translated at the inn.

Besides fresh mountain air, stunning scenery, proximity to the University of Virginia, gracious hospitality, spa services, sports and fitness facilities, and fine dining in the Old Mill Room, you can take a champagne hot-air balloon ride daily (weather permitting) between March and December with Pilot Rick Behr at the controls. Ride over the foothills of the Blue Ridge, see deer running in and around the woods and farmlands, watch people enjoying breakfast on their backyard patios. Even though you might catch them in their pajamas, they'll extend a friendly wave to you. When you're through with your hour-long ride, there's the traditional champagne celebration. Think of it as bed-and-breakfast-and-ballooning; 200 Ednam Dr., Charlottesville 22903; (800) 476-1988; www.boarsheadinn.com.

If you're feeling presidential (from your visits to the University of Virginia and Monticello) and you want to continue in this vein, then visit **Ash Lawn,** home of President James Monroe and called Highland when it was owned by the Monroe family (Monroe lived here from 1799 to 1826). Do leave your UVA feelings in your car; Monroe attended the College of William and Mary. Oh, and leave any "stuffy" feelings in the car as well. Depending on the time of the year, you'll see people (and one hopes you will join them) flying kites, enjoying the Summer Festival of children's shows, listening to traditional music and opera in the Boxwood Gardens, and cutting their own Christmas trees.

Ash Lawn–Highland is open daily 9 a.m. to 6 p.m. Apr through Oct and 11 a.m. to 5 p.m. Nov through Mar. Admission prices are $12 for adults, $11 for seniors (60-plus) and AAA members, and $6 for children ages 6 through 11. Local residents pay $5 or check into the Presidents' Pass if you will also be visiting Monticello and Michie Tavern's Tavern Museum. 1000 James Monroe Pkwy., Charlottesville 22902; (434) 293-8000; www.ashlawnhighland.org.

Albemarle County

The Crossroad Store, just south of Charlottesville, has been welcoming visitors since 1820. The friendly staff will suggest directions, provide brochures, serve breakfast or a hot lunch, sandwiches, and, perhaps best of all, let you sample the house-made fudge (usually at least 15 flavors). The store is open daily from 6 a.m. to 9 p.m. (except Thanksgiving and December 25). 4916 Plank Rd., North Garden 22959; (434) 296-3626.

How Green is my Ark?

Evan Almighty fans traveling through Crozet may notice a familiar look to the Old Trail Village development. It was used as a Washington, DC, suburb during the filming. Why Crozet? You may ask. The apparent reason is that Tom Shadyac, the director/producer, is an alumnus of the University of Virginia, and location director Tom Trigo lives in Crozet. Other buildings and locations around Charlottesville, Waynesboro, Staunton, and Albemarle County were used in the 2007 movie. Much to-do was made about the movie being perhaps the greenest movie ever made. Crew members were provided with bicycles to commute to the set; the lumber, windows, doors, flooring, etc., used in building the set were recycled and the steel framing was sold and the money donated to Habitat for Humanity; and 2,050 trees were planted in the Rappahannock River Valley National Wildlife Refuge in Warsaw, Virginia, and the San Joaquin River National Wildlife Refuge near Modesto, California.

Twelve miles west of Charlottesville, **Crozet Pizza** is the reason people drive out of their way when they're visiting Charlottesville (the burgeoning arts community and arts festival are other reasons). It's an eatery with red clapboard exterior, a wood stove in the middle of the restaurant, and lace curtains covering the country windows. The lines form early, and on Saturday takeout must be ordered hours in advance; but should you find yourself waiting, take a look at the wall with business cards from around the world, or catch a look at family photos or the world map with pushpins indicating where patrons have been—all wearing the Crozet Pizza T-shirts. For lovers of nontraditional pizza, try such seasonal toppings as asparagus spears or snow peas, just two of the almost three dozen toppings available. Open Mon through Fri 3 to 9 p.m., Sat 11:30 a.m. to 10 p.m., Sun noon to 8 p.m. 5794 Three Notch'd Rd., Route 240, Crozet 22932; (434) 823-2132; www.crozetpizza.net.

Orange County

Horton Cellars Winery in Gordonsville is where Dennis Horton has created a winery that's "functional during the winemaking season, someplace wine lovers would visit again and again because of its beauty and atmosphere, and ideal for storage." The 24.5 acres of Viognier grape acreage at Horton is one of the largest commitments to the grape in the country. Horton built underground cellars that fit the contour of the land and provide a constant temperature and humidity that's ideal for wine storage and a very energy-efficient building.

Architect Angus McDonald created an Old English Tudor building that includes a spacious tasting room with an impressive fireplace. The Horton

Cellars are open for tours and tasting. You're invited to stop by daily from 10 a.m. to 5 p.m. 6399 Spotswood Trail, Gordonsville 22942; (800) 829-4633; http://hortonwine.com.

While you're in Gordonsville, stop by the **Exchange Hotel Civil War Museum** to see an 1860 railroad hotel that served as a Civil War hospital for the sick and wounded. Some 23,000 men were treated in 1 year, with 700 Confederate soldiers and 28 Union soldiers who died on the grounds of the former hospital. In addition to medical artifacts and surgical tools, there are weapons, uniforms, and other personal items from Union and Confederate cavalrymen, artillerymen, and infantrymen. It's said to be one of America's most haunted places. Quite an interesting turn of events for a town that has become a great day-tourist stop when once it was almost a ghost town itself.

The museum is open Mon through Sat 10 a.m. to 4 p.m. (except Wed and holidays) and Sun 1 to 4 p.m. Admission is $6 for adults, $5 for seniors (62 and older), and $3 for children (5 to 15). 400 S. Main St., Gordonsville 22942; (540) 832-2944; www.hgiexchange.org.

Just minutes away is **Montpelier** (Montpelier Station), lifelong home of James Madison Jr., fourth president and "Father of the Constitution." Madison was a successful businessman, the primary author of the US Constitution, one of the authors of the Federalist Papers, a key player in negotiating the Bill of Rights, a member of the US Congress, and secretary of state under Thomas Jefferson.

Madison's home was considered a "commodious building," well worthy of entertaining the most important people of the country. The estate sat on 5,000 acres of rolling countryside, woodland, pastures, and cropland. The first portion of the existing building was constructed about 1760. It was renovated, added to, modified, stuccoed, papered, gardened, farmed, and lived in. .

To pay debts incurred by Dolley Madison's son, Montpelier had to be sold, a transaction that could have led to disastrous results. The house changed hands six times until it was purchased in 1900 by William and Anna Rogers duPont. They enlarged the house to 55 rooms, reestablished the gardens, and added new outbuildings. When its last inhabitant, Marion duPont Scott (former wife of the late actor Randolph Scott), died, she left it to the National Trust for Historic Preservation.

The big news from Montpelier is that the mansion has been restored to the 1820s house that the Madisons called home. The project removed alterations made to the mansion, including the wings added by the duPont family in the early 1990s and reduced the home to 22 rooms.

A Montpelier Education Center houses Madison furniture, furnishings, and exhibits.

Gravestones & More

The *Old City Cemetery* has a cemetery records research center; a display of 19th-century mourning clothing, jewelry, and artifacts; and a gift shop. An adjacent caretaker's museum features a display on gravestone carving, a turn-of-the-20th-century hearse, and 19th-century cemetery-maintenance tools and equipment. The cemetery is open daily from dawn to dusk unless ice and snow make the driveway impassable. The Cemetery Center is open daily from 11 a.m. to 3 p.m. Mar through Oct and Mon through Sat and by appointment during the winter. 401 Taylor St., Lynchburg 24501; (434) 847-1465; www.gravegarden.org.

Activities are scheduled throughout the year, including a wine festival (usually late May), celebration of Dolley Madison's birthday, a hot-air balloon festival, and the Orange County Fair. Montpelier is open daily 9 a.m. to 4 p.m. November through March and until 5 p.m. the rest of the year. Admission, which includes a guided tour of the Madison home, access to the gardens and grounds, any seasonal and themed tours on your day of visit, and much more, is $16 for adults and $8 for children from 6 through 14. "Friends of Montpelier" enjoy free admission and National Trust members are $8. A gift shop features books, handicrafts, and decorative items. 11395 Constitution Hwy., Montpelier Station 22957; (540) 672-2728, ext. 140; www.montpelier.org.

Nearby, in the town of Orange, is the *James Madison Museum* (housed in a 1928 Nash automobile dealership), with exhibits that include possessions of James and Dolley Madison, including a campeachy chair, made from a type of mahogany grown in Mexico. The Hall of Agriculture contains antique farming tools and implements from the area. It naturally focuses on Madison's interests in the Constitution, but it also features his involvement in agrarian reform, as illustrated in the 18th-century "cube" house contained in the agricultural display at the museum.

The museum is open Mon through Sat 10 a.m. to 4 p.m. and Sun 1 to 4 p.m. all year except January 1, Easter, Thanksgiving, and December 25. Admission is $5 for adults and $3 for seniors (60 and up) and AAA members. Students are admitted for $1. 129 Caroline St., Orange 22960; (540) 672-1776; www .jamesmadisonmuseum.org.

For lodging and dining in an 18th-century plantation steeped in history, try the *Willow Grove Inn,* complete with period furnishings. Willow Grove began as a modest frame structure built by Joseph Clark in 1778. His son added a brick portion in 1820, and the exterior is an example of Jefferson's Classical Revival style, with a simpler Federal-style interior. Set on 37 acres of rolling hills and pastures, the plantation has been carefully preserved to look the way it would have naturally evolved. Hundreds of ancient trees, Victorian gardens, the original wide pine flooring, fireplace mantels, and wainscoting set the background for your long or short visit.

Dine in the elegant Dolley Madison dining room, enjoy the casual Clark's Tavern bar and pub, relax in the bright and sunny Jefferson Library, or contemplate nature from the antebellum veranda overlooking the Victorian gardens.

The Willow Grove Inn is at 14079 Plantation Way, Orange 22960; (540) 672-7001; http://theinnatwillowgrove.com.

Madison County

With nearly 200 wineries now in Virginia, a place has to be exceptional to be known as exceptional, and *Prince Michel Vineyards and Winery* definitely qualifies. It's set in the heart of Virginia wine country, just east of the Blue Ridge foothills, and is part of the *Monticello Wine Trail.* You can take a free self-guided tour of the winemaking facility, enjoy a picnic on the lawns, stroll through the vines, talk with the knowledgeable staff, and have a complimentary wine tasting of their award-winning wine in the "see-through" room atop the winery, or plan to continue the romantic getaway with a night in one of the one-bedroom suites. Prince Michel is open daily from 10 a.m. to 6 p.m. from Apr through Dec, with more restricted hours Jan through Mar. 154 Winery Lane, Leon 22725; (800) 800-WINE or (540) 546-3707; www.princemichel.com.

The folks at *Graves Mountain Lodge* have been welcoming guests for more than 135 years. They offer all the home-cooked food you can eat, natural beauty, and a wide range of outdoor activities, including hiking, fishing, swimming, and some "good old-fashioned porch sitting." Or you can observe the activities of their fruit and educational farm. There's just too much to mention.

Accommodations range from dormitory to motel style to an old farmhouse to cottages and cabins. When you see an event posted as "Let's Get Naked," they aren't talking about you; they're talking about spring shearing of sheep, goats, alpacas, and llamas. Should you breed fiber animals, professional shearers will be available to have a go at your future clothing and artistic works. Route 670, Syria 22743; (540) 923-4231; www.gravesmountain.com.

Amherst County

After a few years of residing in the 1891 jail, the *Amherst County Museum* moved into the Kearfott-Wood House, a Georgian Revival home built in 1607. You can explore the county's history from the early Woodland Indians to the

Civil War and beyond. The Amherst County Pathways exhibit explores natural history, the bateaus, agriculture, and the Civil War. See Monacan projectile points, a copy of the original legislation creating Amherst County out of Albemarle County, and more. The museum and the genealogy library are free, but donations are accepted. The museum is open Tues through Sat 10 a.m. to noon and 1 to 5 p.m. (closed from noon to 1 p.m.). 154 S. Main St., Amherst 24521; (434) 946-9068; www.amherstcountymuseum.org.

Bedford County

The **Peaks of Otter** overlook the town of Bedford (in Bedford County), "The World's Best Little Town" (population about 6,100), as you take a western approach to the part of the state called Southside. Before entering the town you can hike up the 3,875-foot-high Sharp Top, said by Bedford residents to be Virginia's most famous mountain. A stone from the top of Sharp Top was Virginia's contribution to the Washington Monument in 1852. Milepost 86, 85554 Blue Ridge Pkwy., Bedford 24523; (540) 586-1081; www.peaksof otter.com.

In the middle of the **Bedford City Historical District** is the **Bedford City/County Museum** housed in the 1895 Masonic building on Main Street since 1979. It features two floors of displays, including old photographs, surgical instruments, a 100-year-old wedding dress worn by Miss Anspaugh, daughter of Colonel David Anspaugh, and a Benjamin Franklin printing press used at the *Bedford Bulletin*. The only other press like it is at the Smithsonian Institution in Washington, DC.

The museum's library of historical and genealogical materials is well used by those trying to find their family histories. Special lectures and films are shown in the evening. The library also has a file on the legendary Beale's treasure. There are some who say a treasure (worth about $65 million as of 2010) was buried in a cave near Montvale by a party of adventurers who returned from a trip to the West laden with gold and other valuables "long years prior to the War Between the States." Others say the treasure's been recovered, whereas still others say there wasn't any treasure in the first place. Where was Snopes debunking urban legends when we needed them? The directions to the treasure were left in a sealed box in a Lynchburg bank. When the box was opened, there were three intricate codes describing the treasure and its location. Reportedly, two of the codes have been deciphered, but so far no one seems to have broken the third code. You can come to your own conclusion after looking at the file and checking the maps.

Admission to the museum is free, but a $3 donation is suggested. It's open Mon through Fri 10 a.m. to 5 p.m. 201 E. Main St., Bedford 24523; (540) 586-4520; www.bedfordvamuseum.org.

The *National D-Day Memorial* was dedicated on June 6, 2001, the anniversary of the battle. Thirty-five Bedford residents went ashore at Normandy, and 21 of them died on the spot or soon after. It's said Bedford, which had a population of about 3,500 at the time, suffered the highest per capita loss of any city in the United States.

The sprawling monument sits atop 81 acres at the highest point in Bedford, with a sweeping 360-degree view of the Blue Ridge Mountains and surrounding countryside. It consists of two reflecting pools and an archway with a statue of a soldier titled *The Final Tribute* in the archway. Life-size statues, replicating soldiers approaching the beach, face a story wall that explains the unfolding battle. An education center has exhibits and works on an oral history project and is available for conferences and seminars. The memorial has been overwhelmingly more popular than even its staunchest supporters had imagined. Instead of 150,000 people a year, more than 200,000 had visited in the first months it was open. A gift shop has a variety of D-Day–related items.

If you want to see the invasion pool with water, schedule your visit from mid-March through December (call 540-587-3619 to make sure the pool is operating). Other than on days of inclement weather, the memorial is open daily from 10 a.m. to 5 p.m. and closed on January 1, Thanksgiving Day, and December 25. Admission is $7 for adults and $5 for children 6 through 18. Guided walking and riding tours are available for $2 (student) and $3 (adult) a person. Please buy tickets at the Bedford Area Welcome Center. The D-Day memorial is at 106 Main St., Bedford 24523; (800) 351-DDAY or (540) 586-3329; www.dday.org.

Most people think of Monticello when they think of Thomas Jefferson, but there's another place he called home—the place he went to when he wanted to get away from the crowds of people who filled his Charlottesville home after his presidency. That place is *Poplar Forest,* a home he started constructing in 1806 while still in office. It's an octagonal plantation home, set on 4,800 acres, in Bedford County.

Guided 40-minute tours, covering such topics as the design and construction of the retreat, his landscaping design, the restoration, and the plantation community, are offered daily March 15 through December 15 from 10 a.m. to 4 p.m. except Thanksgiving Day. Admission, including a guided house tour and self-guided grounds tour, is $14 for adults, $12 for active military and seniors (60 and up), and reduced rates for children, students, and AAA members. 1542 Bateman Bridge Rd., Forest 24551; (434) 525-1806; www.poplarforest.org.

Franklin County

Visit the **Booker T. Washington National Monument,** which memorializes the slave childhood of the man who would educate himself and go on to found Tuskegee Institute in Alabama in 1881. He was an important and controversial leader following the end of the Civil War and you can see how the tobacco farm looked and worked when Washington was young. Visitors are invited to step back in time and experience firsthand the life and landscape of people who lived in an era when slavery was part of the fabric of American life. The cabin, one of several reconstructed buildings on the site, is a replica of the slave cabin that Washington lived in as a child.

Within the grounds are living-history demonstrations during the summer and occasionally some costumed interpretation programs. Park rangers offer guided walks of the historic area daily from June 12 through Labor Day, at 11 a.m. and 2 p.m. They vary in length but are rarely two hours long. In the visitor center there are exhibits, an audiovisual program, and a bookstore. There is a living-history farm, trails, and a picnic area. The Plantation Trail is a quarter-mile walking trail through the historic area of the park. Jack-O-Lantern Branch Heritage Trail is a 1.5-mile walk through woods and fields. The visitor center facilities are wheelchair accessible, and the historic area is partially accessible. One wheelchair is available for free loan on a first-come, first-served basis.

Groups of five or more can reserve a tour by contacting the ranger. The park is open daily 9 a.m. to 5 p.m. (it may be closed during inclement weather), with no admission charge. It is closed on Thanksgiving Day, December 25, and January 1. 12130 Booker T. Washington Hwy., Hardy 24101; (540) 721-2094; www.nps.gov/bowa/index.htm.

Within the town **Rocky Mount** is the **Depot Welcome Center,** housed in a late-19th-century Norfolk Southern freight station. Local history is explored at the history museum, and music is enjoyed at jam sessions as this is the eastern gateway to the Crooked Road: Virginia's Heritage Music Trail. Glass blowing demonstrations are available at the grainery and other artists occupy the Artisan Center on the Crooked Road. 2150 Sontag Rd., Rocky Mount 24151; (540) 483-9293; visitfranklincountyva.org.

Campbell County

In 1940 Herman Maril painted **The Growing Community mural** in the Altavista Post Office on Bedford Avenue and 7th Street. It depicts the train station on the right and the Lane Furniture factory on the left. The Lane Furniture Company was opened in 1912 by John and Edward Lane when John

Lane bought a box plant for $500. The company developed the first known moving-conveyor assembly system in the furniture industry during World War I and became known through advertising in such national publications as the *Saturday Evening Post* and the "girl graduate program," which gave miniature cedar chests to some 15 million female high-school graduates between 1930 and just a few years ago.

The **Red Hill Patrick Henry National Memorial** was Patrick Henry's last home and burial place. One of seven different homes he had, this was said to be his favorite as "one of the garden spots of the world." It's the home of the nation's oldest Osage orange tree, estimated to be 350 to 400 years old, with a span of 85 feet and height of 60 feet. Red Hill is open Mon through Sat 9 a.m. to 5 p.m. and Sun 1 to 5 p.m. April 1 through October 31; and Tues through Sat 9 a.m. to 4 p.m. and Sun 1 to 4 p.m. the rest of the year and by appointment. Admission is $6 for adults and $2 for students and children. 1250 Red Mill Rd. (Route 2), Brookneal 24528; (434) 376-2044 or (800) 514-7463; www.redhill.org.

Nelson County

Just a few miles southeast of Charlottesville, over the James River a touch, is the town of **Schuyler** (pronounced Sky-ler), the fictional home of **television's Walton family** and the original home of Earl Hamner Jr., on whose work the television program was based. With such a memorable time of our lives spent watching the trials and tribulations of John-Boy and Mary Ellen and the other Waltons, people just assumed there really was a Waltons Mountain. Visitors came to Schuyler in droves, sometimes as many as 500 a day. There's little resemblance between the real and the fictional town, but visitors wanted to see "Ike's" general store, the Baptist Church, the elementary school, and the Waltons' home.

funfacts

Patrick Henry, of "Give me liberty or give me death" fame, played the violin, flute, and pianoforte.

Not able to do this, they'd stop by the old country store, owned by Rosie Snead, where they could buy a fact sheet detailing the history of the area, a postcard, or a color photograph of the Hamner home. Unfortunately, in 1989 the store burned down.

Waltons Mountain Museum opened in 1992 in the old school, which also serves as a community center. Each of four classrooms holds a re-creation of one of the program's sets. Each display set has an audio interview with Hamner, and he talks about growing up during the Depression; there are also video interviews with the actors.

In the school lobby there's a wall that's covered with newspaper articles of the press coverage of the museum's opening. On the other side local resident Barbara Marks assembled a photographic history of the area. Naturally, you can purchase Walton memorabilia in the museum store, including books by Hamner. Proceeds of the sales and admission fees support the community center, whose activities are held in the other classrooms.

funfacts

James Monroe's younger daughter, Maria Hester Monroe, became the first presidential daughter to have a White House wedding.

The museum is open daily 10 a.m. to 3:40 p.m. from the first Sat in March through the last Sun in November. It's closed on Easter, Thanksgiving, and the last Sat in September, when the annual school reunion is celebrated. Admission is $7 for anyone 6 years old and up. Check the website or call for specific directions because, apparently, online map services and GPS tend to take you elsewhere. 6484 Rockfish River Rd., Schuyler 22969; (434) 831-2000; www.waltonmuseum.org.

Chesterfield County

The Ruritan Clubs of Chesterfield County established the **Chesterfield Museum** in the early 1950s. In 2007 new exhibits were mounted that depict Virginia Indian culture, early settlement of the area, the Revolutionary and Civil Wars, and the first ironworks and coal mines in America. A selection of fascinating lectures is presented on a fairly regular basis, and you may find yourself listening to a "Tavern Talk" with actors Tim Reid and Daphne Maxwell, co-founders of the Ne Millenium Studios in Petersburg. It is located behind the historic 1917 Courthouse. Visiting hours are 10 a.m. to 4 p.m. Mon through Fri and 1 to 4 p.m. Sun. Suggested donations are $2. 10201 Iron Bridge, Chesterfield 23832; (804) 768-7311 or (804) 930-1034 (lecture reservations); www.chesterfieldhistory.com.

Brunswick County

The **Brunswick County Museum,** located in the historic Courthouse Square of Lawrenceville, traces the nearly 300 years of written history (and several thousand of prehistory) of this area, covering just about everything from Native American relics (one arrowhead is estimated to be more than 4,000 years old) to Fort Christanna (1714–18), from Saint Paul's College (founded in 1888) to the life and times of Albertis Sidney Harrison Jr., a local boy who grew up to be governor of Virginia from 1962 to 1966.

Original Home of Brunswick Stew

According to the folks at the Brunswick County Museum, Dr. Creed Haskins went hunting with some friends one day in 1828. While they were out, the camp cook, Jimmy Matthews, shot squirrels and started making a thick stew with butter, onions, stale bread, and seasonings, thus creating **Brunswick Stew.** Because game animals are used, the stew cooks for a long time, much longer than a soup would. Now, you may hear—in other parts of the country and elsewhere—that Brunswick, Georgia, is the home, except they say it happened on St. Simons Island in 1898, so obviously, that's not even in contention. Additionally, some say it originated in Braunschweig, Germany, and that it was a favorite of Queen Victoria. Sure, let the British/Germany conspiracy people take credit for it. Nope. In 1988 the General Assembly of Virginia proclaimed Brunswick County the Original Home of Brunswick Stew.

Two saddles on display—a lady's sidesaddle and a gentlemen's Texas saddle—are more than 100 years old. A real charmer is the showcase of antique dolls wearing authentic clothing of the day. There's also a collection of Civil War artifacts, items from country schools, and household and farm implements.

The Brunswick County Museum is open Tues and Thurs 10:30 a.m. to 1 p.m. and Sat 1:30 to 4 p.m., or by appointment. There is no admission charge, but donations are accepted. 228 N. Main St., Lawrenceville 23868; (434) 848-2638; www.brunswickco.com/html/museum1.html.

Mecklenburg County

Buggs Island Lake, covering 50,000 acres (and 800 miles of shoreline) and straddling the North Carolina–Virginia border, was constructed by the US Army Corps of Engineers between 1946 and 1953 as one of a series of dams along the Roanoke River. It is the largest lake in Virginia. It's really the John H. Kerr Dam and Reservoir (named after a North Carolina congressman who supported its construction), and 169-acre Buggs Island is downstream of the dam.

Besides 800 miles of shoreline, with the expected water fun of fishing (striped bass or rockfish, crappie, and largemouth black bass—said to be the "best bass fishing in the state"—and hybrid muskie, bream, sunfish, carp, and gar), boating, and swimming, there are 5 campgrounds on the Virginia side. On land, you can enjoy picnicking, hunting, horseback riding, and hiking.

If you must be entertained, stop by during the South Hill Chamber of Commerce Beef Festival, Relay for Life, Jazz by the Lake, wine tasting extrava-ganza, live theater, cooking school, or hydroplane challenge. However, the activity that seems to be drawing the most attention here is the three-day July

Don't Return to Sender

East of Clarksville is **Valentines,** a small community of rural Southside Virginia, with an internationally recognized name. Normally it's your typical sleepy country town, but beginning in mid-January every year, there's a loving buzz in the air, particularly at the post office. The story goes that William H. Valentine established the Valentines post office in 1887. In 1951, when Willie Wright became the postmaster of the office in the corner of Wright's General Store, he started stamping envelopes "With Love" and the tradition has grown since then. Business really started booming in 1955 when the "LOVE" stamp was unveiled here. Bags of mail came in shortly after the new year containing some 35,000 to 40,000 letters, all waiting for the postmark with a red heart and several dogwood flowers on the envelope before being sent to that special person. 23 Manning Dr., Valentines 23887; (434) 577-2456.

Pontoon Boat Parade kicking off the annual Virginia Lake Festival (Lakefest). Decorated like parade floats, the boats look like anything from pirate ships to trains. The Lake County Chamber of Commerce is located at 105 2nd St., Clarksville 23927; (800) 557-5582 or (434) 374-2436; www.clarksvilleva.com/recreation/on-the-lake.

Halifax County

Still heading west on Route 360, about 100 miles from Richmond, you'll come to **South Boston** in Halifax County, the fourth-largest county in the state. The land varies from level to gently rolling and is filled with tobacco (Halifax County was for many years the largest tobacco-producing county in the country), commercial forests (the state's largest agricultural revenue producer), and large tracts of seemingly endless land. At one time there were 4,000 active farms, most of them small, and a handful of them produce the sweetest, most delicious cantaloupes, grown only in Wickham soil in a narrow strip along the Dan River. The Turbeville variety is patented and only seven people grow them, and the fruit is honored and celebrated on the fourth Wednesday of each July at the annual **Virginia Cantaloupe Festival** at the Halifax County Fairgrounds, South Boston.

The Halifax County Chamber of Commerce initiated the festivities in 1981, and it's grown since then. The official fun runs from 4 to 10 p.m., but the action clocks in much earlier with the start of the slow-roasted pulled pork taking many hours. It's much like a "big old homecoming," says the chamber of commerce's Nancy Pool. All you have to bring is your appetite, your lawn chair, and the cost of admission, which for 2010 was $30 each, advance purchase only (no door sales).

The cantaloupe is so delicious by itself that it seems logical it would make other foods taste even better, so a cantaloupe cutup recipe contest was held in 1985. The contest brought in recipes for melon with chicken, melon franks (slit a hot dog and stuff with a slice of melon, wrap with bacon, and secure with a toothpick before roasting on the grill), cantaloupe pancakes, melon with Chablis or piña colada mix, and cantaloupe preserves. For more information call (434) 572-3085 or (888) 458-1003; www.valopefest.com.

With so much history here (the county seat dates back to 1777 and two military campaigns—the Retreat to the Dan in the Revolutionary War and the Battle of Staunton River in the Civil War—culminated or occurred in Halifax County), it's natural to have a historical museum. In 1982 the Tuesday Women's Club established the *South Boston–Halifax County Museum of Fine Arts and History,* which houses the permanent collections and loans of items relating to Halifax, including Civil War artifacts, glassware, Indian artifacts, military uniforms, and memorabilia from Halifax County families. A research center is open during museum hours so you can go through newspapers, archives, yearbooks, and other sources for your genealogy work. The museum is open Wed through Sat 10 a.m. to 4 p.m. There's no admission charge, but donations are accepted. The building is at 1540 Wilborn Ave., South Boston 24592; (434) 572-9200; www.sbhcmuseum.org.

You definitely can visit the *Bob Cage Sculpture Garden,* a local artist with an international reputation and you're invited to see his open field

Stars & Stripes Forever

Annin & Company (with plants in South Boston and Cobbs Creek) is the oldest and largest flag manufacturer in the United States and they've been busy making flags since 1847. The company is responsible for the design of the black-and-white POW-MIA flag created by (the late) Newt Heisley, a military man who flew transport planes in the South Pacific during World War II. The company has also designed flags for new United Nations member nations and most recently created the Flag of Honor and Flag of Heroes that honor the victims of the September 11, 2001 attacks. The Flag of Honor includes the names of everyone who died on the planes and in the buildings, the names creating red and blue strips. The Flag of Heroes includes the names of the Emergency Services personnel from the FDNY, PAPD, NYPD, and court officers creating the red strips across the flag. Proceeds from the flags are donated to the Voices of 911, the National 911 Museum at Ground Zero, the Flag of Honor Fund, and the Wounded Warrior Project. The company is located at 3011 Philpott Rd., South Boston 24592. Unfortunately, they do not offer tours, but you can contact them with your flag questions or special requests. (434) 575-7913; www.annin.com.

sculpture display that consists of a lot of found materials, particularly rusty farm machinery parts. And you can watch the llamas, burros, and goats grazing in the field and scampering over the sculptures. He also creates indoor sculptures and paintings. Cage also happens to be a champion tennis player, a community activist, preservationist, and tobacco auctioneer extraordinaire. Drive by, slowly, his place at the intersection of Shanti Road and Cage Trail or you can see his work placed throughout South Boston. www.oldhalifax.com/cage.

Patrick County

Two of the eight *covered bridges* remaining in Virginia (there were more than 100 by the early 1900s) are found in Patrick County, named for Patrick Henry. The **Bob White Bridge** is an 80-foot Theodore Burr–style bridge over the Smith River near Route 8, south of Woolwine. It was constructed in 1921 and served as the main link between Route 8 and a church on the south side of the river. It was used for more than a half century before it was replaced by a newer bridge, but you still can walk up to the old bridge, which has been kept as a landmark. Drive about 1.5 miles south from Woolwine on Route 8 and then east 1 mile on Route 618 to Route 869, then south .1 mile.

Although it is called *Jack's Creek Bridge,* another covered bridge straddles the Smith River on Route 615, just west of Route 8, about 2 miles south of Woolwine. You can see this 48-foot span from Route 8, where it intersects with Route 615, or travel about 0.2 mile west on Route 615. www.virginia.org.

As an effort to preserve and promote the bridges, a covered bridge festival was started in 2005. The June event is in **Woolwine,** with live bands, artists and crafters exhibiting and selling, food vendors, and carriage rides between the bridges. (276) 930-2127; www.visitpatrickcounty.org.

Pittsylvania County

The largest county in the state is Pittsylvania County, where 18th-century houses still stand and where there were more than 30 water mills, and four—Tomahawk, Mt. Airy, Cedar Forest, and Stoney Mill—are still in operation. Genealogy can take on a new dimension in this county, for the courthouse records date from 1747, and the library has in-depth Virginia records and research tools. www.visitdanville.com.

Danville is the place where, on September 27, 1903, a southbound Southern Railroad express mail train left the tracks on a trestle and plunged into the ravine below, killing nine people. This incident was the inspiration for the song "The Wreck of the Old '97" and is recorded on a historical marker on Highway

58 between Locust Lane and N. Main Street. A 46-foot by 74-foot canvas mural was created by Wes Hardin on the side of the Atrium Furniture building at the Gateway to downtown. You can see a slide show of the painting at www .visitdanville.com. A second mural, at 121–125 N. Union St., features the downtown historic area and was created in 2006. Funds were provided by six local residents who paid $500 each to have his or her likeness included in the mural.

The *American Armoured Foundation Tank Museum* takes you to the beginning of military history. Stop here to see reenacters, military model shows, a military bicycle exhibit, and more.

Founded in 1981 and opened in May 2003, the museum has a mission to educate, collect, restore, preserve, and display as varied a collection of military tank and cavalry artifacts as is possible. There are 112 tanks and artillery pieces, the most extensive collection in the world. Some items date from 1509. You'll also find 150 machine guns,

birthplaceof ladyastor

Viscountess Nancy Astor, born in Danville May 19, 1879, was the first woman to sit in British Parliament. Her sister, Irene, inspired the famous "Gibson Girl" artwork done by her husband, artist Charles Dana Gibson. Their birthplace at 117 Broad St. has a historical marker located at the corner of Broad and Main Streets, Danville; (434) 793-4636.

mortars, flamethrowers, recoilless rifles, rocket launchers, tank and artillery optical instruments, small arms, uniforms, and more. Stop by to see an exhibit dedicated to Elvis Presley during his military years. With more than 300 items pertaining to women in the military, the museum needs only money to present an exhibit devoted to women in the military.

Among the other facilities (research library, gift and hobby shop, classroom, etc.), the museum is home to the largest and only under-a-roof radio-controlled-tank battlefield in the world. At this time it's set up to represent a World War II–era town in France. Some exhibits are interactive, including a tank turret trainer with a machine gun attached and a gun sight that shoots out tennis balls using compressed air. The collection includes the largest and only (would have to be largest, then, wouldn't it?) indoor radio controlled tank battlefield in the world!

The museum is open Tues through Sat from 10 a.m. to 4 p.m. from March 14 through the end of Dec and on Saturday only from 10 a.m. to 4 p.m. the rest of the year. Admission is $10 for adults, and $9.50 for children under 12 and adults over 60. 3401 US 29B, Danville 24540; (434) 836-5323; www.aaftankmuseum.com.

Time for a break at the *Little Chef Diner,* an honest-to-goodness 1952 Valentine diner (one of maybe a half-dozen diners still operating in the state).

Order fresh burgers, North Carolina–style pork barbecue, chili and slaw, and a country-style breakfast served anytime. The Little Chef is open Mon through Sat 7 a.m. to 2 p.m. 2337 N. Main St., Danville 24540; (434) 836-2228.

The *Danville Science Center* occupies an 1899 Southern Railway passenger train station and lets you experience science with hands-on exhibits where you can discover how things work. You can make sparks fly while discovering electricity. To understand orbits, you can launch balls. You can also see an astronaut's view of Danville.

If you visit the *Butterfly Station* at the Danville Science Center, you will learn that more than 160 species of butterflies inhabit Virginia. You can also learn that most adult butterflies live from 20 to 40 days, they have footpads that act as taste buds, and butterflies and moths fold their wings differently. You can also learn how to make your own butterfly garden and learn which caterpillar-host plants attract which butterfly species. A guided tour of the butterfly garden is available for $1 a person. The butterfly season is April through October.

The Science Center is open Tues through Sat 9:30 a.m. to 5 p.m. and Sun 1 to 5 p.m. Admission costs $6 for adults and $5 for seniors (60 and over), active military, and children ages 4 through 12; members and children 3 and under admitted free; 677 Craghead St., Danville 24541; (434) 791-5160; www .dsc.smv.org.

As you drive through *Danville,* do take some time to drive or walk through *Millionaire's Row,* 8 blocks of one of the finest collections of Victorian and Edwardian architecture in the South. Look for such details as gables, gingerbread scrollwork, columns, porticos, cupolas, and minarets. You'll also find five architecturally different (Romanesque, Gothic Revival, Tudor Gothic, Neoclassical Revival, and High Victorian Gothic) churches along the row, which helps explain why Danville is frequently called the "City of Churches."

Pick up a *Victorian Walking Tour* brochure at the visitor center. The homes are closed most of the year but are open the second Sunday in December for the Danville Historical Society's annual Christmas Walking Tour. (434) 793-4636; www.visitdanville.com.

Along your tour you'll see the 1857 Italian villa–style Sutherlin house, now the *Danville Museum of Fine Arts and History,* also known as the "Last Capitol of the Confederacy." Confederate president Jefferson Davis resided in this home during the final week of the Civil War, and it was here that Davis and his Confederate government received word that Lee had surrendered at nearby Appomattox. Exhibits depicting the history of the area and revolving art exhibits are featured. Tours are available weekdays at 11 a.m., 2 p.m., and 4 p.m. and on weekends at 2 and 4 p.m. There's also a gift shop.

The museum is open Tues through Fri, 10 a.m. to 5 p.m. and weekends from 2 to 5 p.m. Admission is $5 for adults, $4 for seniors (55 and up), $4 for students, and free to members; 975 Main St., Danville 24541; (434) 793-5644; www.danvillemuseum.org.

Chatham, north of Danville on Route 29, has won several Keep Virginia Beautiful awards and has earned a reputation as the prettiest little town in the Southside. A beautiful view seems to make a beautiful wine, at least that's part of the attraction for the *Tomahawk Mill Vineyard and Winery.* A Confederate soldier built the water-powered gristmill in 1888, and it operated for about 100 years before the first grapes were planted. They also make mead, apple wine, and blends that include a country blush and a Vidal Blanc. They're open for tastings (and picnicking or looking at the restored millpond and dam) Tues through Sat 11 a.m. to 5 p.m., March 15 through December 15. 9221 Anderson Mill Rd., Chatham 24531; (434) 432-1063; www.tomahawkmill.com.

West of Danville is *Martinsville* and in this town you'll find the *Southern Virginia Artisan Center* with a gallery of regional arts, crafts, and related artisan products that encompasses glass, wood craft, ceramics, mixed media, photography, jewelry, and more. If you want to be more active than shopping for wonderful things to buy, check their schedule for lessons in ballroom dancing, basic woodturning, knitting, quilting, glass fusing, jewelry making, and even learning how to make candles. The center is open Mon through Sat 9 a.m. to 5 p.m. 54 W. Church St., Martinsville 24112; (276) 632-0066; www.southernvirginiaartisancenter.org.

Martinsville also is the home of the *Piedmont Arts Association,* a Museum Partner of the Virginia Museum of Fine Arts. You never know what they'll be offering (well, you will if you call or check their website), but it might

Fossils in Focus

Virginia boasts one of the 5 top fossil sites in the world, a proliferation of dinosaur tracks, and modern animals found nowhere else on Earth. Many exhibits at the *Virginia Museum of Natural History* in Martinsville are the result of original research conducted by seven scientists on staff. Exhibits include Rock Hall of Fame, Age of Mammals, Age of Reptiles, and Dan River People. After years of being located in the old Joseph Martin elementary school, the museum moved to new digs and 89,000 square feet of space in 2006 and it's growing again. The museum is open Mon through Sat from 9 a.m. to 5 p.m. It is closed on Sun, Thanksgiving Day, December 25, and January 1. Admission is $9 for adults, $7 for seniors and college students, $5 for children 3 to 18. AAA and AARP discounts are available. 21 Starling Ave., Martinsville 24112; (276) 634-4141; www.vmnh.net.

be an exhibit of paintings and graphics or three-dimensional works and installations in one or more of the five galleries. They also offer the opportunity to see (and purchase) one-of-a-kind craft items in the gift shop. Pottery, jewelry, carved wooden objects, dried flower wreaths, and more come from craftsmen from the region and across the country, with price ranges to fit every budget. Regional artists offer their work for sale in the Lynwood Artists' "Off the Wall" gallery, where visitors can purchase a painting "off the wall" and take it with them.

The Piedmont Arts Association is free and open to the public Tues through Fri 10 a.m. to 5 p.m., Sat 10 a.m. to 3 p.m. Summer hours are extended. 215 Starling Ave., Martinsville 24112; (276) 632-3221; www.piedmontarts.org.

Head north out of Martinsville on Route 220 and, for information and exhibits about the traditional life and culture of the Blue Ridge and its inhabitants; stop by the Ferrum College's *Blue Ridge Institute and Museum.* The institute's programming has an international reputation. Offered are gallery exhibits and a living-history farm/museum of the day-to-day lifestyle of the German Americans who settled here in 1800.

Look for costumed interpreters cooking meals in an open hearth, baking bread in an outdoor bake oven, blacksmithing, and doing other house and farm chores. There are educational workshops, audio and video productions, and an annual folk festival. Historical breeds of sheep, chicken, horses, pigs, and cattle are in the farm buildings, and heirloom vegetables are grown in the gardens around the home and farm buildings. If you'd like, you can inquire about participating in visitor programs in which you wear the costumes and take part in the farm activities and village crafts.

The one-day fall celebration at the institute's *Folklife Festival* (fourth Saturday in October, 10 a.m. to 5 p.m.) shows old customs and competitions, with performers on three stages playing blues, gospel, and string band music. Dozens of artisans show their skills and sell crafts, and antique and contemporary quilts are displayed in the Mountain Comforts Quilt Show. You can also view restored automobiles and farm machines, and you might want to catch the horse pull and coon dog competitions. When you're ready for a bite to eat, try some of the dozens of regional specialties, but don't look for hot dogs or hamburgers.

Located at Route 40, Ferrum, the Blue Ridge Museum is open for walk-in visitors Mon through Sat 10 a.m. to 4 p.m. all year and Sun 1 to 5 p.m. mid-May through mid-August. There is no admission charge. 20 Museum Dr., Ferrum 24088; (540) 365-4416; www.blueridgeinstitute.org.

Where to Stay in Central Virginia

AFTON

Afton Mountain Bed and Breakfast
10273 Rockfish Valley Hwy.
(540) 456-6844 or
(800) 769-6844
www.aftonmountain.com

BEDFORD

Liberty House Inn
602 Mountain Ave.
(540) 587-0966

Otter's Den Bed and Breakfast
8578 Peaks Rd.
(540) 586-2204 or
(877) 968-8377
www.ottersden.net

Peaks of Otter Lodge
85554 Blue Ridge Pkwy
(540) 586-1081 or
(800) 542-5927
www.peaksofotter.com

Reba Farm Inn and Saddle Soar
1099 Reba Farm Lane
(540) 586-1906 or
(888) 235-3574
www.rebafarminn.com

CHARLOTTESVILLE

Clifton Inn
1296 Clifton Inn Dr.
(434) 971-1800 or
(888) 971-1800
www.cliftoninn.net

English Inn of Charlottesville
2000 Morton Dr.
(434) 971-9900 or
(800) 786-5400
www.englishinn
charlottesville.com

Foxfield Inn
2280 Garth Rd.
(434) 923-8892 or
(866) 369-3536
www.foxfield-inn.com

Inn at Monticello
1188 Scottsville Rd.
(434) 979-3593 or
(877) RELAXVA
www.innatmonticello.com

GLEN ALLEN

Wyndham Virginia Crossings Hotel
1000 Virginia Center Pkwy.
(888) 444-6553
www.wyndhamvirginia
crossingsresort.com

GORDONSVILLE

Shenandoah Crossing Resort
174 Horseshoe Circle
(540) 832-9400
www.shenandoah-crossing
.com

HARDY

Ashleigh Manor
430 Hartwell Dr.
(540) 890-3332
www.bbonline.com/va/
ashleigh/

KESWICK

Keswick Hall at Monticello
701 Club Dr.
(888) 778-2565
www.keswick.com

LAWRENCEVILLE

Three Angels Inn at Sherwood
236 Pleasant Grove Rd.
(434) 848-0830 or
(877) 777-4265
www.threeangelsinn.com

LYNCHBURG

Federal Crest Inn
1101 Federal St.
(434) 845-6155 or
(800) 818-6155
www.federalcrest.com

Ivy Creek Farm
2812 Link Rd.
(434) 384-3802 or
(800) 689-7404
www.ivycreekfarm.com

MADISON

Ebenezer House Bed and Breakfast
122 Seville Rd.
(540) 948-3695 or
(888) 948-3695
www.theebenezerhousebb
.com

MONETA

Bernard's Landing Resort & Conference Center
775 Ashmeade Rd.
(540) 721-8870 or
(800) 572-2048
www.bernardslanding.com

NELLYSFORD

Mark Addy
56 Rodes Valley Dr.
(434) 361-1101
www.mark-addy.com

ORANGE

Greenock House Inn
249 Caroline St.
(540) 672-3625 or
(800) 841-1253
www.greenockhouse.com

Holladay House
155 W. Main St.
(800) 358-4422
www.holladayhousebandb
.com

Inn on Poplar Hill
278 Caroline St.
(540) 672-6840
www.innonpoplarhill.com

Mayhurst Inn
12460 Mayhurst Lane
(540) 672-5597 or
(888) 672-5597
www.mayhurstinn.com

RED OAK

CornerStone Farm
525 Barnes Rd.
(434) 735-0527 or
(866) 977-3276
www.cornerstonefarm.net

RICHMOND

Berkeley Hotel
1200 E. Cary St.
(804) 780-1300 or
(888) 780-4422
www.berkeleyhotel.com

Jefferson Hotel
101 W. Franklin St.
(804) 788-8000 or
(800) 424-8014
www.jeffersonhotel.com

Linden Row Inn
100 E. Franklin St.
(804) 783-7000
www.lindenrowinn.com

William Miller House
1129 Floyd Ave.
(804) 254-2928
www.williammillerhouse
.com

ROCHELLE

Ridge View Bed and Breakfast
5407 S. Blue Ridge
Turnpike
(540) 672-7024
www.virginia-ridgeview
.com

ROCKY MOUNT

Hub
245 N. Main St.
(540) 483-9303

Ippy's Restaurant & Lounge
1760 N. Main St.
(540) 489-5600
www.ippysrestaurant.com

SCOTTSVILLE

High Meadows Vineyard Inn & Restaurant
55 High Meadows Lane
(434) 286-2218
www.highmeadows.com

STANARDSVILLE

Lafayette Inn
146 E. Main St.
(434) 985-6345
www.thelafayette.com

WINTERGREEN

Wintergreen Resort
Route 664
(434) 325-2200
www.wintergreenresort
.com

Where to Eat in Central Virginia

CHARLOTTESVILLE

Littlejohn's New York Deli
1427 University Ave.
(434) 977-0588
www.littlejohnsdeli.com

Michie Tavern
638 Thomas Jefferson
Pkwy.
(434) 977-1234
www.michietavern.com

Spudnut Shop
309 Avon St.
(434) 296-0590

LOUISA

Cooper Vineyards
13372 Shannon Hill Rd.
(540) 894-5253
www.coopervineyards.com

PETERSBURG

Brickhouse Run
409 Cockade Alley
(804) 862-1815
www.brickhouserun.com

Outlaw's Bar & Grill
3729 S. Crater Rd.
(804) 862-9277
www.outlawsbarandgrill
.com

RICHMOND

Avalon
2619 W. Main St.
(804) 353-9709
www.avalonrestaurant.com

Berkeley Hotel Dining Room
1200 E. Cary St.
(804) 225-5105

Bill's Barbecue
927 Myers St. (and other locations)
(804) 358-7763
www.billsbarbecue.net

Bogart's
1903 W. Cary St.
(804) 353-9280
www.bogartsinthefan.net

Have A Nice Day Cafe
11 S. 18th St.
(804) 771-1700

River City Diner (other locations)
803 E. Parham Rd.
(804) 266-1500
www.rivercitydiner.com

Strawberry Street Cafe
421 N. Strawberry St.
(804) 353-6860
www.strawberrystreetcafe.com

SANDSTON

Ma and Pa's Diner
5600 Williamsburg Rd.
(804) 226-0329

WASHINGTON

Inn at Little Washington
Middle and Main Streets
(540) 675-3800
www.theinnatlittlewashington.com

WEST POINT

Tony and George's Seafood and Italian
2880 King William Ave.
(804) 843-4448

WILLIAMSBURG

Berrets Seafood
199 S. Boundary St.
(757) 253-1847
www.berrets.com

Dot's Back Inn
4030 MacArthur Ave.
(804) 266-3167
www.dotsbackrichmond.com

Giuseppe's Italian Cafe
5601 Richmond Rd.
(757) 565-1977
www.giuseppes.com

Old Chickahominy House
1211 Jamestown Rd.
(757) 229-4689
www.oldchicahominy.com

Trellis
403 Duke of Gloucester St.
(757) 229-8610
www.thetrellis.com

WESTERN VIRGINIA

We'll explore the western part of Virginia from the northern part of the state and wander down the lush 200 miles of the ***Shenandoah Valley*** and mountains to Roanoke.

Some things you should know about the Shenandoah River and valley:

The ***Shenandoah River*** runs "uphill" from north to south (the mouth empties into the Potomac River, on the north). Yes, there are a few other rivers like that in the world, but not many.

The valley was the main thoroughfare for settlers moving south from Pennsylvania.

More major battles of the Civil War were fought in Virginia than any other state, and this lush, fruitful valley was a grand prize that changed hands dozens of times.

The two-lane ***Skyline Drive*** runs 105 miles through the 194,000-acre ***Shenandoah National Park*** with 75 overlooks and parking areas that lead to trails, waterfalls, and nature areas. There are more than 500 miles of trails in the park (most of them are pet-friendly), and 30 percent of them are designated wilderness. The ***Appalachian Trail*** runs 101 miles through the park. President Franklin D. Roosevelt, in

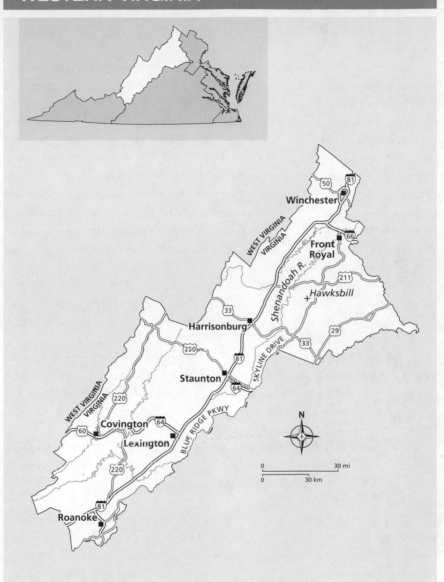

Winchester

Front
Royal

WEST VIRGINIA
VIRGINIA

Shenandoah R.

Hawksbill

Harrisonburg

SKYLINE DRIVE

Staunton

WEST VIRGINIA
VIRGINIA

Covington

BLUE RIDGE PKWY

Lexington

Roanoke

N

0 _____ 30 mi
0 _____ 30 km

dedicating the park in 1936, said visitors would find an experience "good for their bodies and good for their souls." Seventy-five years later, this is even more true.

Admission is $10 per car, or $5 per person (16 and older when entering by other than a private vehicle) Dec through Feb, and $15 per noncommercial vehicle (passenger cars, pickup trucks, RVs, vans, and converted buses) and $8 per person, and the pass is good for the day of purchase and the next six days, from Mar through Nov. Annual passes are available for frequent visitors. The park is always open; however, portions of the Skyline Drive are closed during inclement weather and at night during the deer hunting season. A storm in mid-April 2011 dropped as much as 5.5 inches of rain that resulted in stream and river flooding that damaged park roads and trails. A cautionary warning was posted on the website, so this is an example of conditions that might change depending on the weather. You should check these details before you start hiking. www.nps.gov/shen.

At its southern end it meets with the northern end of the 469-mile Blue Ridge Parkway as it winds along mountain crests toward the North Carolina border. Virginia state parks had their beginning in 1936 also, starting with 6 parks and growing to today's 34.

I call our Virginia mountains friendly because they invite the hiker, the stroller, the skier, the river rafter, the daydreamer, and the explorer into their sanctuary, their tranquility. Perhaps most important to casual visitors, the scenery is breathtakingly beautiful, with each curve and bend in the road more extraordinary than the previous one.

Among the many destination resorts, there are four with skiing facilities, including Bryce Mountain, the Homestead, Massanutten, and Wintergreen. As with other resorts, you'll find many other entertainment, meeting, and pampering options.

We'll travel parallel to I-66, I-81, and I-64. Then we'll skirt and flirt with Skyline Drive and the activities and sights along its path. Stop here for covered bridges, antiques, handmade crafts, maple syrup, and Civil War and historical museums. Taste some of the most delicious apples anywhere, and they're not necessarily Delicious. You might want to stop by an inn filled with antiques or spend some time in a cloistered abbey. And while you're at it, you can catch music ranging from country to classical.

Clarke County

Leaving the northern area of Virginia, head west along Route 7 or Route 50, where you'll detour a smidgeon to enter the world of *Clarke County* and

AUTHOR'S FAVORITES IN WESTERN VIRGINIA

Frontier Culture Museum
Staunton
(540) 332-7850
www.frontiermuseum.org

Humpback Covered Bridge
Covington State Park
(540) 962-2178
www.virginiadot.org/info/faq-covbridge5
.asp

Shenandoah Valley Music Festival
Orkney Springs
(540) 459-3396 or
(800) 459-3396
www.musicfest.org

Virginia Horse Center
Lexington
(540) 464-2950
www.horsecenter.org

Berryville. Although still mostly bucolic, things have changed around here. Gone are the mortuary museum and a general store where your payment was put in a trolley that rode a pulley to the second floor office, and your change was placed in the trolley to be returned to you. (Think a tiny Mister Rogers ski lift.)

Generally, you might say Clarke County people like the status quo. In fact, it's said that one resident put a mock Civil War cemetery in his front yard to keep the state from taking his land for a road-widening project. Supposedly, they never asked him if it was a real cemetery, so he never told them otherwise.

What you can see in Berryville is the **Old Clarke County Courthouse,** designed and built by David Meade soon after Clarke County—named for George Rogers Clark (without the "e")—was formed from Frederick County in 1836. The **Clarke County Historical Association** maintains the museum and archives that are located in the Coiner House. The exhibits tell the unique story of the county and the region. Families have donated papers, photographs, and memorabilia and they encourage you to donate items so they can be shared with historians. If you wish, they'll scan your originals and return them to you, along with a CD of the scans. The museum is open Tues through Sat 11 a.m. to 4 p.m. and by appointment. 32 E. Main St., Berryville 22611; (540) 955-2600; www.clarkehistory.org.

The bread and fruitcake (2 pounds, 4 ounces each) from the cloistered **Trappist Abbey of the Holy Cross Monastery** is legendary. Locally, Safeway and Giant grocery stores carry the baked goods, free of preservatives and made from unbleached and stone-ground flours, spring water, and unsulfured molasses. Or you can order a cake for $29.95. They also sell fraters (fruitcake slices smothered in rich dark chocolate, but not in July and August), honeys, and truffles. The monastery is on the site of the historic **Wormley Estate,** a well-preserved, 200-year-old stone building.

What isn't as well known is that you can stay at the abbey. Accommodations are available for 15 men and women, with no scheduled activities other than meals, and three of them are included each day. Each room has a private bath and a large window that opens onto the scenic beauty of the Blue Ridge Mountains. This is a great, quiet retreat, scheduled from Friday afternoon through Sunday afternoon and Monday afternoon through Friday morning. If you're going off the beaten path to escape or find, this is the place to do it. Oh, and there is a gift shop, open from 9 a.m. to noon and then from 1:30 to 5 p.m., where you can buy the aforementioned goodies. The abbey is on Route 603; 901 Cool Spring Lane, Berryville 22611; (540) 955-9494; www.monasteryfruitcake.org.

The **Burwell-Morgan Mill** is an operating overshot waterwheel with wooden gears. It's made of stone and dates from 1785 (built by former Hessian soldiers who were captured at the Battle of Saratoga in 1777); clapboard was added in 1876. Lt. Col. Nathaniel Burwell and Brig. Gen. Daniel Morgan started the operation, and during the Civil War flour and feed from the mill were sold to both armies. It was an unusual mill in that the abundant water supply and huge 20-foot-diameter wheel achieved 45 horsepower, compared with an average of only 20 horsepower. The mill remained in operation until 1953. The Clarke County Historical Association acquired it in 1964 and spent years doing extensive restoration work. More work must be done to keep up the maintenance, so the Association is requesting donations, which can be made on their website.

Visit the mill Sat from 10 a.m. to 5 p.m. and Sun from noon until 5 p.m., May through Nov. Saturday and most major holidays are grinding days.

Located on Route 624, just north of Route 50/17 in Millwood. (540) 955-2600; www.clarkehistory.org.

It's not exactly in the same league as a historic mill, but if you like prehistoric stuff, **Dinosaur Land** (Route 1, Box 63A, White Post 22663) could be the place to visit. Built in the mid-1960s, nearly three dozen nasty-looking fiberglass critters, from allosaurus to yaleasaurus, roam (statue-wise) the woods waiting to inform you and have their picture taken with you and your youngsters. For your convenience, there's also a little store with souvenirs.

Dinosaur Land is open daily 9:30 a.m. to 5:30 p.m. March 1 to Memorial Day and Labor Day through December 31; 9:30 a.m. to 6:30 p.m. Memorial Day to Labor Day. It is closed on Thurs Oct through Dec and in Jan and Feb. The admission price is $5 for folks ages 11 and older and $4 for children ages 2 through 10. 3848 Stonewall Jackson Hwy., White Post 22663; (540) 869-2222; www.dinosaurland.com.

At the University of Virginia's **Blandy Experimental Farm and the Orland E. White Arboretum** (which is the State Arboretum of Virginia) in Boyce, you can enjoy a bucolic experience as you travel through 170 acres of maintained landscapes and gardens featuring more than 1,000 varieties and species of plants representing 100 generations and 50 families. View the most extensive boxwood collection in North America. Feel free to drive the circular route or take a leisurely walk through a shady dogwood lane. Picnicking is allowed.

Among the types of activities planned by the staff here might be a bus trip to the Maymont Flower and Garden Show, an exhibit of wildflower pictures by Richmond photographer Hal Horwitz, a talk about why some song sparrows are wimps, and an apprentice gardener workshop. Some of these events have an admission fee; some are free. A potluck dinner follows the Wednesday discussions, so bring a dish if you'll be joining them for the meal. The arboretum is open to the public daily from dawn to dusk. There is no charge for admission. 400 Blandy Farm Lane, Boyce 22620; (540) 837-1758; www.virginia.edu/blandy.

Warren County

As you drive west of Washington, on I-66, or the more pastoral Route 55, you're driving through Warren County and apple country (at least until all the orchards are sold for housing or commercial development). One way to sample these succulent gifts of nature is by stopping at the **Apple House** in Linden. I dare you to resist the fragrant aroma and lure of the freshly baked apple-cinnamon donuts. I'm told the mountaintop orchards benefit from rare climatic conditions, and the high altitude produces apples "sweeter and more intensely flavored than valley-grown fruit." Take a taste of the nonalcoholic sparkling ciders (also no added sugar and no preservatives) they've named Alpenglow (a reddish glow seen near sunset or sunrise on the summit of mountains).

They offer the original Alpenglow (red Delicious and Winesap apples); mulled sparkling cider (apple pie in a bottle, they call it); sparkling scuppernong cider (wild grape muscadine from North Carolina and cider); classic blush (Virginia-grown rougeon grapes, muscadine, and various species of apples); and sparkling juice. Sampling is encouraged, they say, because "taste tells all."

They've added so many things to the gift shop selection (including Vera Bradley and leather Baekgaard bags to my favorite, Crocs shoes) that the shop has become an attraction of its own.

The Apple House is open daily 8:30 a.m. to 6 p.m. 4675 John Marshall Hwy., Linden 22642; (540) 636-6329; www.theapplehouse.net.

Year after year and now decade after decade, Patrick O'Connell and the **Inn at Little Washington** continue to garner praise after praise. Just reading notes from the Inn—"The season's first wild morels and local asparagus have arrived"—or, watching the "Dream Dinners" episode of *Avec Eric* on PBS and I'm ready to visit. When participating is your wish, sign up for the two- and three-day Stagiére program that allows you into the kitchen and a chance to "pick up a whisk and join in." If you can't make it for dinner or spending a night or two, you can make pretend at home with Patrick's book, *Patrick O'Connell's Refined American Cuisine.* Middle and Main Streets, Washington 22747; (540) 675-3800; www.theinnatlittlewashington.com.

Fauquier County

Almost before you're out of earshot of the planes from Dulles International Airport, you're in the area of The Plains, and that's where you'll find the award-winning fantastic food of Chef Tom Kee at the **Rail Stop Restaurant,** in a neat, old white building with random-width wooden floor boards.

Join the rest of the regulars, and those who've been sightseeing nearby, in one of the two main dining rooms, or reserve the Red Room, which can accommodate from two to six people. It's beautifully decorated and showcases the outstanding wine selection. You can choose from a special menu. Advance reservations are requested; they're required for the Red Room.

The Rail Stop is open Tues through Sat for dinner and Sunday brunch. 6478 Main St., The Plains 20198; (540) 253-5644; www.railstoprestaurant.com.

Rappahannock County

It's easy to see why people love this area with its forested mountains and bucolic countryside. You're looking at a picture postcard wherever you look. You shouldn't be surprised that more than 50 artisans, artists, and photographers live in the county. You can find their work in the galleries of Washington, Sperryville, and Flint Hill. Or, you can accomplish everything at one time by attending the annual November **Artists of Rappahannock Studio and Gallery Tour** sponsored by the Rappahannock Association for the Arts and the Community. Check the site for a list of participating artists and work samples. 10 Firehouse Lane, Washington 22747; (540) 675-3193; www.raac.org.

You will be excused if you think Rappahannock County should be in the Northern Neck or Eastern part of the state. The Rappahannock River does form the northeastern boundary and separates it from Fauquier County. I'm sure no one's bothered (nor should they), but with 921 students in grades pre-kindergarten through twelfth and a 2000 census of 6,983 people, I'd guess there are

Can You Canoe?

Front Royal, northern gateway to Skyline Drive and Shenandoah National Park, has been officially granted the title *"Canoe Capital"* by the state because of the more than 40,000 people who annually explore the north and south forks of the Shenandoah River. If you want to join them, call the *Front Royal Canoe Company,* 8567 Stonewall Jackson Hwy., Front Royal 22630; (540) 635-5440 or (800) 270-8808; www.frontroyalcanoe.com.

Another canoe, tube, kayak, and raft rental place is *Shenandoah River Outfitters, Inc.* They also have river cabins and a tent campground. 6502 S. Page Valley Rd., Luray 22835; (540) 743-4159 or (800) 6CANOE2; www.shenandoahriver.com.

many more trees than people. Yes, you could spend a lot of time exploring here and not duplicate a single day.

Winchester

Farther west on Route 50 or Route 7 in *Winchester,* you can discover the *Shenandoah Valley Discovery Museum,* which lets you explore the Shenandoah River watershed, experiment with laws of physics, and uncover the relationship among the service, manufacturing, and business sectors of the town. Art materials are available, as are small appliances that you can take apart. And if those muscles need a little stretching, try the 8-foot-high (25-foot-long) climbing wall.

Those who think museums are stuffy should have been here when six original Andy Warhol prints were on display, along with a silkscreen studio where visitors could try their hand at this art form. A fairly permanent (it's there indefinitely) exhibit is entitled Reflections on Mirrors, which explores the nature of them, be they convex or concave, one-way, or otherwise. There are also make-and-take activities.

Based on the motto "To touch is to explore, to explore is to discover, to discover is to learn," there's lots to explore, discover, and learn here. In the natural history section there are "discovery drawers," and one can dig for fossils in the fossil pit or visit a Burmese python named McGuyver. In the Our Town section, there's a hospital with an

grayandblue

The remains of 2,576 Confederate and 4,500 Union soldiers killed in nearby Civil War battles were laid to rest at the *Mount Hebron Cemetery,* 305 E. Boscawen St., Winchester 22601; (540) 662-4868; www.mthebroncemetery.org.

Virginia's Country Classic

Winchester's most famous daughter, Virginia Patterson Hensley Dick (September 8, 1932–March 5, 1963), was buried at the Shenandoah Memorial Park following her plane-crash death in Tennessee. You may know her better as award-winning country singer **Patsy Cline.** A bell tower has been erected here in her memory. Enter the north gate and take the first right to the bench on the left.

Other places of Cline history include her Winchester home at 608 S. Kent St.; the home where she married Charlie Dick on September 15, 1957 at 720 S. Kent St.; Gaunt's drugstore, where she was a waitress at the soda fountain, at the corner of South Loudoun and Valley Avenue; G & M Music, at 38 W. Boscawen St., where she recorded; WINC Radio 520 on N. Pleasant Valley Road, where Patsy often performed; Handley High School on Valley Avenue, where she attended high school; and the Kurtz Cultural Center at the corner of Cameron and Boscawen, where a memorabilia case is on display.

In addition to Patsy Cline Boulevard in Winchester, the 7-mile stretch of US 522 running south out of Winchester is known as the Patsy Cline Memorial Highway. It was dedicated in November 1986. For a brochure highlighting Cline landmarks and historic sites, contact Celebrating Patsy Cline, Inc., P.O. Box 3900, Winchester 22604; www.patsycline.com.

emergency room and ambulance. Children can learn about an integral part of Winchester's history and industry in the apple-packing shed, which also helps teach about physical sciences and mathematics. The handicap obstacle course brings to life the realities and frustrations of navigating in a walking-person's world. The aforementioned climbing wall isn't just a place for exercise; it's an enjoyable way (one hopes) to learn about gravity.

School groups tend to visit the museum on weekday mornings, so call to see if you want to join the crowd or go when it's not quite so busy. The admission fee is $6 per person, with children under the age of 2 free. The museum is open Mon through Sat 9 a.m. to 5 p.m. and Sun 1 to 5 p.m. On the first Fri of each month, the museum stays open until 7:30 p.m. and there is no admission charge after 5 p.m. 54 S. Loudoun St., south end of the Downtown Walking Mall, Winchester 22601; (540) 722-2020; www.discoverymuseum.net.

Frederick County

Now, turning south, along Route 11, 5.3 miles north of Stephens City, is the site of the **Battle of Kernstown,** the only battle in which Stonewall Jackson was defeated (8,000 Federals against Jackson's 3,500 Confederates). Ironically, two years later, in June 1864, the Second Battle of Kernstown was the last Confederate victory in the Shenandoah Valley. You can visit the battlefield on the Pritchard-Grim Farm on Sat from 10 a.m. to 4 p.m. and Sun noon to 4 p.m. from the second weekend in May through Oct. No admission charge. Kernstown Battlefield Association, (540) 869-2896; P.O. Box 1327, Winchester 22604; www.kernstownbattle.org.

America's oldest motor inn, Middletown's **Wayside Inn,** has been in operation since 1797, when it was known as Wilkerson's Tavern. It has always been a marvelous place to dine (7 dining room options, each with colonial-attired waitstaff) and to stay (with 24 rooms). The furnishings make the place an antiques-lover's paradise. Whether you enjoy a meal in the Lord Fairfax Room or the Old Servant Kitchen (both favorites), a walk through the inn, or an extended stay, you'll always receive gracious Southern hospitality. 7783 Main St., Middletown 22645; (540) 869-1797 or (877) 869-1797; www.alongthe wayside.com.

Like stepping back in time to the 1890s, the **Hotel Strasburg** combines Victorian history and charm to make a special place for lodging and dining. Tastefully decorated with many antique pieces of period furniture and an impressive collection of art, the inn's dining rooms and quaintly renovated sleeping rooms invite you to wander through them. Do arrive early so that you can peek into the rooms to view the varied quilts and furniture pieces. There are no elevators and no dedicated staff to take your luggage to your room;

OTHER PLACES WORTH SEEING

DAYTON
Shenandoah Valley Folk Art and Heritage Center
(540) 879-2616
www.heritagecenter.com

FRONT ROYAL
Skyline Caverns
(540) 635-4545 or (800) 296-4545
www.skylinecaverns.com

ROANOKE
Grandin Theatre
(540) 345-6177
www.grandintheatre.com

STAUNTON
Staunton/Augusta Arts Center
(540) 885-2028
www.saartcenter.org

WAYNESBORO
Shenandoah Valley Art Center
(540) 949-7662
www.svacart.com

that means a steep set of stairs to navigate, so pack light. The hotel is at 213 Holliday St., Strasburg 22657; (540) 465-9191 or (800) 348-8327; www.hotel strasburg.com.

Shenandoah County

Yes, that's a basket filled with apples painted atop the water tower along I-81 as you head toward *Mount Jackson.* Hmm, maybe it should be filled with apple cider instead.

For information about the friendly town of Mount Jackson, population about 1,800, the Historical District that's listed on the National Register of Historic Places, the Shenandoah Lanes duckpin bowling alley (ca. 1947), the Union Church that was used as a hospital, and the Our Soldiers Cemetery, call (540) 477-2121; www.mountjackson.com.

Endless Caverns is a vast underground world of caves and tunnels that lets you journey deep into the earth to view remarkable rock formations. A large renovation project enhanced the Caverns' camping and RV area, the grounds, and facilities.

Whether or not it's desirable, the ENDLESS CAVERNS sign on the side of *Massanutten Mountain* was relit a few years ago after being dark for 30 years. It's the largest lighted sign in the United States and the second largest sign (the Hollywood sign is larger). The caverns are open for tours Thurs through Sun during the winter, and daily in the summer, 9 a.m. to 6 p.m. Admission to the caverns is $16 for adults and $8 for children (ages 4 through 12). 1800 Endless Caverns Rd., New Market 22844; (800) 544-CAVE (2283); www.endlesscaverns .com.

Right outside of Mount Jackson and New Market is the *Meems Bottom Covered Bridge,* crossing the north fork of the Shenandoah River, and you can drive through it! It was built in 1893 of materials hewn and quarried nearby and was nearly destroyed by fire in 1976. It was reopened in 1979 and then closed again due to structural problems. It has since reopened. The Mount Jackson community says the bridge is 191 feet long; the Virginia Department of Transportation says it's 204 feet. In any case it's the longest covered bridge in the state and the only one still open for vehicular use.

This single-span Theodore Burr truss, built under the supervision of F. S. Wisler, succeeded at least two other bridges. Records show that one was burned in 1862 as Stonewall Jackson went up the valley ahead of General John C. Fremont prior to the battles of Harrisonburg. Another was washed away during a flood in 1870. ("Up the valley" here is southward, since the river flows northward to join the Potomac at Harpers Ferry.)

The bridge is easily reached by taking exit 269 from the south or exit 273 from the north off I-81 to Highway 11 and turning west on Route 720. Wisler Road, Mount Jackson 22842; (540) 459-2332; www.virginiadot.org/info/faq-covbridge1.asp.

West of Mount Jackson is Orkney Springs, where the **Shenandoah Valley Music Festival,** one of the outstanding events of its type, is held every summer. Their explanation is, "We didn't invent summertime—just the finest way to enjoy it!" First opened in 1962, the festival offers programs that vary from the great masterworks for orchestra to light classical music, lilting pops, vocal music, and big-band sounds. You could not ask for a more beautiful setting in which to hear beautiful music (and it's mountain informal to boot). William Hudson, director of the Fairfax Symphony, is the artistic director and administrator for the nonprofit festival.

Of course you're invited to bring your own picnic to eat on the lawn before the concert. To get there take exit 283 off I-81 and go east on Route 703; then turn right onto Route 11 through Mount Jackson and turn right onto Route 263; follow Route 263 (going west) for 15 miles. Shenandoah Valley Music Festival, P.O. Box 528, Woodstock 22664; (540) 459-3396 or (800) 459-3396; www.musicfest.org.

It's amazing what a little fame will do, or more important, what a great reputation will do to garner that fame. So goes the story with the **Route 11 Potato Chip Factory.** It's been covered in the *Washington Post, New York Times, Winchester Star, Bon Appetite, Gourmet,* and *Southern Living. Today, Good Morning America,* and *The Early Show* have had segments about the yummy products, and perhaps most important, it's been featured on the *Food Finds* show on the Food Network. They note that they use sea salt (real salt) from an ancient Utah seabed (think Salt Lake) on their lightly salted chips and their sweet potato chips. Some of the many steps they've taken toward a green earth are shipping all potato peelings and chip rejects to a herd of cattle down Route 11 and the used chip oil is sold to a company that roasts their horse feed in it. They also recycle the steam from the cookers to help heat the kitchen, and the list continues.

With increased demand for their chips, they had to expand or move so they relocated from Middletown to Mount Jackson in 2008. You're invited to watch them make the chips, but you should call if you specifically want to see the fry-viewing. There are plenty of samples (you are required to taste some if you're going to watch the frying) and a shop full of goodies to buy. Unfortunately, the prices for vegetables has increased so much that they have, at least temporarily, discontinued making the mixed veggie chips. They are open Mon through Sat 9 a.m. to 5 p.m. 11 Edwards Way, Mount Jackson 22842; (540) 477-9664 or (800) 294-SPUD; www.rt11.com.

Shenandoah Caverns (part of a "family" of attractions) has a large (really large) elf statue welcoming you to one of the many caverns available for touring in this part of the state. The hour-long guided tour descends a staircase into the 56-degree cavern system (bring a light jacket and comfortable shoes), or you can take the elevator—the only cavern system in Virginia that has one. The caverns open daily at 9 a.m., with the last tour time varying by season. Admission, which includes the caverns, American Celebration on Parade, the Yellow Barn, and Main Street, is $23 for adults, $20 for seniors, and $10 for children 6 through 14. AAA and group discounts are available. 261 Caverns Rd., Shenandoah Caverns; (888) 4CAVERN; www.shenandoahcaverns.com.

The *American Celebration on Parade* is where you can see, pose by, and even climb on some of the most extensive and glorious parade floats that have graced such events as the Presidential Inaugural, Mardi Gras, Rose, Miss America Pageant, and Thanksgiving parades. You are guaranteed to be amazed at their beauty, complexity, and size. They come from the shop of Hargrove, Inc., a Maryland company that started in the 1940s. The company has been decorating the National Christmas Tree in Washington, DC, since the Pageant of Peace was established in 1954, and some of the lights and decorations from the trees are included in the holiday exhibit. The 40,000-square-foot facility has changing exhibits, and the Shenandoah Jubilee singers perform about a dozen concerts a year at the facility.

Page County

Reportedly the largest bell at the Luray Singing Tower, *Luray Caverns* (a few miles east of Mount Jackson, on Route 211, Luray), weighs 7,640 pounds. The world's largest musical instrument is the Great Stalacpipe Organ in the Cathedral Room of Luray Caverns. The caverns are open daily at 9 a.m., with tours starting about every 20 minutes. The admission fee is $19 for adults, $9 for children (6 through 12), and $16 for seniors (62 and older), and includes admission to the Caverns and the Car and Carriage Museum. The caverns are at 101 Cave Hill Rd., Luray, 22835; (540) 743-6551; www.luraycaverns.com.

Years ago, when I used to publish the *QuickTrips Travel Letter,* I sent a friend to a fly-fishing school weekend to write about the experience. Wife did better than hubs, but they both had a sensational time. You can do something similar at the *Shenandoah Streamers School of Fly Casting* with Allen Campbell (more than 30 years of fly casting and fishing experience) as your instructor. Take an all-day class and learn entomology, knots, fly choice, and more in one-on-one classes. Luray 22835; (443) 924-0067; www.virginia.org/Listings/OutdoorsAndSports/ShenandoahStreamersSchoolofFlyCasting.

Harrisonburg

For a wonderful repurposing story, look to the **Hardesty-Higgins House,** or as they say in **Harrisonburg,** it's "Where History and Hospitality Meet." Today it holds the visitor services offices, the **Rocktown Gift Shoppe, Mrs. Hardesty's Tea Room,** the **Valley Turnpike Museum** (Route 11 or Main Street), the **Harrisonburg-Rockingham Civil War Orientation Center,** and the executive offices for the **Harrisonburg Downtown Renaissance and Harrisonburg Tourism.** It started life when Dr. Henry Higgins began construction in 1848 and was completed in 1853 by Isaac Hardesty (the city's first mayor). Over the years, it has served as an inn, showroom for handcrafted furniture makers, and finally landing the city's hands in 2001. It's open daily 9 a.m. to 5 p.m.; 212 S. Main St., Harrisonburg 22801; (540) 432-8935; www.harrisonburgtourism.com.

You can stroll around or "Do Downtown" with a self-guided tour, shopping (Glen's Fair Price, Oasis Gallery, All Things Virginia, Farmers Market, and the Downtown Books), do something cultural (Court Street Theater, Harrisonburg Children's Museum, or the Virginia Quilt Museum—see below), or dining (27 locally owned restaurants from Thai-fusion to Ethiopian, Greek, and more). 212 S. Main St., Harrisonburg 22801; (540) 432 8922; www.downtown harrisonburg.org.

One dining option is the **L & S Diner** that was opened in 1947, and where they say its pan-fried chicken is the most popular item on the menu. A winning competitor is the Garbage Omelet (need you ask?) with three eggs, cheese, a variety of meats, onions, green peppers, tomatoes, and potatoes. Seems natural, as this is one of Virginia's big poultry centers. Okay, you may have heard that the restaurant was closed. It was. New owner Linda Raines reopened it and hired the former cooks and waitstaff. If you'd like to stop and try some, the diner is open Mon through Sat from 5:30 a.m. to 2:30 p.m. Look for the

Gobble Gobble

Two turkey statues, one at each end of Route 11, welcome you to **Rockingham County,** the top turkey producer of Virginia, signifying the county's status of Turkey Capital. Carl Roseberg was the sculptor and Norwood Bosserman the designer of the bronze sculpture and limestone base. The statues are about 3 feet tall and on a 5-foot base, and they were dedicated in 1955. Gerald Harris, then a sixth grader, originated the idea and three of them were made, with the third located at the Elkton High School. Unfortunately, it was stolen by vandals and, apparently, flew the coop permanently.

TOP ANNUAL EVENTS

MARCH

Highland Maple Festival
Highland
(540) 468-2550
www.highlandcounty.org/maple.htm

APRIL

Annual Fodderstack 10K Classic
Flint Hill
(540) 675-5330 or (540) 675-3670
http://fodderstack10k.com

Virginia Hot Glass Festival
Staunton
(540) 885-0678
www.sunspots.com

Easter Sunrise Service
Natural Bridge
(540) 291-2121
www.naturalbridgeva.com/events

Historic Garden Week
Statewide
(804) 644-7776
www.vagardenweek.org

Shenandoah Apple Blossom Festival and Parade
Winchester
(540) 662-3863
www.thebloom.com

Wildflower Weekend in Shenandoah National Park
(540) 999-3500
www.nps.gov/shen

JUNE

Woofstock Dog Festival
Roanoke
(540) 206-2414
www.woofstockdogfestival.com

Shenandoah Valley Wine and Jazz Festival
Staunton
(540) 332-7850
www.frontiermuseum.org/events.html

JULY

Hot-Air Balloon Rally
Lexington
(540) 463-5071
www.sunriserotarylexva.org/balloon.htm

OCTOBER

Shenandoah Hot Air Balloon Festival
Long.Branch Plantation (Clarke County)
(540) 837-1856 or (877) 868-1851
www.historiclongbranch.com/balloonfestival.htm

International Gold Cup Races
The Plains
(540) 347-2612
www.vagoldcup.com

railway car. 255 N. Liberty Ave., Harrisonburg 22802; (540) 801-0110; http://rockingham.va.golookon.com/listings/l_and_s_diner.

Quilting is a favorite pastime, whether for the wonderful historical patterns created over the years, the heirloom quality, or the physical and mental warmth they create, and you can explore all these facets at the *Virginia Quilt Museum.* Here you'll discover the roles and significance of quilts in American society and be amazed and delighted at the ingenuity, the creativity, and just the beauty of all the quilts on display. You can take lessons, perhaps learn about that beloved quilt that's been handed down in your family for generations, or stop in the gift shop. The museum is open Tues through Sat 10 a.m. to 4 p.m. Admission is $5 for adults, $3 for students (12 to 18), and $2 for young students (5 through 11). Group tours are available; please call to reserve a day and time. Closed during exhibit installation periods. 301 S. Main St., Harrisonburg 22801; (540) 433-3818; www.vaquiltmuseum.org.

The *Daniel Harrison House,* southwest of Harrisonburg and just north of Dayton, also is known as *Fort Harrison.* The front part of this sturdy stone structure was built in about 1748, with the rest of the house constructed in the 1850s. When the nonprofit organization formed by the Harrisonburg-Rockingham Historical Society purchased the property in 1978, the members immediately began restoration, including dismantling and rebuilding the east and west stone walls.

Since then, they've painted the interior and exterior, redone the floors, and reconstructed a 19th-century summer kitchen. Some original cedar shingles were found in the attic and replicated. A 1962 electric map that's 13–feet-by-20-feet has been revised with new electronics and bells and whistles (figuratively, anyway). The map, recalling the campaign of 1862 explains how General Jackson delayed the Union forces on their way to Richmond.

The house is open Tues through Sat 10 a.m. to 5 p.m. and by appointment. A $5 admission fee is charged for adults. 382 High St., Dayton 22821: (540) 879-2616; www.heritagecenter.com.

About 25 miles west of Harrisonburg on US 33, on the Virginia/West Virginia line, is *High Knob Fire Tower* at an elevation of 4,107 feet. World War I veterans started construction in 1939 and it was completed the following year by men in the Civilian Conservation Corps (CCC). It stopped being used as a fire tower many years ago and it was designated a National Historical Lookout in 1994. What's unusual about it is it was built of rocks while other towers were made of wood or metal. You are allowed to climb the tower and just try to absorb the spectacular views. That's easier said than done, for some people anyway. Park along US 33 (limited availability) and hike about 40 minutes to the tower. You will be going through private property, so please stay on the trail. There was another High Knob Observation Tower, farther south in Wise County, that was a 2-story wooden structure and was destroyed by a Halloween arsonist in 2007. So, if you read a website that says it doesn't exist, make sure you're reading about the right tower. (540) 432-0187; www.virginia.org/Listings/HistoricSites/HighKnobFireTower.

The *Natural Chimneys* regional park area in Mount Solon is the home of some towering limestone structures, impressive scenery indeed. Does your mind see 120-foot chimneys or massive castle turrets? Admission to the chimneys is free. 94 Natural Chimneys Lane, Mount Solon 22843; (540) 350-2510; www.visitwaynesboro.net.

Staunton

Because **Staunton** (pronounced Stanton, STAN-tehn or STANT-en) was unscathed during the Civil War, there are plenty of 18th- and 19th-century buildings, many of which have been beautifully restored and preserved. There are six National Historic Districts—Gospel Hill, Stuart Addition, Newtown, Beverly, the Villages at Staunton, and the Wharf District (no, there's no waterfront wharf there; just a reminder that similar warehouses would be associated with a wharf as with the local train station).

Pick up the *Self-Guided Tour of Staunton's Historic Districts* brochure from the visitor center and at many downtown merchants.

On display in the **Staunton firehouse** is Jumbo, a 1911 Robinson fire engine lovingly restored by Billy Thompson's White Post Restorations. Stop by during the day and the firefighters on duty will show you into the room; or if you come at night, you can look through the windows. Because it cost $143,000 to restore the fire truck, they'll accept donations. 500 N. Augusta St., Staunton 24402; (540) 332-3884; www.staunton.va.us.

It's said that the **Frontier Culture Museum** is the only one of its kind in the world. The museum shows four working 19th-century farmsteads. Two of them were brought to the site from European nations—Northern Ireland and Germany—and the English farm was reconstructed (it couldn't be removed because of English preservation law). It is said that although the countless stones that made up the Irish farmhouse were numbered in place, somehow they multiplied like so many wire hangers, and quite a few were left over after it was reassembled here in the United States.

The fourth farmstead was donated by Phyllis Riddlebarger of Botetourt County, Virginia, reflecting the melding of European influences. Her late husband's grandparents bought the farm in 1884. You can see the adaptations in the German V-notched log barn construction, and the A-frame roofed smokehouse has English derivations. The center is amassing and preserving archival and genealogical collections and artifacts. Historical research, academic outreach, intern programs, and the preparation of appropriate materials and publications play a vital role in the museum programs. West Africans were brought to the American colonies by the hundreds of thousands in the 1600s and 1700s, and now there is a West African Farm exhibit depicting the lives of the Igbo people. Their most notable and enduring contributions to American culture are found in foodways, music, folklore, and religious worship.

The museum is open daily 9 a.m. to 5 p.m. mid-March through Nov and from 10 a.m. until 4 p.m. the rest of the year and admission is $10 for adults, $9.50 for seniors, $9 for students (13 through college), and $6 for children ages 6 to 12. 1250 Richmond Ave. (junction of I-64 and I-81), Staunton, 24401; (540) 332-7850; www.frontiermuseum.org.

Wright's Dairy Rite is not the last curb-service (where you order from the speaker on a "Servusfone" at your parking place) hamburger joint in the state (a few Sonic Burgers, at several locations, offer the same service), but it's probably the most historic. F. A. Wright opened this eatery in 1952 and insisted that only the highest-quality and freshest ingredients be used in his kitchen. Mr. Wright created a tradition in Staunton that has existed for more than 50 years. To this day Wright's is still family-owned (Wright's son-in-law James E. Cash and his son, James R. Cash). This is where the Statler Brothers used to hang out and perhaps where they began composing one or more of their songs. Although the '50s have remained here, Wright's now offers free wireless Internet service. 346 Greenville Ave., Staunton 24401; (540) 886-0435; www.dairy-rite.com.

Staunton is a year-round destination featuring a historic downtown, and a hip, culinary, arts, and music scene. The calendar seems to have a different festival every month, so there's almost always something happening in this very vibrant town.

It's time to brush up your Shakespeare, your Ben Jonson, and your Tom Stoppard at the **Blackfriar Playhouse at the American Shakespeare Center** in Staunton. Hoping to duplicate, or go several levels higher than, the annual Shakespeare Festival in Ashland, Oregon, Ralph Cohen has directed the fund-raising ($4 million worth) and construction of the world's only replica of the Bard's favorite theater (the Globe was an outdoor theater; the Blackfriar an indoor facility). It's oak and has wooden benches for about 300 (you can rent a cushion and backrest), and the house lights don't go down when the acting starts so you have a much more intimate relationship with the cast, who can see who the audience is and how you're reacting. And it's jaw-droppingly beautiful.

The Blackfriar Playhouse production days and times vary according to the season, so check their website for sales and packages. 10 S. Market St., Staunton 24401; (877) 682-4236; www.americanshakespearecenter.com.

Augusta County

Anyone serious interested in "beyond organic" farming probably has heard of **Joel Salatin** and his **Polyface Farm** ("the farm of many faces") in **Swoope,** just outside of Staunton, where he uses holistic methods of animal husbandry to raise his livestock. He produces salad bar beef, pigaerator pork, pastured poultry, forage-based rabbits, and forestry products. His farming techniques are environmentally responsible, sustainable, and ecologically advantageous. Salatin is the author of numerous articles and books, including *Everything I Want to Do is Illegal, The Raw Milk Revolution, Folks, This Ain't Normal, Holy Cows and Hog Heaven,* and *Sheer Ecstasy of Being a Lunatic Farmer.* He also spends a fair amount of time lecturing to college students and instructors, and environmental groups, and he attended at least two TEDxMidAtlantic conferences.

You are welcome to take a free self-guided tour of the farm Mon through Sat 9 a.m. to 4 p.m., March 1 through December 14. Two-hour escorted tours may be arranged. Fees vary. If you want to purchase some Polyface products, you can visit the farm Mon through Fri 9 a.m. to noon and on Sat until noon. Or, you can call for an appointment. Additionally, buying clubs in Virginia and Maryland carry his products and you can find a list of local stores that do, too, on the Polyface website. Pure Meadows Lane, Swoope 24479; (540) 885-3590 or (540) 887-8194; www.polyfacefarms.com.

One of the many highlights in the area is the ***Andre Viette Gardens,*** with one of the largest collection of perennial flowers in the eastern United States, as in "more than 3,000 varieties of rare and unusual perennials, trees, shrubs, and evergreens for the sun and shade." The gardens are always open. Or, you can find where Andre will be lecturing or doing a radio or online broadcast, talking about this and that and the monthly flower, etc. The nursery is open Apr through Oct Mon through Sat 9 a.m. to 5 p.m. and Sun noon to 5 p.m. 994 Long Meadow Rd., Fishersville 22939; (800) 575-5538; www.viette.com.

When you want that perfect Virginia souvenir, travel Route 250 east out of Staunton, to visit the ***Virginia Made Shop,*** owned by Terry and Ginger LeMasurier, featuring a wide collection of Virginia products, including Pruden's hams and bacon, wines, crafts, colonial gifts and accessories, and souvenirs. They do a particularly good Christmas-craft business.

Many of the crafts appear more modern than old-timey, but there is a variety of things, such as cornhusk dolls, cornhusk flowers, grapevine and pinecone wreaths, and cotton rugs, the best-selling item in the shop. Everything promotes Virginia, and almost everything is made in Virginia except some souvenirs made elsewhere in the United States (they couldn't find Virginia manufacturers for some of these items). Nothing is foreign-made, and about half the artists are from the Staunton area. The shop is open Mon through Fri 10 a.m. to 7 p.m. and Sat until 6 p.m. This shop has been open since early 1984. 54 Rowe Rd., Staunton 24401; (540) 886-7180 or (800) 544-6118.

Rockbridge County

Captain Joseph Kennedy constructed what is now called **Wade's Mill** some time around 1750, and his family owned it for more than a century. James F. Wade, hence the name, purchased it in 1882, and his family operated it for the next four generations. The 4-story mill is powered by a 21-foot waterwheel from a nearby stream (known originally as Captain Joseph Kennedy's Mill Creek) and is one of the few remaining mills still producing a wide variety of flours on millstones. On your free self-guided tour, you can see all the gears and pulleys used to grind the wheat. It's listed on the National Register of Historic Places.

Jim and Georgie Young now carry on the tradition of the miller and his wife with fresh, old-fashioned, stone-ground grits, grains, and mixes. Then they take things a step further with cooking classes, catered dinners for your special occasions, and more. Check for such events as Mike Lund (formerly of Staunton's Zynodoa Restaurant and the incomparable Inn at Little Washington) teaching how to prepare three special spring meals. Or, you might want to visit while the Youngs' friend and neighbor Jessie Knadler (author of *Tart and Sweet* about growing local crops) talks about local harvests.

Check their website for some mouthwatering recipes that will have you ordering from the catalog immediately, if you don't decide you really want to stop by in person.

Wade's Mill is open Wed through Sat from 10 a.m. to 5 p.m. and Sun 1 to 5 p.m., from early Apr through the middle of Dec. It's closed on Sun from June through Aug and on July 4 and Thanksgiving Day. 55 Kennedy-Wade's Mill, Raphine 24472 (4 miles west of I-81 at the Raphine exit); (800) 290-1400; www.wadesmill.com.

One of the more spectacular sights on the eastern side of the Continental Divide is **Natural Bridge.** It's more than 100 million years old, 215 feet high, and 90 feet wide. It was surveyed by George Washington in 1750 (you can see his initials carved on the wall of the bridge) and once owned by Thomas Jefferson (he bought it and 157 acres of land from King George III of England for 20 shillings in 1774). Seeing the bridge, hiking through nature, stopping in the Wax Museum and taking the self-guided tour of the museum factory, viewing the "Drama," and touring the caverns means you can spend an hour or two here or an entire day.

The nightly illumination of Natural Bridge is a tradition that started on May 22, 1927, when President Calvin Coolidge pressed the start button for the first time. Musical accompaniment was added to this Drama of Creation.

Colonel Henry Parsons explored the caverns in 1889–91, and when modernization took place, some tools, a ladder, a lantern, and rope were found where they had been left almost a hundred years before.

Scenes of Virginia and Natural Bridge history are included in the Wax Museum, with highlights from the lives of such notables as George Washington and Thomas Jefferson.

A combination ticket to Natural Bridge, the caverns and guided tour, Cedar Creek nature trail and Monacan Village, the Wax and Toy Museum, and Drama of Creation show (dusk) is $26 for adults and $14 for children (5 through 12).

Another part of the Natural Bridge collection of interesting things to see is **Foamhenge.** Mark Cline of the Enchanted Castle Studios created, or sculpted, this full-size replica of England's Stonehenge. Yes, it's made of foam and took about six weeks to build. About a mile north of Natural Bridge, on Highway 11, near the Natural Bridge Zoo, the Styrofoam construction is astronomically correct. (540) 291-4655. 15 Appledore Lane, Natural Bridge, 24578; (540) 291-2121 or (800) 533-1410; www.naturalbridgeva.com.

Nelson County

It's always nice to find a good, well-recommended down-home diner, and the **Blue Ridge Pig** northeast of Waynesboro, seems to fit that description to a T. On the be-sure-to-try list are home-smoked pork and beef barbecue (sliced or chopped), ribs, and smoked turkey, all done in a large wood-burning smokehouse behind the restaurant. The homemade lemonade and limeade, spicy baked beans, and potato salad also rate raves. The Pig is popular with locals, skiers from the nearby Wintergreen resort, and truckers going up and down Blue Ridge Mountains. There's carryout and dining inside. It's open daily from 11 a.m. to 8 p.m. 2842 Rockfish Valley Hwy., Nellysford 22958; (434) 361-9170 or (800) 282-8223; www.nelsoncounty.com.

When you want to golf and snow ski in the same day, learn to mountain bike, be pampered in a spa, kayak, rock climb, fish, boat, horseback ride, have some good food, enjoy Blue Ridge Mountain scenery, or just do nothing at all, the place to do it is the **Wintergreen Resort.**

One of the more fascinating programs offered at Wintergreen is **OWLS, the Outdoor Wilderness Leadership School,** where you can enjoy the historic and magnificent Blue Ridge Mountains while developing your biking proficiency with Wintergreen guides to lead you. The OWLS center rides take you through the George Washington National Forest, Walnut Creek Park, or Panorama Farm on their Gary Fisher full-suspension bikes. They provide the rentals, trail maps, and shuttle service—you provide the muscle power. Four-hour tours are offered daily; starting at 10 a.m. and 2 p.m. Reservations are required. (406) 920-2808; www.owlsadventures.com.

You can also take a course in rock climbing and rappelling, and enjoy a fly-fishing retreat. Yes, there are options for those who are more domestic and indoors-oriented.

Wintergreen Resort, Route 664, Wintergreen 22958; (434) 325-2200 or (800) 926-3723; www.wintergreenresort.com.

Be sure to stop by Nelson County's **Crabtree Falls,** about 6 miles off the Blue Ridge Parkway near milepost 27 and the Wintergreen Resort, which has 3 miles of cascading waterfalls. You didn't see them on the TV show *The Waltons,* but the falls were mentioned when it came to a Sunday outing. The falls are said to be the highest waterfall east of the Mississippi River, with a vertical drop of 1,200 feet featuring 5 major and several smaller cascades. You can walk a few hundred feet from the upper parking lot to the first overlook or you can tackle the 2-mile trail along the cascading waterfall, and there are several lookout points. Wooden stairs, gravel paths, railed overlooks, and a 100 foot-bridge over the Tye River (built in 1978) are all part of the trail. The park is open daily from dawn to dusk. Route 56, 11581 Crabtree Falls Hwy., Montebello 24464; (434) 263-7015 or (800) 282-8223; www .nelsoncounty.com/visit/crabtreefalls.

famousresidents

Among the famous people who live or have lived in the Rappahannock County area are painter Ned Bittinger, former columnist James Kilpatrick, music director of the New York Philharmonic Lorin Maazel, former senator Eugene McCarthy, and sculptor Frederick Hart.

Change direction, and drive about 4 miles west of Staunton on US 250 to visit the Jennings Beach Valley, around **Churchville** (named because of all the churches). This is the area where John Trimble, an early Irish settler, was killed in 1764 in the last Indian raid in Augusta County. Visit www.highlandcounty.org.

A few more miles westward and you'll pass the scene of the **Battle of McDowell** (540-396-6169), where you can view Confederate breastworks (low barriers to protect gunners). A forest-walk entrance leads to an area where, in 1862, a military action brought Confederate troops to this mountaintop to build fortifications that would block Union advances into the Shenandoah Valley. So effective were these fortifications that it would be 1864 before Union troops would try again to enter the valley. More than a century later, the trenches of these wartime fortifications are visible. A short ⅓-mile loop trail (about a 20-minute walk that's a little steep and rocky in places) is marked. Travel on the forest walk is one-way and is for the foot traveler only. Three exhibit points along the way tell the story of this small part of Civil War history.

Once you've driven through Highland County, you understand what it means to be the third-least-populated county east of the Mississippi. There's an estimated ratio of five or six sheep to every person living here. Monterey, the county seat, is 50 miles and 4 mountains away, via winding, twisting US 250, from Staunton.

Bath County

Now, you can head down US 220 and along Route 39 for some real solitude.

On one of my exploratory trips, I took off from Hot Springs toward West Virginia on Route 39, a designated scenic byway, and just marveled at this pristine area. A tape of Vivaldi's *The Four Seasons* (what else?) was cranked up fairly high to serenade the woodland creatures through the car's open windows, whether or not they wanted to be entertained. There was no one else on the road for miles. In fact, other than the road, there was barely a sign that a human had happened by this way.

This is Bath County, where the population boasts that there are no traffic lights in the county, no billboards (there are advertising signs on the roads, but no "billboards"), and, because the weather is cool enough, no mosquitoes. I must admit that, in traveling through this area, I have never met a mosquito in Bath County. What Bath has to offer is lots of pretty scenery, some of the oldest rock formations known to geology, and a few pleasant ways to spend some time.

Suddenly, as though from a scene from the movie *Close Encounters of the Third Kind,* I turned a corner, and stretched out below me were the workings and company town of Virginia Power's ***Bath County Pumped Storage Project.*** As I recall, there were about 3,000 people working on this facility. There was on-site housing for 1,000. This meant that another 2,000 were commuting daily, some from as far as 90 miles away. I must have just missed rush hour.

It was my introduction to the pump storage concept. Virginia Power (now Dominion Power) took two streams, the Big Back Creek and the Little Back Creek, and dammed both, creating huge reservoirs. During the day, water is released from the upper storage area to the lower storage area via 1,000-foot-high pipes that are nearly 29 feet in diameter. The upper reservoir is 1,262 feet higher than the lower one. Water gushes through the turbines, generating electricity in the world's most powerful pumped storage generating station. When evening and weekends come, the turbines and the procedure are reversed, and the water is sent back up to the original reservoir area. If you want a visual presentation of that concept, you can watch a short video at www.dom.com/about/stations/hydro/bath-county-pumped-storage-station.jsp.

Why? You might ask. For several reasons. One, the procedure works as both a flood- and drought-prevention program. The water's recycled, so there's no fear of a dry season, and the downstream farmers and residents are assured of a constant supply of water and power. The only water loss is from evaporation. Second, it's a relatively inexpensive means of power generation. Approximately 1 kilowatt is lost (in the return water process) for every 4 generated. This station provides power to millions of homes and businesses across six states, 525,000 of them in Virginia.

You can visit the pump station, but you can't use the two lakes because they can fluctuate in level up to 60 feet in a very short time. There is, however, a 325-acre recreational lake, a 30-site RV campground, a group/family picnic shelter, a sandy beach with swimming area and bathhouse, a hiking trail, and other recreational facilities. The campground doesn't have individual electric hookups (I've always thought that strange), but there is a comfort station with hot-water showers, flush toilets, and a dumping station.

A stocked trout stream, also occupied by smallmouth bass, is available, and the ponds have largemouth bass (18 inches is about the record), red-eared sunfish, bluegill, and channel catfish enjoying the habitat. There's a charge of $2 per vehicle for day-use activities.

Free project tours are available by appointment for groups or on the second Thursday of each month for individuals. You see the upper reservoir and dam, lower reservoir and dam, the second and third floors of the powerhouse, the generating bay, and the control room. Reservations are requested a couple of weeks in advance. The minimum number is one person; the maximum is 40. For reservations and more information, call (540) 279-3123; www.dom.com/about/education/tours-and-educational-programs.jsp.

Garth Newel (Welsh for "new house") **Music Center** is Virginia's only center for studying and performing chamber music. Between Warm Springs and Hot Springs, on 114 acres, with the Allegheny Mountains as a background, you can hear concerts featuring string quartets or a piano trio or sometimes as many as an octet.

Check their website for a concert schedule, cuisine activities, and lodging options. Several spring and fall holiday music weekends are scheduled, and guests can stay for the entire weekend or may obtain lodging elsewhere in the vicinity. Reservations are sometimes made up to a year in advance, particularly for Thanksgiving weekend, but they definitely should be made at least two months ahead. Garth Newel, 403 Garth Newel Lane, Hot Springs 24445; (540) 839-5018 or (877) 558-1689; www.garthnewel.org.

Movie buffs might find the hills familiar looking because Jodie Foster and Richard Gere filmed *Sommersby,* a movie about the struggles of a couple following the Civil War, in these beautiful Allegheny Mountains.

Hidden Valley Bed-and-Breakfast was used in the film. Ron and Pam Stillham are the innkeepers of this bed-and-breakfast with 3 rooms and

18th- and 19th-century antiques. 2241 Hidden Valley Rd., Warm Springs 24484; (540) 839-3178; www.bbonline.com/va/hiddenvalley.

Head east from here to continue on Route 39, one of Virginia's scenic byways, heading eastward to Lexington. This byway goes through Goshen Pass, 3 miles of impressive turns and twists and views (hard to keep your eyes on the road) with jagged cliffs towering a thousand feet on either side. It's necklaced by dogwood, ferns and mosses, hemlock, laurel, maples, mountain ash, pines, and rhododendron. A scenic overlook (built during the repairs from the flood of November 1985) has plenty of parking places, and a picnic area is just yards away.

Head south out of Bacova, and you'll come to what Bath County may be best known for, **_The Homestead_** at Hot Springs (US 220 North, Hot Springs), one of those venerable resorts dating back for what seems forever. It's set on some 15,000 acres, offers three golf courses (one designed by Robert Trent Jones), numerous tennis courts, warm baths, swimming pools, bowling, skiing, ice skating, horseback riding, carriages, stream fishing, children's activities, and countless other amenities.

Playing golf in this area can be devastating to your ego. The courses are tough, but some people say it's the magnificent view (which tends to add a few strokes to your average score) that's so distracting to your concentration.

Although not inexpensive (no one would expect it to be), you can sometimes book packages—such as golfing, wine tasting, tennis, or skiing—that will reduce the overall price. You can stay at the nearby Cascades, which is owned by The Homestead, for a little less and pay a nominal premium to dine at The Homestead or use some of its facilities. As can be expected, fall foliage is a busy time, and you can have trouble getting a shadow in this place without prior reservations. Occupancy is light in July and August. 7696 Sam Snead Hwy., Hot Springs 24445; (540) 839-1766 or (866) 354-4653; www.the homestead.com.

A fairly nearby nature area is **_Douthat State Park_** in Millboro. Some of the cabins and campgrounds that surround the oval-shaped Douthat Lake—as well as the roads, trails, dams, and picnic areas at Douthat State Park—were built by the Civilian Conservation Corps between 1932 and 1942.

Although (or because) it's off the beaten path, more than 180,000 people visit here annually. The 4,493-acre park has some incredible scenery, 24 trails that cover 40 miles of wooded hiking trails (easy to strenuous), waterfalls, boating, camping, environmental center, sandy beach, swimming, and a visitor center. Overnight reservations can be made online or by calling (800) 933-PARK. 14239 Douthat State Park Rd., Millboro 24460; (540) 862-8100; www.dcr .virginia.gov/state_parks/dou.shtml.

The *Lakeview Restaurant* in Douthat State Park is one of only three in the state park system, and the view competes with the food. Generally, the restaurant is open weekends from Easter through Memorial Day and Labor Day through Oct for breakfast, lunch, and dinner; then Wed through Fri for lunch and dinner and weekends for brunch, lunch, and dinner from Memorial Day through Labor Day. Call or check the above website for operating hours. From the screened-in porch, you can see the lake, canoes, paddleboats, and rowboats. Fishing is a major activity, with trout stocked twice a week from April through September. Check at the camp store for fishing permits. 14239 Douthat State Park Rd., Millboro 24460; (540) 862-8100.

Alleghany County

Pick up US 220 going south, where you'll see *Falling Springs,* a leaping cascade of about 200 feet noted by Thomas Jefferson in his book *Notes on Virginia,* written in 1781. The Westvaco Corporation, which owns the land on which the falls and the wayside are located, completed extensive renovations to the overlook in 1997, so you can more safely stop and enjoy the view (than before the upgrade). Take your camera and maybe look for some afternoon sun or early-morning mist. It's beautiful. Not far away are two natural areas where you might want to stay awhile. (540) 962-2178.

Thomas M. Gathright Sr., a landowner, farmer, and avid sportsman, and Benjamin C. Moomaw Jr., executive director of the Covington–Alleghany County Chamber of Commerce, championed the cause for the construction of a water-control project on the Jackson River to protect Covington and other downriver communities from flooding. In their honor are *Lake Moomaw and Gathright Wildlife Management Area.* The 12-mile-long lake, with its 43.5 miles of shoreline, was created by a dam that is 1,310 feet long and rises 257 feet above the Jackson River bed. The dam's appearance is misleading, particularly if you've seen such monumental projects as Hoover Dam. It's a clay and rock structure that you can drive over, and it looks like just another piece of shoreline. Many people ask, "Where's the dam?" It isn't until you go into the visitor center and see the display and then go outside to the overlook that you realize the water at the dam is 150 feet deep (the lake has an average depth of 80 feet). The visitor center, open daily from 8:30 a.m. to 3:30 p.m., has some interesting information.

The 2,530-acre stocked lake created by the Gathright Dam has year-round boating, boat ramps, lighted docks, water sports, sandy beaches, and fishing with its related activities of camping, picnicking, hiking, and hunting (in season). There are some wheelchair-accessible fishing decks. The area is abundant with wildlife, including bald eagle, white-tail deer, and turkey. You must possess a valid fishing license and a free permit from the Gathright Visitor Center. Morris Hill Road, Alleghany County, 24426; (540) 962-2214; www.virginia.org/Listings/OutdoorsAndSports/LakeMoomawandGathrightDam.

Camping in the Gathright Dam and Lake Moomaw area is available in several USDA Forest Service camping areas on a first-come, first-served basis. Furnished cabins are available and reservations can be made by calling (800) 933-PARK. Obviously, there are some peak times when the whoosh of a dog's wagging tail couldn't squeeze into the campgrounds, particularly during fall foliage time. The Morris Hill camping area (with 55 campsites and a dump site, potable water, and restrooms), about a 45-minute drive from recreational facilities at Lake Moomaw, doesn't always fill up when the leaves are changing.

For additional information write to the James River Ranger District, 810-A S. Monroe Ave., Covington 24426; (877) 444-6177, (540) 962-1138, or (540) 839-2521. The dam and lake are about 10 miles north of Covington. Take US 220 to Route 687, to Route 641, to Route 666, which will bring you to the facilities.

Covington

Now, just before you reach civilization, stop for a moment or two by the *Humpback Covered Bridge* in *Humpback Bridge State Wayside Park* (Midland Trail and US 60 West, Covington), a graceful, arched span erected in 1835 just west of Covington. It is said to be the only existing bridge of this type in the country and perhaps in the world, although apparently three of them were originally built within a mile of one another. The bridge received its name because of a rise of 8 feet from the ends to the center. It has no center support. Reportedly, 18-year-old Thomas Kincaid (no, not the "light" painting guy), using an axe as his principal tool, cut the hand-hewn timbers and made the locust pins that join the timbers. No nails were used.

The structure was part of the 200-mile-long James River/Kanawha Turnpike and, when completed, linked the head of bateau navigation on the James River from Covington with the Ohio River at the Kentucky line. Apparently it was saved from destruction by an unwritten agreement between the Confederate and Union soldiers during the Civil War.

The 100-foot, single-span walled structure over Dunlop Creek carried traffic for nearly 100 years before being abandoned in 1929 and, for nearly a quarter of a century, stood derelict near its then-modern successor. Since 1954 it has been maintained as a part of a 5-acre highway wayside 3 miles west of Covington on US 60. At the wayside are several picnic tables, barbecue grills, and 2 portable toilets, and you can wade through the creek for a

The Cyrus McCormick Museum

Cyrus McCormick, the inventor of the mechanized reaper, was born in Steele's Tavern. Visit his farm to discover his achievements through a museum, restored blacksmith shop, and gristmill. Spend a few minutes enjoying a picnic. The 634-acre farm, now known as the *Shenandoah Valley Agricultural Research and Extension Center,* is part of Virginia Tech University. The *Cyrus McCormick Museum* and grounds are open daily from 8 a.m. to 5 p.m., weather permitting. 128 McCormick Farm Circle, Raphine 24472; (540) 377-2255; www.arec.vaes.vt.edu/shenandoah-valley/about/index.html.

better, or at least a different, view of the bridge. Several Civil War cannonballs have been found in the creek and along its banks, as both Union and Confederate troops moved across the bridge with cannons. Graffiti artists have used the walls and roof of the bridge as their canvas, but none of the words seems too objectionable, being mostly love notes from the young at heart and the young in mind.

Unlike most other covered bridges in the state, which take a detailed map to find, this one is easy to locate: There are signs off I-64 at exit 3 (the Callaghan Interchange) directing you to the Humpback. You can also get there by traveling west out of Covington for about 3 miles. Midland Trail, Covington 24426; (540) 962-2178; www.virginiadot.org/info/faq-covbridge5.asp.

About halfway between Lexington on the south and Staunton on the north is Steele's Tavern. The *Sugar Tree Inn* sits about 5 minutes off the Blue Ridge Parkway, half a mile high and surrounded by its own hardwood forest. It was built and designed as an inn (not a readaptive use of an old barn, etc.) by local people using hand-hewn chestnut, oak, and poplar timbers taken from original buildings throughout Rockbridge County. Logs as much as 200 years old were mortised and pegged together without nails, just as in pioneer days.

Its rooms (each with its own wood-burning fireplace) in four buildings and the main lodge are spacious, "with human-size private baths and generous chairs in which to rock or relax." For those who like luxury when they "rough it," they do have "good cell phone coverage, Wi-Fi is available," and some rooms have a whirlpool bath, ceiling fan, and air-conditioning. A full breakfast is provided in a glass-walled dining room, and dinner is available Thurs through Sat if you just can't bring yourself to leave these woods. Sugar Tree Inn is open February through December. 145 Lodge Trail on Highway 56, Steele's Tavern 24476; (800) 377-2197 or (540) 377-2197; www.sugartreeinn.com.

Lexington

Now, it's east to Lexington. The *Virginia Horse Center* (Route 39, Lexington), said to be the largest facility of its type in the East, is fascinating regardless of how much you know (or don't know) about horses. Every weekend, from spring through fall, there are horse sales, 4-H horse-judging competitions, Grand Prix jumping, dressage exhibitions, breed shows, and much more. There's a covered grandstand with seating from which to watch the events in the main rings, or you can stand around the rail and talk to contestants, participants, or others related in a peripheral or major way. Even when the horses and riders are being led through some basic riding events (similar to school figures in ice skating), you can feel the excitement charging through the audience. A 4,000-seat coliseum allows year-round operation and houses an exhibit area, concession concourse, offices, and meeting rooms. 487 Maury River Rd., Lexington 24450; (540) 464-2950; www.horsecenter.org.

Sam Houston was born in a cabin just north of downtown Lexington on March 2, 1793. As commander-in-chief of the Texas army, he won the battle of San Jacinto, which secured Texan independence, April 21, 1836. He was president of Texas, 1836–38, 1841–44; US senator, 1846–59; and governor, 1860–61. He died in July 1863. A 38,000-pound piece of Texas pink granite marks the spot at the *Sam Houston Wayside.* It's open daily, from dawn to dusk. Pets are welcome and the site is wheelchair accessible. Route 11 North, exit 195 off I-81 or exit 55 from I-64, Lexington 24450; (540) 463-3777 or (877) 453-9822; www.lexingtonvirginia.com.

That delicious aroma you smell comes from the *Cocoa Mill Chocolate Company,* started in 1993. They handcraft their chocolates with premium chocolate, natural flavors, fresh cream and butter, and authentic liqueurs. Chocolates are prepared in small batches because they believe freshness contributes as much to flavor as quality ingredients, with each piece hand-dipped, hand-decorated, and hand-packed so that careful attention is paid to every detail. During some times of the year—not around Valentine's Day—you can watch the operation and then buy your favorites after watching them being made. The store is open Mon through Sat from 10 a.m. to 5 p.m. Call Bob Aimone, the owner, for more tour information; 123 W. Nelson St., Lexington 24450; (800) 421-6220 or (540) 464-8400; www.cocoamill.com.

On display at the *George Marshall Museum* are the Nobel Peace Prize bestowed on Marshall and the Oscar won by General Frank McCarthy, an aide to Marshall, as producer of the movie *Patton.* Also in the museum are exhibits tracing Marshall's life and an electric map tracing the significant events of World War II. The Soldier of Peace Gallery illustrates Marshall's contributions in the post–WWII years, as secretary of state, secretary of defense, and as the head of the American Red Cross. The museum is open Tues through Sat 9 a.m. to 5 p.m. and Sun 1 to 5 p.m. and closed on Thanksgiving Day, December 24 and 25, and January 1. Admission is $5 for adults, $3 for seniors, $2 for students, free for children 12 and under, active military personnel, World War II veterans, and Rockbridge County residents with a guest. On Virginia Military Institute grounds, 1600 VMI Parade, Lexington 24450; (540) 463-7103; www.marshallfoundation.org.

About 4 miles east of the visitor center, out US 60 east at the **Ben Salem Lock and Wayside Park** are the remains of the James River and Kanawha Canal. Conceived by George Washington as part of the "Great Central American Waterway from the Rockies to the Atlantic Ocean," this was the earliest canal system in the Western Hemisphere. The wayside is a delightful place for a picnic, swimming, fishing, or a quiet afternoon spent watching the waters frolic over the river rocks. 106 E. Washington St., Lexington 22450; (540) 463-3777.

If your idea of a bed-and-breakfast place is an early Victorian setting, furnished with antiques, wraparound verandas on the first and second floors, with breakfast served on antique Meissen china, a fireplace to relax in front of as you listen to classical music, and a wide trout stream defining the property line, then you might want to stop at the **Hummingbird Inn** in Goshen.

Patty and Dan Harrison purchased the inn from Pam and Dick Matthews in July 2008 and have continued with little upgrades here and there and 2 rooms, Alleghany and Franklin, with a double whirlpool. The inn has been named a "Virginia Green Lodging" property because of their commitment to the environment. 30 Wood Lane, Box 147, Goshen 24439; (540) 997-9065 or (800) 397-3214; www.hummingbirdinn.com.

Craig County

In a Craig County valley is the town of **Paint Bank,** nestled between Peter's Mountain and Pott's Mountain, on the banks of Pott's Creek, not too far from Covington and Roanoke. It consists of **The Paint Bank General Store and Gift Shop** (said to have "the most ambitious worms in the county") with the **Swinging Bridge Restaurant** inside, post office, volunteer fire department, mill (with hopes for restoration), hotel, fish hatchery, and the creek. The General Store opens every morning at 8 with a variable closing time from 3:30 to 9 p.m., depending on the day of the week and month of the year.

In 1907 a train depot was constructed to serve the Norfolk and Western Railway that had just been extended to Paint Bank. The depot has been refurbished and is now available for lodging for hunters, hikers, birders, and

Rolling, Action!

Should you see the Robert Duvall, Stephen Lang, Jeff Daniels, and Mira Sorvino film *Gods and Generals,* you may recognize the VMI campus because part of the film was shot there in the fall of 2001. Ronald F. Maxwell chose the locale for the 1860s historical movie to shoot two scenes in the life of Confederate General Thomas J. "Stonewall" Jackson (Lang), who taught at VMI for 10 years prior to the war. The first scene is when Jackson is leading the VMI cadets to war in 1861, and the second is when his body was returned 2 years later. *Gods and Generals* is a prequel to Maxwell's 1993 movie *Gettysburg* and is based on the 1996 novel by Jeff Shaara. Duvall portrays Robert E. Lee.

others who want to get really off the beaten path. The *Depot Lodge Bed and Breakfast* has 5 rooms, each with private bath and a cast-iron freestanding gas stove. Stephen Cutler, a New Yorker, owns the Depot Lodge (540-897-6000 or 800-970-DEPOT) and the General Store (540-897-5000) and sounds really excited about all the improvements to the area; www.thedepotlodge.com.

Audie Murphy, the most decorated United States soldier of World War II, died in an airplane crash on May 28, 1971, on Brush Mountain. (Reportedly, there are four Brush Mountains and nine Brushy Mountains in Virginia.) You can visit the *Audie Murphy Monument* placed on the crash site by Post 5311 of the Veterans of Foreign Wars.

The monument's plaque reads:

AUDIE LEON MURPHY

JUNE 20, 1924–MAY 28, 1971

BORN IN KINGSTON, TEXAS. DIED NEAR THIS SITE IN AN AIRPLANE CRASH. AMERICA'S MOST DECORATED VETERAN OF WORLD WAR II. HE SERVED IN THE EUROPEAN THEATRE, 15TH INFANTRY REGIMENT, 3RD INFANTRY DIVISION, AND EARNED 24 DECORATIONS INCLUDING THE MEDAL OF HONOR, LEGION OF MERIT, DISTINGUISHED SERVICE CROSS, AND THREE PURPLE HEARTS.

Roanoke

Roanoke (at one time, possibly Rawrenock or Roenoak, an Indian word meaning "white shell beads" or "money") is the largest Virginia city west of Richmond. A huge neon star atop *Mill Mountain,* reportedly the country's largest manufactured star, was erected by the chamber of commerce in 1949. You can see this star from 60 miles away (at least from the air—quite a sight when you're flying into town on a foggy night and 17,500 watts of neon light beam through the mist). It is 88.5 feet high (1,045 feet above sea level) and weighs 10,000 pounds. There are 2,000 feet of neon tubing, and several color combinations are possible. There are two good times to visit the star: first, in the daytime for an overview of Roanoke; second, at dusk, when the star is lit and crackling with electricity. It is illuminated every night until midnight, and it's almost as though Roanoke is saying, "Come on by, we'll leave the star on for you." Webcams have been installed in a lot of interesting places so you can watch eaglets learn to fledge or crabs crawl out of the water and now there's one to see you wave. Yes, a webcam has been installed on the star. When you're on the overlook, the camera is overlooking you at www.roanokeva.gov/WebMgmt/ywbase61b.nsf/DocName/$starcam. Smile!

Mill Mountain is within the city limits, and it's said to be the only mountain in Virginia, and perhaps east of Phoenix, that's located inside a city. Oh, although statistics just don't seem to be available for an accurate account, it's been said that the best and perhaps the most popular place to propose in Roanoke is at the Mill Mountain Star. 210 Reserve Ave., Roanoke 24011; (540) 853-1133; www.roanokeva.gov.

The *Art Museum of Western Virginia,* which was the Roanoke Museum of Fine Arts, which was Roanoke Fine Arts Center, which started as the Roanoke chapter of the American Association of University Women, has been active since 1947, accomplishing so many miracles made purely from hard work and willing it so. They have presented shows covering Thomas Eakins, Andy Warhol, Edward Steichen, and from Howard Finster's Mountain Lake folk art workshop. Its home has moved from pillar to post. In 2000, the city granted money and property and an architectural search was started. Randall Stout Architects, Inc., was selected in 2002, and Georganne C. Bingham was named new executive director in 2003.

It took until September 10, 2005, before ground was broken for the 81,000-square-foot design (16,000 square feet of gallery space) and construction started in May 2006. Two years later, the *Taubman Museum of Art* opened, honoring US Ambassador to Romania Nicholas F. Taubman and Mrs. Eugenia L. Taubman for their generous gift toward the project. The soaring wings seem to fly off into the mountains, or that's how I see the building. What's your opinion?

Admission is $7 for adults, $6 for seniors (65 and up), $3.75 for children (5 through 13). Members are free. The museum is open Tues through Sat 10 a.m. to 5 p.m. (extended to 8 p.m. on Thurs with free admission beginning at 5 p.m.) and Sun noon to 5 p.m. 110 Salem Ave. Southeast, Roanoke 24011; (540) 342-5760; www.taubmanmuseum.org.

Among the interesting shops in the downtown area is the *Historic Roanoke City Market,* which is the oldest in continual use in Virginia. They offer an "Eat Fresh Eat Local" event on the first Saturday of the month from April through October and have cooking demonstrations using the local produce. A number of local artisans also present and sell their creations here. From spring through fall, Haley Toyota, Stellar One Bank, and Downtown Roanoke, Inc., present a showcase of talent every Saturday that might include local chef demonstrations, street performers, and family days. City Market Saturdays run from 11 a.m. to 2:30 p.m. and there is no charge. The market is open Mon through Sat from 8 a.m. to 5 p.m. and Sun 10 a.m. to 4 p.m., however, many vendors take off Sun, Mon, and Tues so they can plant, pick, or otherwise prepare items for sale, Also, during the growing season, the farmers tend to show up around 7 a.m. and depart by 3 p.m. The market is at 1 Market St., Roanoke 34014; (540) 342-2028.

Then venture to the **Center in the Square** and plan to spend some time here. Within this renovated 1914 warehouse building are the Science Museum of Western Virginia and Hopkins Planetarium, the Arts Council of the Blue Ridge, Historical Society of Western Virginia, Opera Roanoke, and the Mill Mountain Theatre. Additionally, the Roanoke Ballet Theatre is supported by the organization but is housed elsewhere. More than 400,000 people visit this unique complex annually, about half of whom are school children. Each component of this celebration of science, history, art, theater, opera, and dance has its own operating hours, so check the site for what you want to see and due. 1 Market Sq. Southeast, Roanoke 24011; (540) 342-5700; www.centerinthesquare .org.

As usual, my favorite is the Science Museum (my high school science teacher, Mrs. Mitchell, would never believe that—surprise!). Whether it's an exhibit called "The Ins and Outs of Anatomy" or summer camp, I want to be there. The museum is open Wed through Sat from 10 a.m. to 5 p.m. Admission starts at $6 for exhibits for children and has a dollar or two added to it when you include the MegaDome and planetarium for up to $13 for adults for all three. Free Friday takes place the second Friday of the month, from noon to 5 p.m. 1 Market Sq. Southeast, Roanoke 24011; (540) 342-5710; www.smwv.org.

When it's time to rest your weary bones, consider the **Hotel Roanoke and Conference Center,** now managed by the Doubletree (Hilton) Corporation. Built for $45,000 in 1882 on a 10-acre knoll overlooking the city, it was constructed in the Tudor style, with hand-rubbed English walnut, carved oak, cherry, and ash woods, gaslight chandeliers, and floors polished to shine like glass. Much of the original Honduras mahogany remains, although part of the hotel burned in 1898. Through its history it has celebrated many firsts. It was the first hotel in Roanoke to have bathrooms with a porcelain or zinc tub, and the first sewer line in town ran from the hotel.

Telephones with multiple plugs (so you could move the telephone around the room) were installed in 1931. It also featured closets with lights that turned on automatically when the door was opened, electric fans, full-length mirrors, and running ice water. In 1937 it became one of the first hotels in the world to be air-conditioned. In 1940 Fred Brown, the hotel's chef, created peanut soup, an item that is still on the menu.

Extensive renovations and additions have been done in the past years, and in the entranceway you can see personalized bricks purchased by local citizens in a fund-raising effort to help the restorations. Residents of the Roanoke Valley (and others) took furnishings, utensils, accessories, and other memorabilia (either via auction or "otherwise") from the hotel when it was closed in 1989. As the hotel celebrated its 125th anniversary in 2007, the management started hunting for these items, encouraging former visitors to search attics and basements for artifacts illustrating the hotel's historical, social, and economic ties to the Roanoke Valley. Items could be given or loaned for the 125 days of celebration. If you missed the notice or the celebration, you can still contact the hotel if you have items you want to return. When you visit these days, you may notice that the hotel features PURE allergy friendly guestrooms. They heard us sneezing. 110 Shenandoah Ave., Roanoke 24016; (540) 985-5900; www.hotelroanoke.com.

The *Harrison Museum of African American Culture* is the only repository of African-American culture in western Virginia. It is "a haven for the arts and treasures of a strong and mighty race." The museum is on the ground floor of the first public high school for blacks in western Virginia. Each year it presents a minimum of 8 art exhibits and 2 performing arts presentations. Art and history lectures, demonstrations, and workshops are offered. The book/gift shop has Afrocentric art, books, cards, and jewelry. The Harrison Museum is open Tues through Sat 1 to 5 p.m. There is no admission charge. 523 Harrison Ave. Northwest, Roanoke 24016; (540) 345-4818; www.harrisonmuseum.org.

The *Virginia Museum of Transportation,* the official transportation museum of Virginia, holds the South's largest collection of steam locomotives, cars, boats, airplanes, and missiles. The exhibits may explain the railroad's part of the circus in America, a composite of rural stations from the last century, and a Norfolk Southern SD-40 Locomotive Cab #1594 that you can climb aboard. There's a gift shop on the premises with railroad memorabilia including hats, goggles, belt buckles, handkerchiefs, patches, pins, recordings, photographs, books, puzzles, train sets, whistles, mugs, decals, and postcards. As much of the collection is outdoors, they suggest (I concur) that you wear comfortable walking shoes and clothing.

The museum is open Mon through Sat 10 a.m. to 5 p.m. and Sun 1 to 5 p.m. It is closed on Easter Sunday, Thanksgiving, December 24–26 and 31, and

January 1 and 2. Admission is $8 for adults, $7 for seniors (60 and over), and $6 for children (3 through 11). Discounts are available for AAA, National Railway Historical Society, and other memberships. 303 Norfolk Ave. Southwest, Roanoke 24016; (540) 342-5670; www.vmt.org.

Where to Stay in Western Virginia

BASYE

Bryce Resort
1982 Fairway Dr.
(540) 856-2121 or
(800) 821-1444
www.bryceresort.com

COVINGTON

Cliff View Golf Club & Inn
410 Friels Dr.
(540) 962-2200 or
(888) 849-2200

EDINBURG

Inn at Narrow Passage
30 Chapman Landing Rd.
(540) 459-8000 or
(800) 459-8002
www.innatnarrowpassage
.com

FRONT ROYAL

Killahevlin Bed and Breakfast
1401 N. Royal Ave.
(540) 636-7335 or
(800) 847-6132
www.vairish.com

Lackawanna Bed and Breakfast
236 Riverside Dr.
(540) 636-7945
www.lackawannabb.com

Woodward House on Manor Grade
413 S. Royal Ave.
(540) 635-7010 or
(800) 635-7011
www.acountryhome.com

GOSHEN

Hummingbird Inn
30 Wood Lane
(540) 997-9065 or
(800) 397-3214
www.hummingbirdinn.com

HARRISONBURG

Stonewall Jackson Inn
547 E. Market St.
(540) 433-8233 or
(800) 445-5330
www.stonewalljacksoninn
.com

Village Inn
4979 S. Valley Pike
(540) 434-7355 or
(800) 736-7355
www.thevillageinn.travel

HOT SPRINGS

The Homestead
1766 Homestead Dr.
(540) 839-1766 or
(866) 354-4653
www.thehomestead.com

KEEZLETOWN

Old Massanutten Lodge
3448 Caverns Dr.
(540) 269-8800
www.oldmassanuttenlodge
.com

LEXINGTON

Applewood Inn & Llama Trekking
242 Tarn Beck Lane
(540) 463-1962 or
(800) 463-1902
www.applewoodbb.com

Brierley Hill Bed and Breakfast
985 Borden Rd.
(540) 464-8421 or
(800) 422-4925
www.brierleyhill.com

House Mountain Inn
455 Lonesome Dove Trail
(540) 464-4004
www.housemountaininn
.com

Stoneridge Bed and Breakfast
246 Stoneridge Lane
(540) 463-4090 or
(800) 491-2930
www.stoneridge-inn.com

LURAY

Mimslyn Inn
401 W. Main St.
(800) 296-5105
www.mimslyninn.com

South Court Inn
160 S. Court St.
(540) 843-0980 or
(888) 749-8055
www.southcourtinn.com

Victorian Inn
138 E. Main St.
(540) 860-4229 or
(866) 937-3466
www.victorianinnluray.com

Woodruff Inns
330 Mechanic St.
(540) 743-1494
www.woodruffinns.com

MCGAHEYSVILLE

Massanutten Resort
1822 Resort Dr.
(540) 289-9441 or
(800) 207-6277
www.massresort.com

NEW MARKET

Apple Blossom Inn
9317 N. Congress St.
(540) 740-3747
www.appleblossominn.net

STANLEY

**White Fence Bed &
Breakfast**
275 Chapel Rd.
(540) 778-4680 or
(800) 211-9885
www.whitefencebb.com

STAUNTON

**Frederick House Bed and
Breakfast**
28 N. New St.
(540) 885-4220 or
(800) 334-5575
www.frederickhouse.com

Inn at Old Virginia
1329 Commerce Rd.
(540) 248-4650 or
(877) 809-1146
www.innatoldvirginia.com

**Stonewall Jackson Hotel
and Conference Center**
24 S. Market St.
(540) 885-4848
www.stonewalljackson
hotel.com

STRASBURG

Hotel Strasburg
213 S. Holliday St.
(540) 465-9191 or
(800) 348-8327
www.hotelstrasburg.com

WARM SPRINGS

**Anderson Cottage Bed
and Breakfast**
Old Germantown Rd.
(540) 839-2975
www.bbonline.com/va/
anderson/index.html

WINCHESTER

George Washington
103 E. Piccadilly St.
(540) 678-4700 or
(877) 999-3223
www.wyndham.com/
propertyfinder/ratessearch/
main.wnt

Where to Eat in Western Virginia

CATAWBA

Homeplace
4968 Catawba Valley Dr.
(540) 384-7252

HARRISONBURG

Village Inn
4979 S. Valley Pike
(540) 434-7355
www.thevillageinn.travel/
dining.html

LURAY

Rainbow Hill at Parkhurst
2547 US 211 West
(540) 743-6009
www.rainbow-hill.com

MIDDLEBURG

Market Salamander
200 W. Washington St.
(540) 687-8011
www.marketsalamander
.com

ROANOKE

Alexander's
105 S. Jefferson St.
(540) 962-6983
www.alexandersva.com

**Arzu Mediterranean
Restaurant**
213 Williamson Rd.
Southeast
(540) 982-7160
www.arzurestaurant.com

Carlos Brazilian International
4167 Electric Rd.
(540) 776-1117
www.carlosbrazilian.com

Coach & Four
5206 Williamson Rd.
Northwest
(540) 362-4220
www.coachandfour.com

Famous Anthony's
221 Crystal Spring Ave.
Southwest (other locations)
(540) 981-0200
www.famousanthonys.com

Kabuki Japanese Steak House
3503 Franklin Rd.
Southwest
(540) 981-0222
www.kabukiva.com

Nawab
118-A Campbell Ave.
Southwest
(540) 345-5150
www.nawabrestaurant.com

Norah's Cafe, Taubman Museum of Art
110 Salem Ave. Southeast
(540) 204-4154

SALEM

Awful Arthur's Seafood
1302 W. Main St.
(540) 387-1004
http://awfularthursseafood
.com/awful-arthurs/salem

Famous Anthony's
1716 W. Main St. (other locations)
(540) 389-4502
www.famousanthonys.com

Mac "n" Bob's
316 E. Main St.
(540) 389-5999
www.macandbobs.com

Mamma's Pizza
151 S. Electric Rd.
(540) 444-9994

STAUNTON

Mockingbird
123 W. Beverley St.
(540) 213-8777
www.mockingbird123.com

Staunton Grocery
105 W. Beverly St.
(540) 886-6880
www.stauntongrocery.com

Zynodoa
115 E. Beverly St.
(540) 885-7775
www.zynodoa.com

STRASBURG

Hotel Strasburg
213 S. Holliday St.
(540) 465-9191 or
(800) 348-8327
www.hotelstrasburg.com/
dining.html

WHITE POST

L'Auberge Provencale
13630 Lord Fairfax Hwy.
(540) 837-1375 or
(800) 638-1702
www.laubergeprovencale
.com

SOUTHWESTERN VIRGINIA

Ah, Southwestern Virginia. This is where mountains form the skyscrapers, not buildings; where canyons are really canyons (the deepest this side of the Mississippi), not the canyons created by tall structures.

You will note that interstate highways here are more serpentine than ironed-ribbon straight. If you're observant, you'll even notice that one stretch of I-77 and I-81 overlap, and you can be going south on one and north on the other and still be on the same side of the road. This is called a wrong-way concurrency, one of maybe a handful of such roadway designs on the continent.

Enjoyable scenery notwithstanding, this span of I-77 includes two tunnels, one through East River Mountain and the other through Big Walker Mountain. Each tunnel is about a mile long and saves the traveler from 10 to 20 miles of meandering and hilly roadway along Route 21. On the other hand, if you're interested in off-the-beaten-path options, saving time and miles may not interest you.

This is where Mother Nature's awe-inspiring works are yours for the looking and hiking and exploring. You will find the frontier spirit and revitalizing natural beauty. You will be

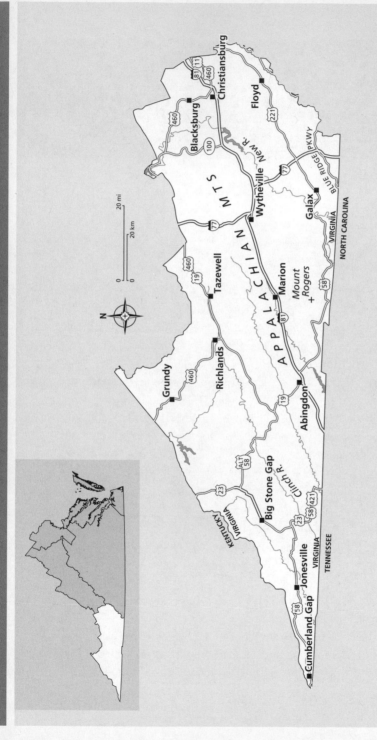

SOUTHWESTERN VIRGINIA

able to take time for camping, fishing, and swimming in numerous state and national parks. You will find quaint old mills and summer outdoor dramatic offerings that retell the history and life of mountain days decades and centuries ago. And you will find unusual ways to enjoy yourself, including trekking via llama.

In 2004, the *New River Heritage Coalition* was formed to improve the coordination and collaboration of the numerous historical sites along New River. These include testaments to explorers, Native Americans, European settlers, and industrial developers. They are working to help you understand how the people and events preceding us have made us and this area what it is today. Its members include the Blacksburg Museum, Cambria Depot, Christiansburg Institute, Coal Mining Heritage Park, Floyd County Historical Society, Giles County Historical Society, Glencoe Museum, Historic Smithfield Plantation, Montgomery Museum and Art Center, Raymond F. Ratcliffe Museum, Virginia Tech Museum of Geosciences, and the Wilderness Road Museum. Some of these are highlighted in this book and you can learn about all of them at www.newriverheritage.org.

Many of Virginia's 35 *state parks* and 33 natural areas are located in the Southwest area, with cabins, campsites, trails, waterways, and picnic shelters all available for your outdoor pleasure.

Among the parks, preserves, and management areas are Breaks Interstate Park (276-865-4413), Buffalo Mountain Natural Area Preserve (276-676-5673), Claytor Lake State Park (540-643-2500), Clinch Mountain Wildlife Management Area (276-944-5024), Grayson Highlands State Park (276-579-7092), Hungry Mother State Park (276-781-7400) with the Hemlock Haven Conference Center (276-781-7425), Natural Tunnel State Park (see more details in the Scott County listings; 276-940-2674) and the Cove Ridge Center (276-940-2696), Pinnacle

AUTHOR'S FAVORITES IN SOUTHWESTERN VIRGINIA

Cumberland Gap
(606) 248-2817
www.nps.gov/cuga

Harry W. Meador Coal Museum
Big Stone Gap
(540) 523-9209
www.bigstonegap.org/attract/coal.htm

Historic Crab Orchard Museum and Pioneer Park
Tazewell
(540) 988-6755
www.craborchardmuseum.com

Natural Area Preserve (276-676-5673), Shot Tower and New River Trail State Park (see more details in the Pulaski County section; 276-699-6778), Southwest Virginia Museum Historical State Park (276-523-1322), and the Wilderness Road State Park (276-445-3065).

For more information about these facilities, call the Virginia Department of Conservation and Recreation, 203 Governor St., Richmond 23219; (804) 786-1712 or (800) 933-PARK; www.dcr.state.va.us.

The Crooked Road: Virginia's Heritage Music Trail, (851 French Moore Jr. Blvd., Suite 146, Abingdon 24210; 276-492-2085; www.thecrooked road.org) created in 2004, connects legendary bluegrass and traditional mountain music venues together in a 250-mile driving tour through the mountain towns of Southwest Virginia. The trail is a driving route that features some of Virginia's significant contributions to the music world, promoting Appalachian Virginia's cultural heritage. Starting on the eastern end, it goes through Ferrum (Blue Ridge Institute and Museum), Floyd (Floyd Country Store and Country Records), Galax (Blue Ridge Music Center and the Old Fiddler's convention at the Rex Theater), Bristol (Birthplace of Country Music Alliance Museum), Hiltons (Carter Family Fold), and Norton (Country Cabin), until it reaches Clintwood (Ralph Stanley Museum) on the northwestern end.

Obviously, you can visit as much or as little as you wish, depending on where you're driving or how you like your blend of gospel, bluegrass, and mountain music. Look for annual festivals, weekly concerts, live radio shows, and informal jam sessions throughout the area.

You'll also have a chance to appreciate (and buy, in some cases) traditional handcrafted woodwork, weaving, and pottery.

We'll start our tour after leaving Salem and Roanoke to the northeast and head southwest along I-81, then along Route 460 back down to Radford and Wytheville, then north and south on I-77 up to Bluefield and down to Galax, over to Bristol, and just weave back and forth until we arrive at Cumberland Gap, a truly spectacular and amazing place to end any trip.

Montgomery County

The history of a place helps us see how the people of today arrived here and understand what they think, how they act, and where they're going. A good place to visit is the *Montgomery Museum and Lewis Miller Regional Art Center.* It focuses generally on southwestern Virginia, particularly Montgomery County, and the works of primitive and 19th-century country folk artist Lewis Miller as well as contemporary art displays. There's also a genealogical research area.

The museum is housed in a mid-19th-century Presbyterian church manse of American and Flemish bond brick, made with local materials and hand-hewn oak beams and rafters. There are two satellite branches in Riner and Shawsville.

Admission is free to members, $2 for adults, and $1 for children under 12. The museum is open Tues through Sat 10:30 a.m. to 4:30 p.m. 300 S. Pepper St., Christiansburg 24073; (540) 382-5644; http://montgomerymuseum.org.

The *Oaks Historic Bed-and-Breakfast Country Inn* is the focal point of the E. Main Street Historic District in Christiansburg. Construction began in 1889 and was completed in 1893. Modern bathrooms and other amenities have been added, and the original floor plan and elegant interior have been carefully restored and preserved. 311 E. Main St., Christiansburg 24073; (540) 381-1500 or (800) 336-6257; www.theoaksvictorianinn.com.

Floyd County

South of Christiansburg is *Floyd* and the *Floyd Country Store,* where, every Friday at 7 p.m., folks bring their banjos, fiddles, guitars, and harmonicas, their old-timer's memories, and the music of Floyd County. The store is open Tues through Thurs 10 a.m. to 5 p.m., Fri until 11 p.m., Sat to 5:30 p.m., and Sun noon to 5:30 p.m. Floyd's is located at 206 S. Locust St., Floyd 24091; (540) 745-4563; www.floydcountrystore.com.

To learn about the political, geological, and natural history of this area, head north of Christiansburg on Route 460 to *Blacksburg,* to stop at *Virginia Tech,* home of the Hokies and the largest university in Virginia. There are a number of interesting places to see, the first of which is *Smithfield Plantation.* When Colonel William Preston constructed it back in 1772, it would have been difficult to predict the influence he would have on the area. Let it suffice to say that the Preston family was a founding family of Blacksburg and Montgomery County. William Preston, born in 1730, arrived here from Ireland in 1738 and served in the militia in the French and Indian and Revolutionary Wars. He then went on to serve in the House of Burgesses, representing several different counties. He built Smithfield in the Tidewater Plantation style and named it in honor of his wife, Susanna Smith.

The plantation is open for tours (beginning on the hour and half-hour) with costumed interpreters on Mon, Tues, Thurs, Fri, and Sat 10 a.m. to 5 p.m., Sun 1 to 5 p.m. April 1 through the first week of Dec. Admission is $7 for adults, $4 for students 13 and up or with college identification, and $3 for children ages 5 through 12. Ask about AAA membership discount. 1000 Smithfield Plantation Rd., Blacksburg 24060; (540) 231-3947; www.smithfieldplantation.org.

All Roads Lead to Floyd . . .
or Away From It

If you're looking for a particular place in the town of Floyd, directions will start with "Begin at 'the stoplight'" in the center of town at the intersection of Route 8 and Route 221. You should also note that there's no turn on red. If you go north on Route 8, you're aiming toward I-81 and Christiansburg. Go south and you head toward Stuart. Go west on Route 221 to I-77 toward Galax, or east toward the south side of Roanoke. Because they are all long and winding roads, you need a good map, a GPS system, or a sense of adventure because using the sun for a compass just won't work.

Driving through this country could stir your interest in the earth sciences, and, fortunately, Virginia Tech has a **Museum of Geosciences** to satisfy your curiosity. Included in its collection is a full-scale model of an allosaurus (a huge carnivorous North American theropod dinosaur of the Later Jurassic period, about 150 million years ago). And if that means nothing to you, just check with the children; they're sure to know. It also has fossils, gemstones, a seismograph, and the largest display of Virginia minerals in the state.

The museum is open Mon through Fri 8 a.m. to 5 p.m., and there is no admission fee. 2062 Derring Hall, Virginia Tech, Blacksburg 24061; (540) 231-6894; www.outreach.geos.vt.edu/museum.

Nancy's Candy Company has stores in Salem, Floyd, and Meadows of Dan, and in the latter location you can see (through viewing windows) how chocolate is molded into sweet morsels of smooth, velvety candy and watch fudge being made. Skilled craftspeople and candymakers take special care to ensure quality and superior confections. There are at least 40 different flavors of fudge made daily and 60 varieties of chocolates on display, ready for you to sample. Can you even imagine a half-pound Grand Marnier truffle? Nancy's has it. Call ahead to request a "chocolate talk" and candy-making video presentation.

Open Mon through Sat 10 a.m. to 5 p.m., and Sun 1 to 5 p.m. with

funfacts

In May 1808, Thomas Lewis and John McHenry were involved in the first duel with rifles known to have taken place in Virginia. Both men died. This duel led to the passage of the Babour Bill in January 1810, which outlawed dueling in Virginia. Dr. John Floyd was the attending physician and later went on to become governor of Virginia and a member of Congress. A marker in Christiansburg at Routes 11 and 460 designates the site of the duel.

extended hours in Oct and closed Jan through Mar. 2684 Jeb Stuart Hwy., Meadows of Dan 24120; (276) 952-2112 or (800) 328-3834; www.nancys homemadefudge.com.

Head northwest out of Blacksburg and you're touring through Giles County. Near Newport are located two of the seven (some references say eight) remaining **covered bridges** (Sinking Creek and C. K. Reynolds) that are accessible to the public in Virginia. There used to be more than 100 covered or "kissing" bridges. They are modified William Howe truss bridges (in 1840 he combined iron uprights with wooden supports, creating the forerunner of the steel bridge) and cross Sinking Creek. The first is a 55-foot bridge, which used to be along the Appalachian Trail near Route 700 (Mountain Lake Road) but was bypassed by a realignment of the trail. The bridge was left in place so that the property owner could use it when a new bridge was built in 1949. The second, a 70-foot span, was left in place when a new bridge was constructed in 1963. The bridge indicates it was constructed in 1912; the state says circa 1916. (540) 921-5000.

Farther up Route 700 in Pembroke is the **Mountain Lake Conservancy and Hotel,** which has been catering to summer visitors for years. Although former manager Joseph "Mac" McMillin used to say that people would tell him they or their relatives stood on the fire line fighting the blaze that destroyed the old (1850s) wooden structure, in fact it was torn down and rebuilt in 1936 with stone cut from the property.

Even if you have never visited **Mountain Lake,** you may feel you know the place, for it was featured in the 1986 movie *Dirty Dancing,* with Patrick Swayze and Jennifer Grey. Word has it that they were fighting Mother Nature toward the end, with crew members spraying the turning autumn leaves green.

In Lee County You Can . . .

- be farther west than Detroit

- be farther west than all of West Virginia

- be closer to eight other state capitals than to Richmond

- see five states at once

- see "black diamonds" (coal)

- walk the "Trail of the Lonesome Pine" (see Big Stone Gap)

- visit the University of Virginia's College at Wise, a place that grew from a home for indigents and the homeless into the only branch of the University of Virginia.

The Preston Dynasty

Virginia Tech's original name was Preston and Olin Institute, named for **William Preston.** Colonel William Preston and his wife, Susanna, of Smithfield Plantation (Blacksburg) fame, raised and educated their 12 children at Smithfield.

Smithfield Plantation was the birthplace of two Virginia governors, James Patton Preston and John Buchanan Floyd, and briefly home of a third, John Floyd Jr. (grandson of William). Their progeny and other relatives would go on to serve in Congress and achieve positions of high rank through various state governments. Among the relatives was Montgomery Blair, the postmaster of the United States in President Lincoln's cabinet.

Apparently, a British reality show, *Dirty Dancing: The Time of Your Life* and a documentary entitled *Seriously Dirty Dancing* were shot at the resort. In honor of those films, a Dirty Dancing Weekend is scheduled periodically and includes tours, lessons, and a dance.

The dining room offers gracious service, a pleasant house wine, and fairly good food. Of course, after a day of fresh air and exercise, anything is likely to taste good. About 25 non-hotel guests can be seated in the dining room, but reservations are essential.

Mountain Lake is said to be the highest lake in Virginia (4,000 feet) and the highest inhabited mountain in the state. Activities abound, including fishing on the 250-acre lake (the chef will cook your catch of the day, which might be a largemouth bass, rainbow or palomino trout, or even a 4-inch bream), tennis, and golf in summer. Photography is marvelous all year, with wild azaleas and rhododendrons in spring, blazing leaves in fall, and crystal snow scenes as winter starts its visit. The resort is open from the first Fri in May to the last Sat night in Oct with weekends and Thanksgiving in Nov. The cottages at Blueberry Ridge are open all year. 115 Hotel Circle, Pembroke 24136; (540) 626-7121 or (800) 346-3334; www.mountainlakehotel.com.

The *George Washington and Jefferson National Forests* blanket 1.8 million acres across Virginia, West Virginia, and Kentucky, and an entire book could be compiled on the various trails and activities within the system. As a sampling I'll use the part of the forest in the area around Giles County that is supervised from the New River Valley ranger district. A visit to the Blacksburg office will find the rangers eager to help you with all your questions and suggest things you'll enjoy doing. (540) 552-4641; www.southernregion.fs.fed.us/gwj.

Among the activities is a 2-mile hike to view the *Cascades,* a spectacular 60-foot waterfall. The approach is via *Little Stony Creek* (stocked with trout), past a steam boiler from an old sawmill (1918–22) and an awesome look at **Barney's Wall** (a sheer bluff rising from the creek bed to a height of 3,640 feet) from the bottom of the bluff. The hike along this easy-to-moderately-difficult trail should take 3½ hours (round-trip).

Up from Mountain Lake is **Minie (or Minnie) Ball Hill,** a great place to find Civil War souvenirs. According-ing to legend, General George Crook, pressed by Confederate troops and bogged down by muddy trails, was forced to abandon an extra weight of ammunition and perhaps even a can-non full of gold (which some say is at the bottom of Mountain Lake). Lead bullets, or "minié balls," left behind on May 12, 1864, are still found by those who search this area. Actually, minié balls do not refer to size, but to French army captain Claude Étienne Minié, who developed the bullet-shaped projectile that could be shot from the muzzle-loading rifle.

Take a hike along **Sinking Creek Mountain,** named for a streambed that tends to dry up in summer months, or go up to **Hanging Rock** for a 360-degree look at the world. An old fire tower is good for watching the spring (April) and fall (mid-September to mid-October) migration of redtail, broad-wing, and sharpshinned hawks.

Recreation, illustrated trail, Appalachian, Ramseys Draft Wilderness, St. Mary's Wilderness, and Lake Moomaw maps, in the George Washington and Jefferson National Forests, can be purchased online and at various retail stores.

cool waters

Mountain Lake (near Blacksburg), one of only two natural freshwater lakes in Virginia, was formed when a rock slide dammed the north end of the valley. Debris of organic matter filled around the rocks to form a watertight seal. The lake is fed by underground streams that rarely allow the water temperature to rise above 72 degrees.

Lake Drummond in the Great Dismal Swamp is the other natural lake in Virginia.

Go with the Flow

The **Eastern Continental Divide** runs through the Christiansburg and Blacksburg areas. All the water to the east of this divide flows through the Roanoke River into the Atlantic Ocean. The water to the west runs into the New River and eventually to the Ohio and Mississippi Rivers and on to the Gulf of Mexico before spilling into the Atlantic. Unfortunately, there are no signs indicating the location of this ridge. Look instead for where the New River (which runs south to north, by the way) has etched through limestone, leaving spectacular towering formations hundreds of feet tall.

Radford City

Driving back down Route 460 and then I-81, you come to **Radford,** the home of **Radford University.** Assuming it's a nice day, or if you're too early or too late for other attractions to be open, stop by the **Corinna de la Burdé Outdoor Sculpture Court,** which features permanent and temporary collections. You'll find contemporary pieces in metal, wood, and cement by artists from the region. Between Porterfield and Powell Halls; (540) 831-5754; http://rumuseum .asp.radford.edu/pages/sculpture.html.

The Court is next to the **Flossie Martin Gallery,** also at the university, in Powell Hall 200. You most likely will see something different each time you visit, with works representing regional and national artists. Among the more famous names represented are John Cage, Christo, and Dr. Jehan Sadat (widow of the former president and Nobel Peace Prize recipient Anwar al-Sadat of Egypt) with her own Egyptian art collection.

The gallery is open Mon through Fri 10 a.m. to 5 p.m. (4 p.m. during summer sessions) and on Sat and Sun from noon to 4 p.m. The gallery is closed during university breaks and between installations. (540) 831-5754; http:// rumuseum.asp.radford.edu/pages/exhibition.html.

Pulaski County

A mile or less off I-81 and away from the rush of today's traffic is **Newbern,** a town from yesterday. The entire 1-mile-long linear town, basically located on the Olde Wilderness Road, was declared a historic district in 1979. The land was granted to early settlers by King George III in 1772, and it was founded as a town in 1810, acting as the Pulaski County seat from 1839 to 1893. At an altitude of 2,135 feet, the town, with its beautiful sunsets and surrounding mountains, reminded the settlers of Bern, Switzerland.

Daisy Williams, born in 1905, was a major force in bringing the past to our present in the form of the **Wilderness Road Regional Museum,** covering Floyd, Giles, Montgomery, and Pulaski Counties and the city of Radford. It includes rooms furnished in period style and several outbuildings. A log kitchen has been constructed behind the museum, on its original foundation. The museum committee is always looking for such artifacts as paintings, letters, photographs, and documents from 1810 to 1865 to further document the growth and development of the area. The museum is open from Mon through Sat 10:30 a.m. to 4:30 p.m. and Sun 1:30 to 4:30 p.m. Admission is $2 for adults and $1 for children 6 through 12. Visit them at 5240 Wilderness Rd., Newbern 24126; (540) 674-4835.

OTHER PLACES WORTH SEEING

ATKINS

Settlers Museum of Southwest
Virginia
(276) 686-4401
www.settlersmuseum.com

DUNGANNON

Scott County Lavender Farm
(888) 222-3715
www.scottcountylavender.com

GATE CITY

Wilderness Road Blockhouse
(276) 386-6665

MEADOWS OF DAN

Mabry Mill
(276) 952-2947
www.virginia.org/Listings/HistoricSites/
MabryMill/

RURAL RETREAT

Cedar Springs Trout Farm
(276) 686-4505
www.virginia.org

The historic district contains original log and wooden buildings, including a jail, hanging house, store, churches, private residences, and an inn that served as a stagecoach stop. You also can see the waterworks, a slave-built flagstone sidewalk, a pre–Civil War church, the community center, and other points of interest. The original *Newbern Reservoir,* constructed in 1870, also remains. The water system, more than 110 years old, is still intact, and a piece of the original pipe is shown as part of the reservoir display. Various fires destroyed the courthouse in 1893, the Methodist church in 1912, and 11 of the original houses in 1924, but 26 of the original log or wooden buildings constructed between 1810 and 1895 still stand.

A walking-tour brochure about Pulaski County and Newbern (listing accommodations, restaurants, campgrounds, entertainment, a calendar of events, maps, tours, and attractions) is available from the Pulaski County Chamber of Commerce, 4440 Cleburne Blvd., Suite B, Dublin 24084; (540) 674-1991; www.pulaskichamber.info.

The *Fine Arts Center for the New River Valley,* in Pulaski, offers music shows, exhibitions, poetry and literary readings, lectures, private collections, and shows by amateur and professional artists. The Virginia Historic Landmark building, constructed in 1898, is considered an excellent example of Victorian commercial architecture. Free concerts are presented at Pulaski's Jackson Park throughout the summer.

The center is open Mon through Fri 10 a.m. to 5 p.m. and Sat 11 a.m. to 3 p.m. There is no admission charge. A gift shop is on the premises. 21 W. Main St., Pulaski 24301; (540) 980-7363; www.facnrv.org.

The *Pulaski Railway Station* was erected by the Norfolk & Western Railroad in 1886 when passenger service existed here and Pulaski was one of the major stops along its route. The railroad donated this remarkable example of railway stations of the late 1800s to the town in 1989. It was restored in 1994 and included the *Raymond F. Ratcliffe Memorial Museum.* Unfortunately, a fire in 2008 ravaged the building. The station and museum are on the mend, so give a call to see if it's been restored enough for you to visit. 124 S. Washington Ave., Pulaski 24301; (540) 980-2055; www.newriverheritage.org/members-ratcliffe.htm.

As you'll learn when you visit the *Shot Tower and New River Trail Historical State Park,* Colonel John Chiswell discovered lead and zinc deposits in this area in about 1757 while he was hiding from the Cherokees. Shot was made from those deposits for firearms for frontiersmen and settlers at the Jackson Ferry shot tower, constructed by Thomas Jackson in about 1807, with walls that are 2½ feet thick on a 20-foot square base. Shot was made by dropping the molten lead from a pouring kettle, through a sieve at the top of the 75-foot tower, down to a kettle of cold water that was 75 feet belowground. The size of the holes in the sieve determined the size of the shot. This is one of only a handful of such towers in the United States.

The shot tower was designated a National Historic Mechanical Engineering Landmark in 1961 by the American Society of Mechanical Engineers. There are 77 steps up the winding staircase. The tower is open weekends from 10 a.m. to 6 p.m., April 1 through Memorial Day and Labor Day through October 31; Memorial Day to Labor Day weekends, open daily from 10 a.m. to 6 p.m. It is closed Nov through Mar. There is a $2 parking fee on weekdays and $3 on weekends. Route 1, Box 81X, Austinville 24312; (276) 699-1791 or (276) 699-6778; www.dcr.state.va.us/parks/newriver.htm.

The state park itself is a linear park paralleling for the most part the Norfolk & Western Railway bed. It winds 57 miles along the New River, through four counties; Carroll, Grayson, Pulaski, and Wythe. You're invited to use the trail for hiking, biking, horseback riding, cross-country skiing, and access to the river. NOTE: Some parts of the trail are quite steep, and most of the trail is isolated. Check at one of the stations for information about water releases during the rainy months.

Galax

Head out of the Fort Chiswell area and you're on your way to *Galax* (which also is the name of a mountain evergreen, by the way), passing by Hillsville on your way.

TOP ANNUAL EVENTS

APRIL

Historic Garden Week
Statewide
(804) 644-7776 or (804) 653-7141
www.vagardenweek.org

Blue Ridge Kite Festival
Salem
(540) 387-0267
www.roanokecountyva.gov

MAY

Whitetop Mountain Ramp Festival
(276) 388-3422
www.graysoncountyva.com/Whitetop_
Mountain_Ramp_Festival.aspx

JUNE

Grayson County Fiddler's Convention
Elk Creek
(276) 655-4866
www.ecvfd.net

JULY

**Smoke on the Mountain Barbecue
Championship**
Galax
(276) 236-2184
www.smokeonthemountainva.com

FloydFest
Floyd
(540) 745-3378
www.floydfest.com

AUGUST

**Fairview Ruritan Old Fiddler's
Convention**
Galax
(276) 236-5725
www.fairviewruritan.com/
bluegrassmusicvirginia.aspx

Virginia Peach Festival Week
Stuart
(276) 694-6012
www.patrickchamber.com

AUGUST-SEPTEMBER

**Virginia Mountain Crafts Guild Claytor
Lake Fair**
Dublin
(540) 725-9570
www.artandcrafts.com/virginia/

SEPTEMBER

Virginia Highlands Festival
Abingdon
(276) 623-5266
www.vahighlandsfestival.org/

Labor Day Flea Market & Gun Show
Hillsville
(276) 728-2911
www.hillsville.com/fmarket.htm

OCTOBER

**White Top Mountain Molasses
Festival**
White Top
(276) 388-3480
www.graysoncountyva.com

In Galax the place for crafts is the ***Rooftop of Virginia Craft Center.***
Housed in a cathedral-type setting, it is part of Rooftop of Virginia CAP, a community action agency that hosts senior citizen activities as well as Head Start programs. The center offers for sale such authentic handmade items as pottery, wood carvings, quilts, and needlework, and the work is done by native

craftspeople. If you're stopping at either Grayson Highlands State Park or the Mount Rogers National Recreation Area during summer, you'll find some of these crafts available as well. The center is open Mon through Fri 9 a.m. to 6 p.m., Sat and Sun 9 a.m. to 5 p.m. 206 N. Main St., Galax 24333; (276) 236-7131; www.rooftopofvirginia.com.

The *Jeff Matthews Memorial Museum* is housed in two pioneer cabins (one built in 1834). Among the things you'll see are more than 1,000 different knives collected by Matthews, newspapers dating to January 4, 1800, covering George Washington's burial, and 40 mounted heads and animal rugs from other parts of the country collected by Glenn Pless.

funfacts

Word has it that the *Hillsville Diner,* established in 1946, now in Hillsville, was transported from Mt. Airy, North Carolina, and that a young Andy Griffith either worked or visited there (when it was in Mt. Airy, of course). It is also said to be the "oldest continuously operating streetcar diner in the state." 525 N. Main St., Hillsville 24343; (276) 728-7681; www.virginia.org/Listings/Dining/HillsvilleDiner.

With today's ever-more-painless dentistry, you might want to notice a collection of old dental equipment from local dentist Dr. Paul Katt, who was still practicing dentistry at the age of 80 when he died in 1988. Among the equipment are his chair, an X-ray machine, and tools of the trade from an earlier generation. A Confederate soldier display in two rooms shows pictures of all the men they could locate from Galax, Grayson, and other nearby towns who fought in the Civil War.

The museum is open Wed through Sat 11 a.m. to 4 p.m. and occasionally on Sun (call for specific information). The visit is free, but donations are accepted. 606 W. Stuart Dr., Galax 24333; (276) 236-7874; www.jeffmatthewsmuseum.org.

The Bottle House

In 1941 or 1948 (depends on who you ask) pharmacist John "Doc" Hope had a large playhouse (about 15 feet by 25 feet, estimated by the current owner) built for his daughter out of about 10,000 medicine, wine, and other bottles. I did not realize there are "conventions" about building a bottle house or wall, but apparently there's at least one, and that's the concept of building with both the neck facing outdoors so the inside wall is flat, and building with the necks inward so the exterior is a flat wall. The *Bottle House* is on N. Main Street in Hillsville.

It's hard to believe that it's been a decade (October 6, 2001) since the $5.2 million **Blue Ridge Music Center,** an outdoor stage and amphitheater just off the Blue Ridge Parkway, about 12 miles east of Galax, enjoyed its first concert. Located at milepost 213 on the Blue Ridge Parkway, an interpretive center helps preserve, interpret, and present the unique American music tradition of the Blue Ridge Mountains. An interactive exhibit about the Roots of American Music opened to huge fanfare over Memorial Day weekend in 2011. The complex includes an interpretive center, and a 2,000-seat hillside amphitheater, picnic facilities, and a luthier shop (people who make or repair stringed instruments). The visitor center is open daily from 9 a.m. to 5 p.m. from late May through Oct and Thurs through Mon in late May. 700 Foothills Rd., Galax 24333; (276) 236-5309; www.blueridgemusiccenter.org.

independence

Located 15 miles west of Galax, the town of Independence came into being in 1850 over a dispute between residents of two towns about where to locate the county seat. In a Solomonesque decision, adjacent county commissioners chose a site favored by a group of "independents."

Grayson County

West of Galax is **Independence,** the Grayson county seat. There, at the **1908 Courthouse,** is the art and cultural center of Grayson County. The former county courthouse also houses the **Vault Museum,** formerly the court clerk's vault room, and has a display of an early mountain home, barn, and blacksmith shop, complete with tools and farm implements. There's also the Grayson County Tourist Information Center and an arts and crafts shop featuring Grayson County artists and artisans. The building is open from Mon through Fri 10 a.m. to 4:30 p.m. and until 4 p.m. on Sat. 107 E. Main St., Independence 24348; (276) 773-3711; www.historic1908courthouse.org.

Wytheville

It's back north now to **Wytheville,** where you can see exhibits from the old mining camps, Civil War artifacts, and antique farm machinery at the (Colonel) **Thomas J.** (Jefferson) **Boyd Museum,** the Father of Wytheville. Its collection includes Boyd's surveyor's instruments, Wytheville's first firefighting equipment, minerals, paintings, tools, musical instruments, antiques and clothing, books, and racks of photographs of early people from and places in the county. Large items, including a buggy, a moonshine still, and business equipment, are in the basement. The Museum Resource Center, of interest to genealogists and researchers, is on the first floor. The Discovery Center provides hands-on learning opportunities for children.

The Boyd Museum is open Mon through Fri and the third Sat of the month 10 a.m. to 4 p.m. Admission is $4 for adults and $2 for children ages 6 through 12 or admission to the Boyd and the Haller-Gibboney Rock House Museum for $6 for adults and $3 for children. 295 Tazewell St., Wytheville 24382; (276) 223-3330; http://museums.wytheville.org/museums.htm.

trivia

Elizabeth Brown Memorial Park is the site of the largest festival in Wytheville, the annual Chautauqua Festival in the Park, attended by thousands. You should be there for the concerts, shows, arts and crafts, hot air ballooning, and lots of other activities and food. (276) 223-3355.

Next to the Thomas J. Boyd Museum is the ***Haller-Gibboney Rock House Museum,*** an old Pennsylvania gray limestone house that has seen a lot of history. The home was built in 1824 and served as a hospital to both Confederate and Federal troops. Included in its exhibits are furnishings that were transported by oxcart from Pennsylvania, possessions of the Haller, Gibboney, and Campbell families, who lived in the house from 1820 until 1967. Dr. John Haller, the second occupant of the Rock House, was Wytheville's first resident physician.

The furnishings are displayed in a parlor, dining room, reception room, and some bedrooms. There are also displays of coins, rocks, and Indian relics of the area, among other regional artifacts. Another Rock House souvenir of the Civil War time is a bullet hole in the wall of the front parlor.

trivia

One of the fascinating items about Wytheville history is its place in medical journals. It was considered a "polio" town in 1950 and suffered the largest number of polio cases per capita in the country. Of the 1,200 cases reported throughout the state, about 190 cases were reported in Wythe County with most cases in Wytheville, which had a population of 5,500 at the time.

The museum is open Mon through Fri and the third Sat of the month from 10 a.m. to 4 p.m. Admission is $4 for adults and $2 for children. A combination ticket to both museums is $6 for adults and $3 for children. 205 E. Tazewell St., Wytheville 24382; (276) 223-3330; http://museums.wytheville.org/museums.htm.

Beagle Ridge Herb Farm and Environmental Education Center, operated by Gregg and Ellen Reynolds, includes a formal walled herbal display garden; a lavender walk; thyme,

Virtus in Virginia

So, **George Wythe,** for whom Wytheville is named, never visited the town. He did, however, sign the Declaration of Independence and design the original great seal of Virginia. It's circular, with a figure of Virtus, the goddess of virtue, dressed as a warrior in the center. She holds a spear in her right hand, with its point held downward touching the earth. In her left hand is a sheathed sword pointing upward. Her left foot rests on the chest of the figure of tyranny, who is lying on the ground. Above the figure is the word "Virginia," and under the figures is the state motto "Sic Semper Tyrannis" or "Thus Always to Tyrants." The seal was adopted in 1776 and modified in 1930.

Wythe also was the first professor of law in an American college, the College of William and Mary in Williamsburg.

oregano, and lavender collections; a pergola that shades the medicinal herbs; nursery beds; a water garden; and a shrub border with rugosa roses. Other special areas are being added. They grow organic garlic and herbs to make delicious herbal vinegars and seasonings and manufacture a line of herbal bath products. You can take a workshop, hike, or talk with Gregg and Ellen about your garden and theirs.

Ellen, who was named the 2006 Virginia Project Learning Tree Outstanding Educator, reports exciting news that's almost obvious with their new, longer name. They have started FAWN Inc., a nonprofit foundation for environmental education on a part of their property. "We believe being a good steward to the land begins at a young age, and as environmental educators it is our mission to give back to the community."

Self-proclaimed as "Your Outdoor Classroom in the Blue Ridge," the programs they offer vary from pre-K to high school, women in the outdoors, and just about everything in between.

Beagle Ridge Herb Farm is open from late Apr through the fall, Thurs through Sun 10 a.m. to 5 p.m. and by appointment. Call (540) 962-2247 during the week and (276) 621-4511 on weekends; 1934 Matney Flats Rd., Wytheville 24382; www.beagleridgeherbfarm.com.

When you head north out of Wytheville, you come to Big Walker Mountain, and the **_Big Walker National Scenic Byway and Big Walker Lookout,_** at an elevation of 3,405 feet, in the Big Walker National Forest. The Appalachian Trail goes through this area, affording many vistas of the farmland below to the north and mountain wilderness to the south. The lookout, with a 100-foot tower, is at the halfway point of the byway.

There also is a commercial tourist shop. Of course, the main attraction is the view. In spring it's highlighted by the newborn blossoms; in fall, by the flaming foliage. There's a beginners hiking trail, Monster Rock Trail that begins behind Big Walker Lookout and follows the ridge of the mountain.

The chair lift is open daily during the summer and weekends only in spring and fall. The byway is open year-round; the lookout is open daily 10 a.m. to 6 p.m. Memorial Day to Labor Day and until 5 p.m. in the spring and fall. The overlook is free. 8711 Stoney Fork Rd., Wytheville 24382; (276) 663-4016; www .scenicbeauty-va.com.

Bland County

For an unusual activity you certainly can write home about, try trekking with the *Virginia Highland Llamas.* With advance reservations, Cathy Davis and Jay Cox will lead you and your party, along with a herd of llamas, up Big Walker's old Appalachian Trail section. On special saddles the llamas will carry a picnic lunch you can enjoy after hiking through lush green meadows up to a beautiful vista.

The hike, which costs about $60 per person, is about 3 hours up and 2½ hours down. All you need are sturdy footwear, a camera, and film. Everything else is furnished. Llama treks are available Apr through Oct. 10325 Echo Lane, Glade Spring 24315; (276) 688-4464 or (703) 944-4674; www.llamaweb.com/ llfarms/vhl/vhl.html.

Continuing north on I-77, you'll come to Bastian and the *Wolf Creek Indian Village and Museum* (exit 58, 1,000 feet north on Route 52, Bastian). The living-history museum is a 24.5-acre re-creation of an American Indian community with a population of about a hundred persons that existed nearby approximately 800 years ago.

The remains of the original village site came to the attention of state archaeologists in 1969 after highway workers began excavating the area to

Skeeterdogs

Since 1920, Skeeter's E. N. Umberger store has been serving its self-proclaimed "world-famous hot dogs" or *"skeeterdogs."* More than eight million have been sold so far "without a dissatisfied customer." They've been shipped to customers from Singapore, Amsterdam, Germany, and Great Britain. By the way, Edith Bolling Wilson, a descendant of Pocahontas and wife of President Woodrow Wilson, was born in the residence above the store. 165 E. Main Street, Wytheville 24382; (276) 228-2611.

build I-77. Archaeologist Howard MacCord mapped the area before it was flooded by the rerouting of Wolf Creek, and the catalog of artifacts includes 14 Indian skeletons, signs of 11 wigwams, and several storage pits.

The reconstructed village includes wigwams, fire pits, a perimeter fence, and other facilities. Costumed interpreters help you understand the skills that these Indians probably used and how they created their pottery and weavings.

A picnic area with 14 tables and grills, a shelter, and hiking trails are available.

Wolf Creek is open Mon through Sat 10 a.m. to 5 p.m. The admission fee to the museum and the Indian Village is

funfacts

Llama fibers can be used in fine clothing (when mixed with 30 percent sheep wool for elasticity), felt cowboy hats, rugs, ropes, and for making dry-flies.

$10 for adults and $6 for children ages 5 through 16; a family pass (2 adults and 3 or more children) costs $35 (AAA discounts are honored). 6394 N. Scenic Hwy., Bastian 24314; (276) 688-3438; www.indianvillage.org.

Tazewell County

The **Historic Crab Orchard Museum and Pioneer Park** displays photographs, multimedia presentations, and artifacts dating from millions of years ago to the present in a 110-acre area near **Tazewell** (it's a short "a") designated as a prehistoric and historical archaeological area. Among the regular exhibits are a leg bone and teeth of a huge mastodon that roamed the area millions of years ago, the double palisades (protective fortification wall of tree trunks) of the Native Americans, and relics from the Revolutionary and Civil Wars. Many of these "souvenirs" of the past were uncovered during the construction of US 19 and US 460.

A **"lepidodendron tree,"** which is really sandstone rock, might be the first thing you see as you enter the museum. The lepidodendron was a popular growth item about 300 million years ago and grew in the water that then covered the area. Eventually the trunk would break off, and water would rot the interior, which would then fill with sand and form a cast of the inside of the tree trunk. Some of the wood would adhere to the stone, carbonize, and form bituminous coal. I'll admit it, the Historic Crab Orchard Museum and Pioneer Park in Tazewell is one of my favorites, no qualifiers attached.

Crab Orchard, however, is more than what's past and gone. There's a new exhibit every quarter: perhaps photographs, a history of railroading, German Expressionistic art, or the paintings of local artist Tracy Ratliff. The activities

Just Cuz . . .

Find your way to Pounding Mill and *Cuz's Uptown Barbeque, Cabins and Resort,* located in a renovated dairy barn, where Mike and Yvonne Thompson are the inn-keepers. Since 1979, they've been fixing huge steaks, smoked prime rib, fresh fish, Thai curry, and pit-smoked barbecue. Stop in on weekends and listen to live blue-grass music. There are two hand-hewn cedar cabins, each with a fireplace and a two-person hot tub, and one brightly colored beach-style bungalow. Enjoy breakfast served on your porch, play tennis on the clay court, take a dip in the pool, or just relax.

Open Wed through Sat from 2 to 9 p.m. from Mar through Dec. US 460, Pounding Mill 24637; (276) 964-9014; www.cuzs.us.

calendar is filled with such items as a May Civil War reenactment and, on July 4, a community festival that's attended by several thousand people with crafts and home-baked goods. In September there's a storytelling festival.

Crab Orchard is open Tues through Sat 9 a.m. to 5 p.m. and Sun 1 to 5 p.m. Memorial Day to Labor Day. Admission is $4 for adults, $3 for seniors and AAA members, and $2 for children 7 through 12 (yes, that's a huge discount from previous years, so the museum is more accessible to visitors) for full site privileges. It's even less if you're just visiting the gallery or the park. Event day demonstrations may have an extra charge. 3663 Crab Orchard Rd., Tazewell 24651; (276) 988-6755; www.craborchardmuseum.com.

Not too far from Tazewell is *Burkes Garden,* which was surveyed in 1748 and is now designated a Virginia Scenic Byway. This beautiful valley is unique because it is surrounded by only one mountain. It's also the highest, coldest, greenest, and maybe the prettiest in Virginia. James Burke discovered the area in the 1740s when he followed a wounded elk there. Legend says he planted the potato peelings that provided food for the Irish surveying party that came through in 1749, who jokingly named the place "Burkes Garden." To get there, take Route 623 east and south out of Tazewell for about 15 miles; (276) 322-1345 or (800) 588-9401; www.tazewellcounty.org/tourism/broch8.html.

Smyth County

Just as your back (or whatever) is about to give out from hours of driving and riding while you're exploring the back roads and beautiful mountain scenery, along comes *Saltville,* the Salt Capital of the Confederacy. Suddenly, out of what appears to be almost nowhere, is the *Saltville Fitness Trail,* running along the railroad tracks to help you work on your tired muscles and brain cells. The first salt mine in America opened here in 1795. The "mining" operation removed the salt from the ground in liquid form, which was then boiled. Four million bushels of salt were produced in 1864. You can see examples of the big salt kettles around the town.

Time in Saltville goes back a long way. Each summer a dig is conducted by the Virginia Museum of Natural History and the Smithsonian Institution for prehistoric bones, and finds have included a musk ox skeleton and the track of a giant ground sloth. It's possible they've also found evidence of human life in our hemisphere from 14,000 years ago. The floor of the Saltville valley has a flat layer of mud, which is why so many artifacts and fossils have been preserved and not washed away.

The town continues this prehistoric theme during the Labor Day celebratory parade, which includes a gigantic (man-made) wooly mammoth and a baby mammoth, complete with trunks that blow water. In addition to the annual dig in the Well Fields, a visit to Saltville could include a tour through the town, where you can learn more about the history of this "salt town." Saltville Town Hall, 217 Palmer Ave., Saltville 24370; (276) 496-5342; www.saltville.org.

A tour of Saltville begins at the **Museum of the Middle Appalachians,** which contains memorabilia of Saltville's rich history and of the industries that manufactured salt and salt by-products for almost 200 years. The museum is housed in what was an office of one of the early salt companies. The surrounding park includes two 1890s steam locomotives that were used by local industry; tramway buckets that were part of a 7-mile tramway used to carry limestone; and huge iron kettles, used during most of the 19th century for boiling down salt brine. In the museum's main hall, you can see an interactive model of the Valley with historical and geological points of interest, fossils

funfacts

The soft drink Dr Pepper was created in Rural Retreat. It didn't exactly put the town on the map, but it helped. Dr Pepper's Drug Store closed a few years ago, and then the building burned down. But talk to the locals for the real story about Dr Pepper.

trivia

Writer *Sherwood Anderson* lived in this area for a while, owned two newspapers here, and is buried in Roundhill Cemetery, next to his wife, Eleanor Copenhaven Anderson. The Smyth-Bland Regional Library in Marion houses the Anderson archives, including many first editions of his books, some correspondence, and some *Life* magazine photographs of him. A Sherwood Anderson Short Story contest is held annually. Contact the Sherwood Anderson Association at P.O. Box 1161, Marion 24354; or call (276) 783-8230.

from the late Pleistocene Epoch, Woodland Indian artifacts, relics from the two battles that occurred in the Saltville Valley, and other items of historic importance.

The museum is open Mon through Sat from 10 a.m. to 4 p.m. and Sun 1 to 4 p.m. Admission is $3 for adults and $2 for seniors and children 6 to 12. 123 Palmer Ave., Saltville 24370; (276) 496-3633; www.museum-mid-app.org.

Next to the **Madam Russell Methodist Church** is the **Madam Russell House.** The church and home are named after Elizabeth Henry Campbell Russell, sister of Patrick Henry. She was a leader of the Methodist Church in the region and is considered by some as the "Mother of Methodism." Construction of the church was begun in 1898, using local sandstone. 207 W. Main St., Saltville 24370; (276) 496-5342; www.saltville.org.

Washington County

Probably the best-known historic and tourist area in Washington County is **Abingdon,** the oldest incorporated town west of the Blue Ridge Mountains. One of the better-known attractions in Abingdon is the world-famous **Barter Theatre** (open February through December), with such comic and lightly serious traveling company presentations as the marvelously funny *Greater Tuna* by Jaston Williams and Joe Sears. Other productions might include *Disney's Beauty and the Beast, Elvis Has Left the Building, Eye of the Storm, Circumference of a Square,* and *Saving Old Smokey.* Bob Porterfield gathered the first production company together during the Depression, when they bartered their presentations in exchange for food and services from area residents. 127 W. Main St., Abingdon 24210; (276) 628-3991; www.bartertheatre.com.

The Barter Cafe serves sandwiches, salads, soups, and hot lunches, starting at 11 a.m. and open late after evening performances. It's located on Porterfield Square, next to Barter Stage II. 110 W. Main St., Abingdon 24210; (276) 619-5462; www.bartertheatre.com.

Gregory Peck, Ernest Borgnine, Patricia Neal, Ned Beatty, Hume Cronyn, Gary Collins, and Larry Linville are among more than 100 well-known stars of stage, screen, and television who launched their careers at **Barter Theatre** in Abingdon.

The sculptures surrounding the lighting fixtures were created by Mary Filapek, in the Barter production building. Payton Boyd designed the seat covers, based on the Charles Vess design of the Barter logo. There are about 40,000 stitches on each embroidered pattern, with the embroidery donated by Lebanon Apparel. The lobby drapes were designed by Amanda Alridge, Pat Van Horn, and Amy Fansler of the costume shop, and the stained-glass circular window on the building's facade was crafted by Abingdon artist Allen Boyd.

The **Historic District of Abingdon** is about 20 square blocks of restored 100- to 200-year-old homes and buildings, each with its own story. The **Arts Depot** (inside an 1890s railroad freight station) has artists' studios, changing exhibits, and classes at 314 Depot Sq.; (276) 628-9091. **Heartwood Southeast Virginia's Artists Gallery** is the latest and largest stab at packaging local artists and their works as a tourist attraction. The facility, housed in a "deconstructed barn" design opened in June 2011. 851 French Moore Jr. Blvd., Abingdon 24210; (276) 492-2095; http://heartwoodvirginia.org.

It's said that on the night of the full moon, haunting violin melodies can be heard from the third floor of the **Martha Washington Inn** in Abingdon. Traditional lore says that during the Civil War, Captain John Stoves, a Union officer, was captured near the inn, which was a girls' finishing school at the time. As he lay dying, a "Martha Girl" who was known as Beth played a comforting melody on her violin. Soon after he died, she came down with typhoid fever and died. They're both buried in Abingdon's **Green Springs Cemetery.** More cheerful times at the inn today could include a visit to the year-round indoor swimming pool or the spa. 150 W. Main St., Abington 24210; (276) 628-3161; www.marthawashingtoninn.com.

The **Virginia Creeper Trail** is a 35-mile rail trail running from Abingdon to Whitetop along an old railroad bed. There is an abundance of beautiful scenery as the trail passes through farmland, a small mountain range, and over creeks and gullies. Thanks to the assistance of the Jacobs Creek Job Corps and the Seabees, there are four trestle bridges, which have been floored for pedestrian use and are provided with handrails. Motorized vehicles, firearms, and alcoholic beverages are not permitted. The trail passes through private property, and you are asked to remain on the trail itself, not trespass, and to please close the gate behind you. A shuttle is available from the top of Whitetop (which at 5,525 feet is the second tallest mountain in the state, after Mount Rogers) for those who bike or hike up and want an easier or faster way down. Although there's an official website, www.vacreepertrail.org, I think the one at www.vacreepertrail.us provides better information. What is new on both sites is the construction of an "old time" railroad station, the Alvarado Station, which has 2 restrooms for public use and a community room. It's 9 miles from Abingdon and 25 miles from the North Carolina/Virginia border.

Russell County

The old **Russell County Courthouse** at Dickensonville on Copper Creek was the first landmark in Russell County to be nominated to the National Register of Historic Places. The courthouse was used from late 1799 to 1818, when a new county seat was designated. To see the courthouse, take Route 58/19 out of Abingdon to the Hansonville split and follow Route 58 to the left about 4 miles to Dickensonville; (540) 762-7254; www.virginiaheritage .org/russell_co.htm.

Bristol

Going south out of Abingdon, you come to **Bristol,** the "twin cities" whose State Street is the dividing line between Tennessee and Virginia. The famed BRISTOL—A GOOD PLACE TO LIVE sign, with arrows pointing to the Virginia and Tennessee sides of State Street, is right outside the train station.

With the thought of observing a solar eclipse on August 7, 1869, an astronomical observatory was built on the highest piece of land in the Bristol area where a near total eclipse was predicted. Thought to be an ideal residential neighborhood, the area was named Solar Hill and the street running along the top of the hill was named Solar Street. The area reached its peak in the early 1900s. Many homes are huge, representing "one of the finest collections of historic residential architecture in the region," and date from the 1800s to early 1900s. You'll see Colonial, Victorian, Neoclassical, and Craftsman style homes. In 2001 it became the first Bristol neighborhood listed on both the Virginia Landmarks Register and the National Register of Historic Places. The Solar Hill Historic District Association was formed in 2003 to provide improvements that include replacing sidewalks, installing decorative post street lights, burying overhead cables, erecting a gateway monument, installing historic markers and landscaping, and offering walking tour maps. Peter Lawrie, grandson of sculptor Lee Lawrie (designer of the *Atlas* statue in Rockefeller Center in New York City), was named the architect for the monument. You can download a walking map tour on the Solar Hill website. (276) 669-6457; http://solarhill .tripod.com.

The **_Birthplace of Country Music Alliance Museum_** (BCMA) is based in Bristol, where it focuses on the history of country, bluegrass, and other music that's such a vital part of this area, its influences, and how it has affected the local and national population. The BCMA works to help preserve and promote this musical heritage by showing historically significant artifacts and teaching about the history of country music. Although there's information from colonial days, it mostly concentrates on the period starting in 1927 through the mid-1970s. 110 Piedmont Ave., Suite 202, Bristol 24201; (276) 645-0111; www .birthplaceofcountrymusic.org.

Scott County

West of Bristol, near Duffield, is the **Natural Tunnel,** part of Natural Tunnel State Park. The tunnel is 850 feet long and as high as a 10-story building that began more than a million years ago in the early glacial period through the limestone rock of Powell's Mountain by Stock Creek's persistence. It's large enough for trains to go through. William Jennings Bryan called it the "Eighth Wonder of the World."

Other scenic features include a wide chasm between steep stone walls surrounded by several pinnacles, or chimneys. Facilities include picnic areas and an amphitheater. The park also offers cave tours and canoe trips on the Clinch River, and the Cove Ridge Center, which offers environmental education, conference facilities, and overnight dorm accommodations.

A visitor center sits atop the mountain And is open weekdays from 10 a.m. to 5 p.m. and weekends from 10 a.m. to 6 p.m. from Memorial Day through Labor Day and weekends from 10 a.m. to 4 p.m. in Apr, May, Sept, and Oct. The only chairlift in Virginia state parks is at Natural Tunnel. It runs daily from Memorial Day through Labor Day and on weekends in May, Sept, and Oct. Cabins and a campground were added in 2007. Each campsite has a campfire ring grill, with firewood and ice sold at the park. RV sites are up to 38 feet and have electric and water hookups. Summer swimming in a 5,400-square-foot pool is free to campers. 1420 Natural Tunnel Pkwy., Duffield 24244; (276) 940-2674 or (800) 933-PARK; www.dcr.virginia.gov/state_parks/nat.shtml.

Nashville, Tennessee, may claim to be the home of country music, but the Carter Family Fold claims that A.P. Carter, his wife, Sara, and her cousin Maybelle (mother of June, Helen, and Anita Carter) were the pioneers of this music form. The Carter family recorded 300 songs between 1927 and 1942, 100 of them written by A.P.

Now the **Carter Family Museum, Memorial Music Center, and Music in the Fold** on Saturday nights at 7:30 p.m. show what country music, clogging, and buck dancing are about in a rustic country setting. A 1,000-seat music "shed" is the site for traditional country music every Saturday night.

The museum, cabin, and the Family Fold are open Mon through Wed from 10 a.m. to 2 p.m. during the season. You can see displays about the role the Carter family played in developing and promoting traditional bluegrass and country music, shown through instruments, original records, photographs, and personal family items. The museum is their old home, and A.P. Carter's general store is "the fold" where the shows are held. Admission is free although donations are gladly accepted. Concert tickets are $7 for adults and $1 for children 6 to 11, although some special concerts have a higher price.

An annual festival, with only acoustic music, celebrating the first recordings by the Carter family, is held the first weekend in August.

The Carter Family Fold, Hiltons (Route 614, 3 miles east of Weber City) 24258; (276) 645-0035 or (276) 386-6054 (for a recorded schedule of upcoming performances); www.carterfamilyfold.org.

Wise County

The *University of Virginia's College at Wise* is the only branch of the University of Virginia. It was founded in Wise in 1954 after local citizens petitioned UVA to build a college here. Until then, access to public higher education in far southwest Virginia was minimal, limited to a few extension courses.

Wise County donated the land and two old stone buildings (still standing and in use) that had served as the Wise County Poor Farm, a home for the indigent. The state offered up a total of $5,000 in appropriations for the first year. Local citizens contributed twice that to furnish and equip the school. One hundred students entered the first class in 1954.

Until 1968 the school was a two-year "feeder college" for UVA (and other universities). Many of the area's most prominent citizens got their start at Clinch Valley College (CVC) during its two-year phase.

Now called UVA at Wise, this is the only four-year state college in Virginia west of Radford (the college became a four-year school in 1968; it was never a community college). Ties with UVA have strengthened considerably in past years. As with any college, there are numerous cultural activities, including recitals, exhibits, and an international movie series. 1 College Ave.; Wise 24293; (276) 328-0100; www.wise.virginia.edu.

Dickenson County

Northeast of Wise (north on Route 23, east on Route 83) is Clintwood, the Dickenson County seat. This is where Ralph Stanley, noted bluegrass and mountain singing legend, grew up, and helped establish the *Ralph Stanley Museum and Traditional Mountain Music Center.* The $1.4 million complex is at one end of the Crooked Road Music Heritage Trail that starts in Floyd, goes by Galax, through Grayson County, Bristol, Hiltons, and then to Clintwood. Stanley donated old musical instruments and memorabilia collected since he started in the business as a teenager.

The museum is open Tues through Sat 10 a.m. to 4 p.m. and Sun 1 to 4 p.m. Apr through Dec, and Wed through Sat 10 a.m. to 5 p.m. and Sun 1 to 5 p.m. the rest of the year. Admission is $7.50 for adults and $5 for seniors

(55 and over), students, and Dickenson/Wise/Buchanan County residents. 249 Main St., Clintwood 24228; (276) 926-8550; www.ralphstanleymuseum.com.

Big Stone Gap

The ***Harry W. Meador Coal Museum*** at E. 3rd Street and Shawnee Avenue in Big Stone Gap is operated by Big Stone Gap Department of Parks and Recreation. The museum exhibits artifacts collected by the late Harry Meador Jr., who went from being a union laborer to the vice president of coal development for a local coal company. Other items have been painstakingly assembled from private homes and public buildings, which illustrate the coal-mining heritage of the area and coal mining's profound effect on the local lifestyle.

> ## funfacts
>
> This area may look familiar to those of you who've seen the movie *Coal Miner's Daughter.* Some filming for the movie was done in Bee, Haysi, and Wise (fairground scene).

Among the more interesting exhibits are photographs, mining equipment and tools, and coal company items. There's also a 1900s dentist office tucked in there. The museum is open Wed through Sat 10 a.m. to 5 p.m., Sun 1 to 5 p.m., and by appointment. There is no admission fee. E. 3rd and Shawnee Avenue, Big Stone Gap 24219; (276) 523-9209; www.bigstonegap.org/attract/coal.htm.

For the longest continuing outdoor drama in the United States, see ***The Trail of the Lonesome Pine*** (the official outdoor drama of Virginia), telling the story of the romance of a mountain girl during the development of the coal industry. The drama is adapted from a book by John Fox Jr., which was the nation's first million-selling novel (and was later made into a movie), and it has been presented every year since 1963. Performances are given at 8 p.m. Thurs, Fri, and Sat, June through Aug. Ticket prices are $15 for adults, $12 for seniors, and $8 for students. 518 Clinton Ave. East, Big Stone Gap 24219; (276) 523-1235; www.thetraildrama.org.

June Tolliver was the heroine of Fox's book, and her home is open as the ***June Tolliver House and Folkart Center*** for tours Tues through Sat from 10 a.m. to 5 p.m. Fantastic local craft offerings from the gift shop, again open only until the last week before Christmas, are a must.

> ## funfacts
>
> John Fox Jr., a Rough Rider with Teddy Roosevelt, and author of *The Little Shepherd of Kingdom Come* and *Trail of the Lonesome Pine,* used the building that is currently the coal mine museum as his study and library.

522 Clinton Ave. East, Big Stone Gap 24219; (800) 362-0149 or (276) 523-4707; www.junetolliverhouse.org.

The Big Stone Gap welcome center, *Interstate 101 Car and Visitor Center,* is located in an 1870 Pullman Company passenger train car. It had two staterooms, a dining area, kitchen, and an observation room. The president of the Interstate Railroad Company used it when they purchased it in the 1920s. The car was retired in 1959 and used as a hunting cabin on Dorchester Lake on Black Creek in Wise County. Eventually, it was donated to the Gap Corporation in 1988 when it was restored. Stop by the center to learn about sights and activities in this area and about the car's history. 619 Gilley Ave., Big Stone Gap 24219; (276) 523-2060; www.bigstonegap.com.

To see authentic Fox family furnishings, visit the *John Fox Jr. Museum.* The house was opened in 1970, and is open Thurs through Sat 2 to 6 p.m. from the Thurs following Memorial Day until the Sat before Labor Day. Admission is $3 for adults, $2 for seniors 65 and older, and $1 for students. 118 Shawnee Ave. East, Big Stone Gap 24219; (276) 523-2747; www.bigstone gap.org.

The *Southwest Virginia Museum* is in a 4-story mansion bequeathed in 1946 by Congressman C. Bascom Slemp. Opened in 1947, it strives to preserve a picture of the early southwest Virginia pioneer lifestyle and the boom and bust times of the late 19th century. You should note the use of local materials, including locally quarried and hand-chiseled sandstone and limestone and the extensive use of red oak in the interior and as decorative flourishes on the doors and windows. You can also see custom-made china commissioned by Queen Victoria of England and Oriental antiques. The museum is open from Tues through Thurs 10 a.m. to 4 p.m., Fri 9 a.m. to 4 p.m., Sat 10 a.m. to 5 p.m., Sun 1 to 5 p.m. Mar through Memorial Day and Labor Day through December 31. Monday hours are added during the summer. Closed Jan and Feb. Admission is $3 for adults and $1.50 for children (6 to 12). 10 W. 1st St., Big Stone Gap 24219; (276) 523-1322; www.swvamuseum.org.

Cumberland Gap

Our tour ends in Lee County, the most southwestern of Virginia's counties, where Virginia borders Kentucky and Tennessee at Cumberland Gap, named for the Duke of Cumberland, son of King George II. Getting there along Route 58 is an experience that can just about make you forget there's a highly industrialized civilization just a few miles away. Once you leave Duffield (Scott County), it's a pleasant drive past serene, checkerboarded pastures, little towns, white churches of assorted denominations, tobacco-drying barns, livestock

barns, wildflowers, and cemeteries. Norman Rockwell couldn't have painted
anything more idyllic.

Historical markers along the road
relate the comings and goings of Native
Americans, such as the June 1785 mas-
sacre of the Archibald Scott family by
a notorious Native American known
as Benge. Two miles west of Rose Hill
is an Indian burial mound, most likely
Cherokee.

Once you reach the Gap, you have
to go into Kentucky to reach the visitor
center where there are displays on the
Civil War and about Daniel Boone and the 30 axemen who cut the Wilderness
Trail in 1775. The Cumberland Gap is both a scenic wonder of the world and
a lesson in the significance of geography to history. From 1775 to 1800 some
300,000 settlers traveled this way to get to the other side of the Appalachian
Mountains as the Gap evolved into the primary track of an immense trans-
Allegheny migration.

Leaves start turning in this neck of the woods as early as 125 days before
Christmas, but the peak is late fall. During fall you're likely to find the view
fogged much of the time, but at the visitor center you can buy slides of what
the view would look like on a clear day.

The trail was an evolving process. Deer and buffalo migrated across the
Gap, and Indians followed their path. The Cherokees, leading strategic battles
against other tribes, had made the trip on foot from their native North Carolina.
An occasional courageous person wandered through, and there was talk of
the marvelous bluegrass country and the riches of food, livestock, and logging
trees on the western side of the Gap. Eventually coal would be discovered
here as well.

Then, Richard Henderson, a lawyer and land speculator, formed the Tran-
sylvania Co. to establish trade with the Indians. Daniel Boone was hired to cut
and mark the trail known as Boone's Trace, or the Wilderness Road, between
areas now known as Kingsport, Tennessee, and Fort Boonesborough, Kentucky. It wasn't very wide in places: In some areas it was barely a horse path;
in others just large enough for a wagon to get through. Some say it was littered
with the bleached skeletal bones of history.

Then the Revolutionary War began, and the Gap just wasn't on anyone's
front burner for a while. In fact, because the British stirred up the Indians

choochoo

Supposedly the **Bee Rock Tunnel,**
at 47 feet, 7 inches, is the second
shortest railroad tunnel in the world
(reportedly, the Westmoreland
Tunnel in Gallatin, Tennessee, is
the shortest, at 46 feet). At one
time the town of Appalachia was
the center of eight coal camps
constructed by the Louisville &
Nashville Railroad and the Southern Railroad: (276) 565-3900.

against the settlers during the American Revolution, Kentucky was a downright dangerous place at the time.

The Wilderness Road eventually became a two-way thoroughfare. As some settlers trekked westward, others brought cattle, sheep, pigs, and turkeys eastward to the markets along the Atlantic Ocean. At the turn of the century, other means of transportation were developed, including the Erie and Chesapeake and Ohio Canals, the Pennsylvania Main Line, and even steamboats up the Mississippi. The Gap was of extreme strategic value during the Civil War and changed hands a few times, but mostly it languished.

On June 11, 1940, the area was declared a National Historical Park, and no matter how many people are visiting the park when you're there, you're bound to think you're one of the first to discover its rugged beauty. It's one of two historical parks in the state and of 45 in the country, which are different than historic sites because the park includes multiple components. The National Park Service says the 24,000-plus acres of the Cumberland Gap area is one of the "lesser-used" areas in the system and therefore offers an above-average park experience.

There are more than 85 miles of hiking trails (from 1 mile to the scenic 21-mile Ridge Trail), a developed campground and primitive camp areas with summertime campfire programs and daytime activities, Hensley Settlement, caves, and the ***Pinnacle Overlook.***

The Pinnacle is reached via a 4-mile drive from the visitor center. The drive is off-limits to trailers and vehicles more than 20 feet long because the road can give a new meaning to the term hairpin turn. Additionally, due to inclement weather (ice, snow, lightning), the road to the overlook may be closed. Depending on available staff, a shuttle runs to the overlook; the charge is $5 per person. As staffing and crowds fluctuate throughout the year, you might want to let the staff know you'll want a shuttle ride so they can try to schedule you on your desired day.

On a clear day at the Pinnacle you can easily see the three states of Kentucky, Tennessee, and Virginia, and, of course, the Gap, approximately 1,000 feet below you. On exceptionally clear days you can see the Great Smoky Mountains of North Carolina, and possibly even South Carolina and Georgia. More likely, you'll see a lot of mist and will have to rely on purchasing slides and pictures of the spectacularly sweeping vistas.

The plants and wildlife here are seldom seen elsewhere, and they abound in much the same setting as when the gap was first described. There are hardwoods (majestic virgin hemlock, oak, and magnolia) and pines. There are clumps of mountain laurel and rhododendron, so spring and early summer fill the eyescape with fragrant wildflowers and brilliant redbud and dogwood.

Although you'll periodically come across some rocky outcroppings, the area is fully clothed in greenery because the glaciers never came this far south, so the hilltops weren't denuded of valuable plant-supporting dirt. Because of the various elevations, each season's exotic blooms last a very long time, and you need only climb up or descend a few feet for a different botanical view.

From 1903 to 1951 the Hensley and Gibbons families (who intermarried) occupied the *Hensley Settlement,* a plateau that is almost 1,000 feet higher than the Pinnacle Overlook. It was unreachable by our current standards of accessibility. Everything had to be made or grown there or carted in on mule-drawn sleds or by hiking. They lived without roads, electricity, or other conveniences. Sherman Hensley was the last to depart. The Park Service has been re-creating this last settlement, and several buildings and farms have been restored.

Tours, including a shuttle bus and a 1-mile walk through the settlement are offered daily at 9 a.m. and 1:30 p.m. from late May through October 31. Tickets are $10 for adults, $5 for seniors with a Senior Passport, and for children under the age of 12. Bring a light snack and drink. Reservations are strongly suggested because the tour has a limited capacity.

The biggest change to come to Cumberland Gap National Historical Park is the completion of two 2-lane, nearly 1-mile-long tunnels that cut off 3.2 miles of curving, dangerous winding roads. This is allowing the old Wilderness Road (now US 25E) to be restored and revert roughly to the way it was in Daniel Boone's days. First, the trail will be narrowed down to a 10-foot wagon path. Native seeds of grasses, shrubs, and trees have been collected and propagated to be used to restore the gap. This method is less expensive than buying nursery stock and is a lot more natural. It probably will be well into the 21st century before the area looks the way it did 200 years ago, but the work is providing a major head start.

You can join park rangers on a moderately strenuous 1.5 mile, 2-hour hike through the Gap Cave, looking at stalagmites and flowstone cascades, maybe seeing a bat. Should your passion include spelunking, note that the White Nosed Syndrome is killing hundreds of thousands of bats, incredibly handy animals that eat thousands and thousands of nasty insects and bug. Therefore some caves may be closed or you may be requested to wear appropriate clothing and footwear that either has not been in another cave or has been decontaminated. Check with the Rangers to see whether that cave is open to the public or if they have specific requirements in place.

Hike tickets are $8 for adults, $4 for seniors with a Senior Passport, and for children 5 through 12. Be sure to wear appropriate hiking boots. The tours are offered at various times of the day (sometimes once a day; sometimes twice) depending on the season and day of the week. Call or check the website to confirm a hike reservation.

The visitor center has films, exhibits, overnight camping passes, and general information. It is open daily 8 a.m. to 5 p.m., except December 25; (606) 248-2817; www.nps.gov/cuga.

Where to Stay in Southwestern Virginia

ABINGDON

Inn on Town Creek
445 E. Valley St.
(276) 628-4560
www.innontowncreek.com

Summerfield Inn Bed and Breakfast
101 Valley St. Northwest
(276) 628-5905 or
(800) 668-5905
www.summerfieldinn.com

Victoria and Albert Inn
224 Oak Hill St. Northeast
(276) 623-1281 or
(800) 475-5494
www.abingdon-virginia
.com

BIG STONE GAP

Ivy Inn
207 Shawnee Ave. East
(276) 523-0070
www.ivyinnbsg.com

FANCY GAP

Inn and Cottages at Orchard Gap
4549 Lightening Ridge Rd.
(276) 398-3206
www.bbonline.com/va/
orchardgap

FLOYD

Hotel Floyd
120 Wilson St.
(540) 745-6080
www.hotelfloyd.com

MEADOWS OF DAN

Primland Resort
2000 Busted Rock Rd.
(866) 960-7746
www.primland.com

PEARISBURG

Inn at Riverbend Bed & Breakfast
125 River Ridge Dr.
(540) 921-5211
www.innatriverbend.com

RADFORD

Nesselrod on the New River
7535 Lee Hwy.
(540) 731-4970
www.nesselrod.com

WIRTZ

Manor at Taylor's Store
8812 Washington Hwy.
(703) 721-3951
www.innsite.com/inns/
A031645.html

WOOLWINE

Mountain Rose Inn
1787 Charity Hwy.
(276) 930-1057
www.mountainrose-inn.com

Where to Eat in Southwestern Virginia

ABINGDON

Alison's Restaurant
1220 W. Main St.
(276) 628-8002

Huddle House (other locations)
986 E. Main St.
(276) 628-1900
www.huddlehouse.com

The Tavern
222 E. Main St.
(276) 628-1118
www.abingdontavern.com

CHRISTIANSBURG

Crab Creek Seafood Restaurant
9 Radford St. Northwest
(540) 382-6100
www.crabcreek.info

Farmhouse
285 Ridinger St.
(540) 382-4253
www.thefarmhouseonline
.com

HOT SPRINGS

Sam Snead's Tavern
2849 Main St.
(540) 839-7666

Index